Diderot

Updated Edition

Twayne's World Authors Series

French Literature

David O'Connell, Editor
Georgia State University

TWAS 425

Portrait of Diderot, by Fragonard.
Cliché des Musées Nationaux—Paris.

Diderot

Updated Edition

By Otis Fellows

Columbia University

Twayne Publishers
A Division of G. K. Hall & Co. • Boston

PQ
1979
,F44
1989

Diderot, Updated Edition

Otis Fellows

Copyright 1989 by G. K. Hall & Co.
All rights reserved.
Published by Twayne Publishers
A Division of G. K. Hall & Co.
70 Lincoln Street
Boston, Massachusetts 02111

First Edition copyright © 1977 by G. K. Hall & Co.

Copyediting supervised by Barbara Sutton
Book production by Gabrielle B. McDonald
Book design by Barbara Anderson

Typset in 11 pt. Garamond
by Williams Press, Inc. of Albany, New York

Printed on permanent/durable acid-free paper
and bound in the United States of America

Library of Congress Cataloging-in-Publication Data

Fellows, Otis, 1908–
    Diderot / by Otis Fellows.—Updated ed.
        p. cm.—(Twayne's world authors series ; TWAS 425. French
    literature)
    Bibliography: p.
    Includes index.
    ISBN 0–8057–8225–7 (alk. paper)
    1. Diderot, Denis, 1713–1784—Criticism and interpretation.
I. Title. II. Series: Twayne's world authors series ; TWAS 425.
III. Series; Twayne's world authors series. French literature.
PQ1979.F44   1989
848.509—dc19   88–33276
                                                                           CIP

To John Pappas, Sim Copans and in memoriam, *to Norman L. Torrey*
Loyal friends all

Contents

About the Author

Otis Fellows, Avalon Foundation professor emeritus in the humanities, Columbia University, has studied at Amherst College, the American University, the Université de Dijon (France), and Brown University. He has taught at the École Normale de Savenay (France), St. Dunstan's School, Brown University, and the University of Pennsylvania as well as at Columbia. He has given lectures in some thirty universities on both sides of the Atlantic. For six years he represented the humanities on the *Members of the Corporation Visiting Committees* of the Massachusetts Institute of Technology. He was chairman of Columbia's Department of Italian for three years and received "The Casa Italiana of Columbia University Merit Award."

During World War II he was with the Office of War Information as an intelligence officer. At the time, besides on missions for the U. S. Army, he lectured at such institutions as the Sorbonne, the Institut Catholique, the Lycée Henri IV, and the Lycée Condorcet. He has been decorated twice by the French government and also received the bronze medal of the Quinzaine Anglo-Américaine (Paris, February 1945).

A Guggenheim Fellow, he is founder and coeditor of *Diderot Studies,* now in its twenty-fourth volume. He is also author of such books as *French Opinion of Molière, From Voltaire to "La Nouvelle Critique," The Periodical Press in Liberated Paris, The Age of Enlightenment* (with Norman L. Torrey, first and second edition), *Buffon* (with Stephen F. Milliken), *Look and Learn Italian* (with G. N. Laidlaw), as well as numerous articles in periodicals, compendia, and encyclopedias. *Essays on Diderot and the Enlightenment in Honor of Otis Fellows,* edited by John Pappas, was published by Droz of Geneva, Switzerland, in 1974.

He was *invité d'honneur* of *La Société Diderot* during *La Promenade Diderot* (Paris, Sèvres, Reims, Langres) in July 1984.

Foreword

Diderot's current place in the vernacular of intellectual discourse is to no small extent attributable to the work of Otis Fellows at Columbia University over the past decades. Converts being the best proselytes, we who were privileged to attend Professor Fellows's seminars can bear witness to the change they effected in our lives and scholarship. Diderot's subtle, robust, and unpredictable mind was revealed to us by a master practitioner of eighteenth-century urbanity. Out along the vertiginous ziggurat of Diderot's imagination we were guided with a steady hand. As a result, we were eventually able to perceive the balance inherent in that dazzlingly complex dynamic and the centricity of those wonderfully eccentric peregrinations.

Diderot emerges—no, explodes—from the Procrustean purism of the French aesthetic as he does from the philosophical entraves of his tradition and seems at first glance a chaos of contradictions. His insatiable imagination appeals immediately to our own agonized eclecticism. But as recent scholarship has recognized and as the readers of this book will see, Diderot was a self-unifying force. His major achievement is, perhaps, his serene atheism, unhaunted by any remnant of religious or antireligious hysteria, an ongoing ontological vision full of vibrant life-giving energy.

His social philosophy, too, was well integrated. From the social and political world in which he was immersed and from the classical world that provided his angle of vision, he forged for himself a moral terra firma—again with no credits to deity. Of course, putting together a purely human humanism was no great effort after the mid-eighteenth century. Diderot was able to take for granted the anticlerical and antimetaphysical bias of his peers—battles won in his youth. But it remained for his broad and sympathetic historical mind to chart new connections between the good and the possible. As Professor Fellows shows, Diderot's last work, the *Essay on the Reigns of Claudius and Nero* is a great summa of sagacity and experience, a powerful fusion of pragmatic idealism.

Not content to play Montaigne in his old age, Diderot further demonstrates a passion for social justice that we usually associate with fiery youth. It blazes out from his defense of Abbé Raynal in the merciless letter of 1781 to Grimm, old friend and perpetual toady, who, he taunts, has suffered attrition of soul in the antechambers of the great. Outspoken, yes, but still pragmatic: Diderot, in defending truth against tyranny, is also defending his own unsigned contributions to Raynal's book—a covert operation after all.

And so, to the end, this man of tenacious courage and bold elusiveness continues to intrigue us with his infinite complexity, as he awes us with his drive, dedication, energy, passion, love, curiosity, appetite, erudition, and vision. He dissipated himself in a million pursuits, squandered his genius on demand, risked his valuable time in the service of importunate friends, spent his enormous powers at the mill of daily necessity, mortgaged himself to a despot for the price of his daughter's dowry. Yet he found the time to deal with fundamental questions of man, mind, and matter, to raise many that no one had thought of, and to engage in speculations so advanced that words to express them had not yet been coined.

Every day we encounter some problem whose essentials he somehow touched. Alienation in the *Neveu,* the life-potential of basic matter in the *Rêve,* the creative process almost everywhere. At any great theatrical performance the controversy of the *Paradoxe* inevitably revives in our minds. Only recently, in the course of some theater work, I was watching actors develop their roles. Sure enough, even the method actors— *especially* the method actors—were busily creating for themselves those "fantômes" postulated by Diderot. Working with great concentration, they were able to slip in and out of their roles with perfect ease. Having "objectified" their creations for themselves, they were able to project them at will. In short, they were doing the paradox. No wonder Diderot found these arch-dissemblers endlessly fascinating. Emblem of man's prismatic consciousness, embodiment of the persona Diderot created for himself as artist-observer, Diderot's actor also reflects our social selves in the multiple roles we must play.

Multiplicity, facets, reverberations, adumbrations, roles, data, masks, mystifications, aspirations—in the laboratory, the theater, the salon, the bedroom, from the Homeric world to the Shandyan, from the age of Pericles to the court of St. Petersburg to the tribunal of posterity— Diderot is everywhere, a whirlwind controlled by the complex principles of order that control all natural phenomena. In this smooth, lively little book Professor Fellows has given us a vivid account of the life and works of this protean genius, this bourgeois bohemian. No small feat this—slipping the genie back into the bottle. With the skill of an epic miniaturist, the author reproduces a universe for us in a format we can grasp. In the final synthesis, Diderot had it all together. In this book, so do we.

June S. Siegel

New York

Preface

When in 1971 the first edition of this slim volume on Denis Diderot appeared, a well-known *Diderotiste,* the late J. Robert Loy, in a review of the monograph, emphasized that it was simply an introduction but a good one "to one of France's greatest writers."

This, the updated edition, is still an introduction to the life and works of the philosophe. Like the first, it seeks to meet the requirements of the general reader. If the specialist finds in its pages an original suggestion or two suitable for further development, so much the better.

More than a century ago Karl Rosenkranz wrote his two-volume *Diderots Leben und Werke.* Despite its qualities, with the passage of time its limitations became increasingly apparent. But, since there was no major biography devoted exclusively to Diderot to replace it, Rosenkranz was again published—still only in German—well over a hundred years later.

Shortly after (in 1972), however, an American, Arthur Wilson brought out the 900-page *Diderot* of inestimable value as a carefully laid groundwork upon which present and future scholars might build for years to come. It has been internationally acclaimed, and is now available in French as well as in English.

Toward the beginning of the present century a professor of English at the University of Edinburgh was prone to refer to the "systole and diastole of the human heart in history." He was thinking chiefly of two literary trends that succeed one another down through the years, the classical and the romantic.[1] The turn of expression was decidedly arresting, but the concept of action and reaction or the swinging pendulum was more common. The principle of alternance in natural phenomena must have been apparent to man from the start: the light of day and the darkness of night, the rise and fall of the tides, and the changing seasons.

Races, peoples, nations, and governments also rose and fell to rise again. France, during the reign of Louis XIV, the "Sun King," who declared that "L'Etat c'est moi," eventually gave way to the period of the French Revolution with its violent reaction to the protracted abuses

of the privileged classes and the subsequent return to absolute power
vested in Napoleon as Emperor.

However, throughout Europe in general and France in particular a
noteworthy span of time extended, roughly, from 1740 to the outbreak
of the French Revolution in 1789. This period has gone down in history
as the Age of Reason, the Age of Ideas, the Age of Humanism and,
more luminously, the Age of Enlightenment. Norman L. Torrey and
I have defined this point of time as follows:

"Enlightenment" is a term applied to a definite revolution in the history
of thought and especially to its manifestations in eighteenth-century France.
It signifies not only the popularization and dissemination in literary form of
scientific knowledge but also an all-pervasive philosophic and critical spirit.
The leaders of the movement were called "philosophers," although few of
them established definite systems of philosophy. The main tenets of the
group were a sincere belief in the idea of progress, the application of the
experimental method in science, the free and unfettered use of the God-
given faculty of reason in all affairs, human and divine, and the ardent faith
that reason, controlled by experience, was, with all its limitations, the final
judge and the best guide available for the conduct of life.[2]

With the twentieth century drawing to a close, there is more or less
agreement that it is difficult for the well-read *dix-huitiémiste* to say
with unqualified assurance whether Voltaire, Rousseau, or Diderot had
made the greatest contribution to our appreciation of the French Enlightenment. Voltaire was clearly the most representative writer of the
age with a hand in every conceivable event of the day. With persuasive
eloquence, Rousseau inflamed readers' imaginations and thinking, whether
pro or con, on education, politics, or nature. Because of his writings
he was often referred to as the father of romanticism and the French
Revolution. Diderot saw the *Encyclopédie,* the first of its kind, through
to a fruitful conclusion: a vast compendium of knowledge, this work
by Diderot and his fellow *encyclopédistes.* And it gave forth, upon
occasion, ill-timed and ill-disguised criticism of critical, social, and
institutional malpractices then prevalent. Contrary to Voltaire and Rousseau, however, Diderot's greatest work, his masterpieces, appeared after
his death—some well after. For over a century after they had come to
light there were few readers to appreciate or denigrate such works as
*Jacques le fataliste (Jack the Fatalist), Le Neveu de Rameau (Rameau's
Nephew), La Religieuse (The Nun),* or *Le Rêve de d'Alembert (D'Alembert's
Dream).*

As Diderot the personality evolved throughout his lifetime so did his works. His unorthodoxy in philosophical and scientific speculation as well as in literary forms was part and parcel of the man himself. The approach here, then, is that of a life and works presented chronologically.

Diderot, along with Voltaire, was for years France's foremost example of *l'homme engagé*—the intellectual man of action. The *Encyclopédie* was his great work of commitment to the age. But most of his boldest writings, too heady for his day, appeared posthumously as manuscripts. He had dedicated them to posterity. Thus it seems that in a thin-bodied volume such as this, two movements should be considered: 1) the unfolding of Diderot's life along with his works, and 2) the reactions of posterity to his writings. In this second development it is often the concept of Diderot's modernity that has gained the upper hand. Both movements have been taken into account in this study.

When one is obliged to treat a man as complex as Diderot in extremely limited space, it is imperative to pick and choose what aspects of the man and his work are to be underscored and which ones must be scanted or even ignored. The choice cannot meet the approval of all. Certain interpretations will appear commonplace to Diderot scholars; they are nevertheless essential for those comparatively unfamiliar with the subject.

The author dealing with a man as complex as Diderot also has the right, even the duty, to leap into the fray with interpretations of his own, though some of these will surely conflict with those of other *Diderotistes* whose numbers are growing by leaps and bounds in the second half of the twentieth century. I try here to show that Diderot was in his day a presence of formidable proportions whose influence was felt—often unknowingly—in psychology, in religion, in education, in new art forms, in sociology, in science, and in the systematic accumulation of knowledge, and to demonstrate that this presence is still with us. Diderot was an exciting writer; we have attempted to impart some of this excitement to the present-day reader.

Otis Fellows

Columbia University

Acknowledgments

To those friends who were formerly students of mine, June S. Siegel, Frederick A. Spear, Maurice Posada, Arnold Miller, Lenore Kreitman, Thelma Richman, and Martha Ivaldi, I wish to express my appreciation for the help and encouragement they have given me. I am also grateful to a new member of Columbia's French Department, Vincent J. Errante, for his kindness in discussing textual problems with me. To all of them it is a real pleasure to offer my heartfelt thanks.

Chronology

1713   Denis Diderot born 5 October, in Langres, son of a master cutler.

1728   Breaks off studying with Jesuits at Langres; leaves for Paris. Resumes studies either at the Collège d'Harcourt or Louis-le-Grand.

1732   Awarded "maître ès arts" at the University of Paris 2 September.

1732–1735   Studies for the doctorate in theology at the Sorbonne.

1743   Marries Antoinette Champion against father's wishes 6 November. Becomes close friends with Rousseau, Condillac, and others, and is obliged to seek steady employment.

1745   Publishes free translation of Shaftesbury's *Inquiry concerning Virtue and Merit.*

1746   Composes first original work, *Pensées philosophiques.* Commissioned, along with d'Alembert, to direct what was first to be a translation from the English of Chambers's *Cyclopaedia,* a project which evolved into the great *Encyclopédie.*

1748   Denounced to the police as author of a licentious novel, *Les Bijoux indiscrets.* Brings out a memoir on various mathematical subjects.

1749   Because of his writings, is condemned to some three months of prison at Vincennes.

1750   Publishes prospectus to the *Encyclopédie.*

1751   *Lettre sur les sourds et muets;* first voume of the *Encyclopédie.*

1752   Attempted suppression of the *Encyclopédie.* Reconciled with father.

1753   Birth of daughter, Angélique, his only surviving child. Publishes *Pensées sur l'interprétation de la nature.*

1755   Attends Montesquieu's funeral. Begins correspondence with Sophie Volland.

1756   Begins collaboration on Grimm's confidential periodical, *Correspondance littéraire, philosophique et critique.*

1757   Publishes drama, *Le Fils naturel,* and discusses his theories on the theater through his *Entretiens sur le Fils naturel.* Friendship with Rousseau ends.

1758   D'Alembert withdraws from the *Encyclopédie.* Diderot's play, *Le Père de famille,* is published, as is his *Discours sur la poésie dramatique.*

1759   The *Encyclopédie* continues despite opposition of the court. Writes his first formal art criticism with commentaries on the biennial salons. Father dies.

1760   Violently attacked in Palissot's play, *Les Philosophes.* Writes novel, *La Religieuse* (published in 1796).

1761   The satirical dialogue, *Le Neveu de Rameau* (first published in retranslation from the German in 1821). *Le Père de famille* coolly received at the Comédie Française.

1762   The Paris Parlement pronounces a decree for the expulsion of the Jesuits from France.

1765   Sells his library to Catherine the Great of Russia, who also grants him a pension.

1766   Distribution both abroad and in the provinces of the last ten volumes of the *Encyclopédie.*

1767   The fifth *Salon* on painting.

1769   Writes *Le Rêve de d'Alembert* (published in 1830).

1772–1778   *Jacques le fataliste* and the *Supplément au Voyage de Bougainville* (both published in 1796).

1773   Sets out for Russia at invitation of Catherine the Great.

1778   *Essai sur les règnes de Claude et de Néron.*

1784   Death of Sophie Volland 22 February: 21 July, death of Diderot.

Chapter One
Then and Now

When Diderot was thirty-six the police inspector, Joseph d'Hémery, noted more than once in his journal that the budding encyclopedist was a clever young fellow and downright dangerous. This judgment paled beside the torrent of opprobrium Diderot eventually picked up during his lifetime. Such criticism followed his memory down through the nineteenth century and into the twentieth. Neither Montesquieu, nor Voltaire, nor Rousseau have been objects of such scathing commentary while alive or in the hands of a sizable segment of posterity. Even some of our most respected critics, taking a leaf or two from the police inspector's journal, have treated Diderot as a bright but wayward, even naughty boy who, from time to time, merits a smart intellectual spanking. Others find he can do no wrong. Edna Frederick seems to have struck, at least, for the present, an admirable kind of balance in assessment of Diderot's genius. She writes: "He seems to have had an enormous capacity for assimilation; although his impressionable nature was likely to be influenced by the work of his predecessors, Diderot was at the same time endowed with enough creative genius, enough independence of thought to enable him to give to struggling tendencies a more original, more positive interpretation."[1]

Not until the middle of the twentieth century was there gathering recognition that perhaps Denis Diderot deserved a place of rare distinction among French writers and thinkers of his age. At last it had become slowly evident that, upon occasion, his pen could be more analytical than Montesquieu's, more scintillating than Voltaire's, more eloquently personal than Rousseau's, more grandiose in its flights than Buffon's. In short, could he have had the most original, the most daring, the most imaginative mind of the Enlightenment?

Whereas at the beginning of the twentieth century few among the intelligentsia held such an opinion, by the mid-1950s there had sprung up on all continents and in most countries certain eminent *Diderotistes,* any one of whom could speak for the rest. The summarizing remark Robert Niklaus, then of the University of Exeter, made in 1970, does

1

just that. He writes, "Perhaps the greatest genius of the century of
brilliant men, Diderot fulfilled his total promise within his lifetime, but
it is only in our time that he has been understood."[2] Nevertheless, let
us retrace our steps or, rather, briefly touch upon his rise in the esteem
of others.

To many in his own day, Diderot had been a garrulous though
learned bourgeois, the author of two or three undistinguished plays and
of an indiscreet brochure or so that had resulted in an inopportune and
unpleasant prison sentence; but he was also the competent though
occasionally imprudent editor of a multivolume encyclopedia. Then, too,
he was a man whom the French Academy disdained to honor, yet
whom Catherine the Great would invite to her court in Saint Petersburg
when old age was upon him.

Still, there were those among his compeers who were well aware of
his merit. Voltaire, in scattered references throughout his letters, recognized that here was no ordinary man, and watched the unfolding of
this "pantophile," this "Plato," this "Socrates," as he called him in
turn, with disquiet but open admiration. And Rousseau, despite his
long-standing enmity toward this once-close friend, suggested that Diderot's nature was exceptional and could be fully appreciated only by
future generations.

In nineteenth-century Europe it was Germany that sensed the philosophe's very real genius. Goethe toiled over some of the French writer's
manuscripts and knew them well. Near the end of his life the illustrious
German poet told his friend Muller: "So the French will never have
another eighteenth century no matter how hard they try. Where do
they have anything they could compare to Diderot?" Then on 9 March
1831, a year before his death, Goethe wrote to Zelter: "Diderot is
Diderot, a unique individual; he who is too fastidious in his criticism
is a philistine, and they are legion. Human beings are incapable of
finally appreciating what is of inestimable value, handed down from
God, from nature or from their fellow men." Schiller would have
agreed.

In nineteenth-century France a chosen few—Delacroix, Balzac, and
Stendhal—were quick to delve into and profit by what this seminal
mind had to offer. And, at almost the same time, that dour Scotsman
from across the Channel, Thomas Carlyle, while finding Diderot "utterly
unclean, scandalous, shameless," felt obliged to add, "Nevertheless,
Nature is great; and Denis was among her nobler productions."[3]

But the notion of Diderot's lack of personal decency and the belief that his intellectual and literary gifts were as meager as they were undisciplined, persisted in academic minds, sometimes in high places, even during the first third of the twentieth century.

Thus, in the 1920s that distinguished, erudite, witty but conservative scholar and Frenchman, the late André Bellessort, wrote informatively on and lectured entertainingly about figures of the Enlightenment at the famous Lycée Louis-le-Grand. He was periodically invited to give these lectures at the Sorbonne as well. Each time his Sorbonne lecture on the man whom he designated as that philosophe, that *encyclopédiste*, that intellectual rapscallion rolled around, M. Bellessort, it appears, introduced his subject with the selfsame formula: "Diderot, gentlemen!" then, after a brief pause, "Open the windows!"

Bellessort's reactions were motivated less by ignorance than by self-acknowledged prejudice. It was a time when Diderot was often a victim of both ignorance and prejudice, especially in the English-speaking world. A scholar in one of the prouder citadels of higher learning in America—the professor and the institution shall remain nameless—was able to publish unchallenged the following statement: "On account of his lack of artistic talent and self discipline, Diderot has left behind no literary masterpiece." At almost the same time, a British scholar over whom it would also be well to cast the cloak of anonymity, asserted for all to read that Diderot squandered what little genius he had, in much the same way he had squandered his time, health, and money.

There were, even then, notable exceptions, particularly among the more discerning. Carl Becker, whose mind was that of a trained historian, writing in the *Philosophical Review* as early as 1915, was able to say: "Diderot was the century itself: in him all the currents of that age, deep and shallow, crossed and went their separate ways." This is quite true, and there are those now willing to agree that it is much more so than in the case of either Voltaire or Rousseau. Moreover, at present, with the recent discovery or rediscovery of Diderot's manuscripts, and a better understanding than ever before of his great posthumous works, the bright complexity as well as modernity of the man's insights in a variety of fields has become increasingly apparent.

Despite the quickened interest on diverse fronts and in different corners of the world, still some well-known and seasoned scholars show a tendency to assume a somewhat disenchanted attitude toward Diderot. The philosophe continues to be chided for his "intellectual anarchy," his "affected disorder," his "lack of clarity," his "willful confusion," and his "distorted logic." He is also taken to task for his incompetence in dealing with the ancients, especially Plato and Aristotle. And so it goes! Others, however, agree with Elizabeth Potulicki that these are opinions conditioned by the traditional analytic demands for comprehensibility and lucidity at all costs.

Diderot's disorder, Professor Potulicki observes, is a refreshingly new, unrestricted procedure squarely facing a reality that, in its complexity, stretches to infinity and is never finally or totally perceived. She wonders whether one should continue to be dismayed by the confusion of Diderot's writings, or overwrought by his cogitations and speculations. And indeed, among the more spritely and perhaps more youthful minds, there appears to be a steadily growing awareness that Diderot has glimpsed a new conception of reality—a reality that, in its complexity, as Dr. Potulicki puts it, faces up to the concept of infinity or the totally perceived. Ultimately, and perhaps prudently, Potulicki accepts the criterion proposed by Roland Barthes that, after all, "literature is always the question devoid of the answer."[4]

Reevaluations of Diderot's significance have also come in from other academic disciplines. The philosopher M. W. Wartofsky tells us that too often Diderot's place in the history of philosophical writings of eighteenth-century France has been more or less grudgingly situated as a necessary evil between Kant and Hegel, or between Descartes and Bergson, or as a weak reflection of British mechanism and empiricism.

While acknowledging the philosophe's debt to Descartes and the mechanist tradition in France and England, he declares that Diderot stands out as a creative and revolutionary force in a much maligned and neglected philosophy of eighteenth-century France. He notes that Diderot struggled to break through the limits of reductionist mechanism, to cope with the contradiction in the materialism of the mechanists, which gave rise to the idealist critique of mechanism and to the idealist solution of vitalism and hylozoism. And he concludes: "The logic of change, motion, transformation, which had been developed in the main by the idealist philosophers and whose absence was the Achilles' heel, mechanism is grasped by Diderot not in its idealist form, but rather, as the logic of a material universe, which itself changes, moves, is in constant transformation. In a sense, Diderot puts the idealistic logic of change back on its feet, starting from the outermost limits of mechanism."[5] In short, Diderot develops a materialist philosophy of change, a fact that could have intrigued Engels.

In his review of Wilson's *Diderot: The Appeal to Posterity* the eminent historian Emanuel Chill gives the reader an idea of Diderot's "labile, multiform thought." It has, he tells us, opened up new paths in the philosophy of science, in aesthetics, and inspired some of the beginnings of romanticism. But more important, he finds, is the fact that our philosophe prefigures up to a point "some of the typical dilemmas and preoccupations of modern bourgeois intellectuals with their dependence on, yet uneasiness with established powers." These middle-class intellectuals, Professor Chill concludes, in their regard for worldly rather than spiritual matters, are committed "to an empirically given world but simultaneously to a better one; and the search for a social definition of reason that will endow the intellectual with an emancipatory function within the human community. To the extent that twentieth-century conditions force us to compare alternative modes of social existence, to take society as the most serious object of thought, we are linked to the Enlightenment and preeminently to Diderot."[6]

Now that we have seen three American scholars expressing their views, one as a literary critic, another as a philosopher, and a third as a historian, we begin to discern why Diderot is viewed with increased interest as the twentieth-century comes to a close. It might also be well to consider the findings of a fourth scholar representing modern American scholarship in an entirely different domain. What Soviet scholars think of Diderot is very proper in the interests of objective scholarship.

Diderot, late in life, remained an empiricist, a materialist (matter in motion), an atheist, and far more politically minded than heretofore. In the first volume of the *Encyclopédie* (1751) he had declared, some ten years before Rousseau's *Contrat social* appeared (1762), that sovereignty resided in the people who should decide how and to whom it should be delegated. In the mid-1770s now, with pen in hand, he studied Catherine II's *Nakez* (Russian word for "instruction"), and so wrote his *Observations sur Nakez*. In these comments on Catherine's instructions to her political delegates Diderot notes that the empress said nothing about liberating serfs. He also expressed his disapproval of a ruler willing to submit political institutions to religious sanction. In his opinion, there was no true sovereign except the nation, and there can be no true legislator but the people.

Surprisingly or not, critics of yesterday as well as of today submit that both Rousseau and Diderot can be seen as forerunners of Marxist totalitarianism. By the mid-twentieth century specialists of the French

Enlightenment were generally of the opinion that such outstanding scholars of the period as Jacques Proust of France, Roland Mortier of Belgium, and Franco Venturi of Italy might throw considerable light on the reception of Diderot by that giant totalitarian state to the east. What had been the general attitude of Soviet scholars to that eighteenth-century encyclopedist, humanist, and would-be adviser to Catherine II of all the Russians? How has Diderot been judged by Marxist standards?

Prominent *Diderotistes* such as Venturi, Mortier, and Proust had not, it seems, carried investigations far enough to satisfy sufficiently today's unjaundiced historians, philosophers, and political scientists. It turns out, however, that an American has a considerable amount of impartial information to offer.

Arnold Miller has studied Soviet reactions to and interpretations of Diderot. The 464-page book resulting from the research constitutes the fifteenth volume of *Diderot Studies*. Of almost equal importance is the fact that he has had occasion to return to the Soviet Union thereafter. I am most grateful to him for what follows.

In the eyes of Soviet scholars, we are told, Diderot ranks as one of the leading eighteenth-century French materialists, who in turn formed part of the larger group known as the philosophes. These men, according to the prevailing Marxist view, he points out, constituted a progressive force, since they helped prepare the way for a new stage of history, in which the domination of the bourgeoisie would in due course call forth its dialectical nemesis, the proletariat. In short, the French Revolution was the necessary prelude to the October Revolution.

As a result, according to Professor Miller, Soviet scholars thus consider Diderot an intellectual ancestor in this very general sense. But they have devoted much study to him for another reason as well: the interest, sympathy, and esteem manifested toward him by their principal authority figures, especially Marx and Engels, whose positive attitude has served to sanction what Roland Mortier would refer to upon occasion as a "volonté d'annexion" by the scholars.

This "annexion" of Diderot by Soviet scholarship, Miller informs us, begins in the 1920s and extends with time into ever new domains. What Soviet scholarship tells us, in effect, is that Diderot was a precocious traveler along the road that led to Marx and Engels, and onward to the Soviet state: in philosophy, a materialist; in religion, an atheist; in aesthetics, a realist; in literature, a precursor of "critical realism." Moreover, he was a great admirer of Russia, for which he predicted a brilliant future.

Nevertheless, says Miller, Soviet scholars emphasize what they consider two fundamental and inevitable shortcomings of Diderot. The low level of the biological sciences in the eighteenth century, compared with the relatively highly developed state of physics, did not permit our philosopher to transcend mechanistic materialism and rise to an understanding of dialectical materialism. And the darkness in which the social sciences languished before the advent of Marx made it impossible for Diderot to reach irreproachably correct conclusions in the fields of politics, religion, ethics, and aesthetics.

In sum, Diderot, as seen through the prism of Soviet scholarship, is a respected ancestor, admired in spite of his historically conditioned flaws; he helped advance a progressive historical movement, and in many fields came very close to the truth of things.

Present-day Marxists are impressed by Professor Miller's industry and conscientiousness. But they hold that his efforts fall short since only a dyed-in-the-wool Marxist would be capable of completely understanding the Marxist point of view.[7]

Because of the peculiar quality of Diderot's mind we are apt to learn as much about those who write on him as about Diderot himself. Outstanding in the nineteenth century was Rosenkranz whose interpretation was colored by Hegelianism. In the first half of the twentieth century we had been provided with a Marxist interpretation by I. K. Luppol and Jean Luc as well as by Jean Stewart and Jonathan Kemp, the editors of *Diderot, Interpreter of Nature,* and Henri Lefebvre. We also have a humanistic Diderot interpreted by Jean Thomas, and even a Diderot, prey to "le naturisme mystique," as viewed by Baron Seillière from his eminence in the Institut de France. Moreover, we have a highly creditable presentation of two aspects of the philosophe's thought— ethics and aesthetics—by Lester Crocker. Each evaluation is, in its way, a tribute to Diderot and a contribution to an understanding of the eighteenth-century "Pantophile," as Voltaire called him.

Toward the middle of the twentieth century there was a vivified interest in Diderot the man and writer that gathered momentum as the years continued to file by. It might be well to touch upon some of the factors involved.

At the outbreak of World War II, for instance, Herbert Dieckmann succeeded in rediscovering and rescuing from an invading army valuable manuscripts in Diderot's handwriting. Some had not been published during the author's lifetime and others had not been published at all.

They are known as the Fonds [or "stock"] Vandeul and are almost priceless to interested publishers, librarians, and scholars. They are now, for the most part, in France's Bibliothèque Nationale.

The late Arthur Wilson plays a significant role in the present kindling interest in the philosophe and we have already mentioned his *Diderot* appearing a full century after that of Rosenkranz. Wilson had the same stamina, intellectual courage, and breadth of knowledge to write a penetrating and deadly serious history of Denis Diderot's life and works as the German savant.

Wilson dug in archives from Philadelphia to distant Leningrad and found a wealth of material of which Rosenkranz and others had never dreamed. At the same time Wilson was familiar with almost everything that had been written on Diderot. Here his training as a historian served him well; he judged with critical eyes and, whenever possible, verified all available evidence. The work, which took thirty-six years of his life to complete, were years extremely well spent. The Wilson book assures the specialist and the general reader alike that their intuitive attraction to Diderot is justified. As such, written to satisfy many needs, *Diderot* is richly informative, and essential to all who are, these days, delving into Diderot scholarship whether they be neo-Freudians, neo-Marxists, structuralists, diacritics, or merely old-fashioned literary historians.

Another recent development in our knowledge of Diderot that heightens our interest in the man and his work is to be found in those years (1731–43) that have been relatively obscure for historians. We do know that for two years he had worked in a solicitor's office, that he had briefly been a tutor for the children of a well-to-do financier, had done a certain amount of hack work, was not above accepting an occasional loan from some acquaintance or friend, and had begun translating a work or two of English into French. Then, too, the registers of the University of Paris revealed that he—the only "philosopher" to do so—had earned the *maître ès arts* degree within its walls. Mathematics and philosophy were his chief subjects. Three more years spent studying theology and he was well on his way to earning a doctorate in theology. Was it his intention to become a monk or a priest?

Years later he wrote in the *Salon de 1767,* "I arrived in Paris. I was to take the fur (i.e., holy orders) and install myself among the doctors of the Sorbonne. I meet a woman beautiful as an angel. I want to sleep with her, I do so. I have four children by her" (*AT,* 11:265–66).

It is Blake T. Hanna who had ferreted out the evidence showing that Diderot had studied theology for three years at the Université de Paris. It is true, though, that Arthur Wilson and, in particular, Robert Salesses had surmised that Diderot had studied in the faculty of the Sorbonne.

Hanna's discovery clearly reveals for the first time that Diderot had been a serious student in theology and that his thoughts on the subject in the *Encyclopédie* and elsewhere were not, after all, simply drawn from hearsay or were borrowings from respected authorities. In the light of this revelation new interpretations of Diderot's comments and reflections on theology may invite reexamination by future generations.[8]

Have there been other indications of a changing evaluation by interested parties in France and the world at large? Two unquestionable giants, Voltaire and Rousseau, died two months apart in 1778. In each instance the bicentennial was recognized and even dutifully feted. And so, in 1878, there was a new burst of interest concerning the contributions of each to France and various other countries. Historians and especially *Diderotistes,* but few others, were well aware that 1984 would mark the bicentenary of the philosophe's death. What would it bring?

One well-known Belgian scholar, Raymond Trousson, had already treated in two articles the reception accorded in France, first for the centenary of his death, in 1884, then that which he received in 1913 for the bicentenary of his birth. In both instances Diderot was praised by the leftist republican party and other anticlericals but condemned by the acerbic pens of such rightist writers as Maurice Barrès and Charles Maurras.[9] The posterity Diderot had hoped for did not seem to be entirely in hand. But much water has gone over the dam since then.

Manuscripts composing the *Fonds Vandeul* and the Leningrad Collection are now at the disposal of scholars. When examined with care they sometimes reveal inaccuracies by editors rather than by Diderot himself. One example from many might suffice. The *Oeuvres Complètes de Diderot* (in twenty volumes, 1875–77) had, until recently, been the main standby of historians despite occasional lacunae or careless editing. With the original manuscript in hand, Assézat brought out the unpublished memoir *Sur les probabilités,* which Diderot had written in 1761 (*AT,* 10:192–206). The brief essay caused much puzzlement among mathematicians and even led some to believe that Diderot was deficient in that science. Professor O'Gorman and I, having obtained a photostat of the original manuscript, found that the "obscurities" and "repetitions" laid to Diderot's door, were caused by two serious errors in editing and an uncalled-for addition supplied by Assézat himself.[10]

Halfway through the twentieth century several significant steps were taken to present Diderot's works to their best advantage. From 1951, beginning with the Niklaus edition of the *Lettre sur les aveugles* and ending with Jacques Rustin's *Les Bijoux indiscrets* in 1981, there appeared some twenty editions of Diderot's individual works admirably prepared. One example drawn from many is Jean Seznec and Jean Adhémar's edition of the *Salons* (Oxford: Clarendon Press, 1957–67).

As far as new sets of Diderot's works are concerned there was a decided step in the right direction when Le Club français du Livre brought out (1969–73) the first chronological edition in fifteen volumes. The ten thousand handsome sets were published under the highly competent direction of Roger Lewinter. Besides his own commentaries he had the happy idea of utilizing texts already established and commented on: Jean Fabre's edition of *Le Neveu de Rameau,* for instance, or Robert Mauzi's edition of *La Religieuse.* One of Lewinter's chief aims was to restore Diderot's works as literature rather than as history or science.[11]

Another *Diderot, Oeuvres complètes,* a true edition of the philosophe's complete works, was a natural consequence of the Bibliothèque Nationale receiving the entire collection of manuscripts comprising the Fonds Vandeul in 1952. The set will unquestionably be the standard edition scholars throughout the twenty-first century will turn to time and again. This critical, annotated edition got under way in 1975 with the first of what is expected to be thirty-four volumes presented chronologically and published in deluxe form by Hermann of Paris.

The original committee launching this important enterprise consisted of Arthur M. Wilson, Blake T. Hanna, Roland Desné, Jacques Roger, Alain Seznec, John S. Spink, and Paolo Casini, under the watchful eye of Jean Varloot. Readers are told that the edition is chronological, critical, modernized, with commentaries, introductory essays, footnotes, and the like. It will have an all-inclusive index begun by Herbert Dieckmann and being completed by his widow, Jane Marsh Dieckmann. There are some fifty collaborators for the volumes involved.

When 1984 rolled around, it bore little resemblance in mood and substance to the centenary of Diderot's death one hundred years before. Not only France but the whole world seemed aware that the approaching date was harbinger of things to come in memory of the philosophe. Already, periodicals in various countries were devoting entire issues to Diderot. Congresses had been planned in different parts of the world to honor the occasion. Anne-Marie Chouillet, in collaboration with other members of the Société française du dix-huitième siècle, filled more than 120 pages of the book titled *1984 L'Année Diderot* giving detailed accounts of colloquiums and expositions on all six continents and in dozens of cities in more than twenty countries.

Perhaps what had the greatest impact on *Diderotistes* was the Colloque International Diderot, also known as La Promenade Diderot. Some 2,500 interested parties gathered at the Sorbonne for the opening session, then the following day at the Conciergerie. From there, close to two hundred members spent several days (from 6 to 10 July) at Sèvres, Reims, and Diderot's birthplace, Langres. The volume of 551 pages resulting from this, includes more than fifty articles and communications gathered together by Mme Chouillet and the Comité scientifique with its twelve members, all outstanding authorities on Diderot. The Secrétaire Général of the Congress was M. Jacques Chouillet of Paris III. Through the efforts of these and other scholars the international Société Diderot was formed in 1986, and the first issue of its semiannual publication, *Recherches sur Diderot et sur l'Encyclopédie*, became a welcome reality. Thus, *Recherche* came to be the second serial publication devoted to Diderot. The first had been *Diderot Studies*.[12]

With the publication of the *Bibliographie Instructive* (1763) by Diderot's contemporary, William De Bure, the term *bibliography* would no longer simply mean the writing and copying of books. Soon thereafter it represented the process of tabulating and classifying both books and articles. With time it included those works devoted to a given author or a specific subject. More often than not, they took the form of "selected bibliographies" appended to a particular book, essay, or article.

Specialists of the French Enlightenment have in recent years been fortunate in being able to consult two works. The first is *A Critical Bibliography of French Literature: The Eighteenth Century*, edited by George R. Havens and Donald F. Bond (1951). The second is its *Supplement*, edited by Richard S. Brooks (1968). With the research of Arthur and Mary Wilson covering the years 1952–67 at his disposal, Brooks was able to devote thirty double-columned pages to Diderot bibliography coupled with pithy evaluations. The list of references itself indicates the unusual interest in Diderot during the fifteen years following mid-century.

It was in 1968 that Professor Frederick A. Spear began research for his *Bibliographie de Diderot: Répertoire analytique international* (1980), a work covering essentially the period 1743–1975. This finest of research tools thus represents a labor of twelve years and has required frequent travel to major libraries both in the United States and abroad. That it is a truly international bibliography is attested by the fact that books and articles appear in more than twenty languages and represent publication in more than forty different countries. For the first time it brings together substantial but formerly little-known studies from Eastern Europe and Japan. Its 3,968 entries present an astonishingly complete coverage. The work is eminently usable and useful: and the extraordinarily conscientious table of contents combined with an extensive index and a multiplicity of cross-references throughout can lead to unexpected discoveries and often suggest new areas of investigation.

Professor Spear has since published in *Diderot Studies* supplements to this exceptional work. In order to accommodate the phenomenal growth in the number of studies devoted to *Diderot* in recent years, however, a growth given new impetus by the approach and subsequent fitting recognition of his death, Spear is in the final stages of a second volume covering the period 1976–86.

The writer who clings only to the inclinations, tastes, and prejudices of the day is more preoccupied with himself than with his writings, Jean de La Bruyère hints in his *Caractères* published a few years before Diderot's birth.

And what did Diderot think of himself, his writings, and posterity? Was he justified in counting on the understanding, the appreciation, the acclaim he failed to receive while alive? Maurice Posada reminds us that "as author proposes, posterity disposes" and, with the Falconet debate in mind, adds, "In this case, Posterity seems to have been particularly jealous of its prerogatives towards these two authors who presumed to question its powers and sought to dictate how it should dispose of themselves."

And with this, a twist of irony enters the picture. The correspondence suppressed by Diderot's veto and the Vandeuls' nolle prosequi nevertheless survived. It was preserved for posterity through the efforts of the sculptor-author who was indifferent to posterity. It is Falconet who had originally collected all the correspondence and prepared the first manuscripts.[13]

Irony takes another turn with the passage of time. On the one hand, there was a sculptor athirst for contemporary acclaim and adulation while holding posterity in disdain. Opposed to this view was a friend chiefly known as a mere encyclopedist who could not bask in the approbation and touch of fame he longed for from his contemporaries, but still hoped against hope for posterity's acceptance and acclaim. Interestingly enough, relatively few in today's world could name the artist responsible for the imposing equestrian statue of Peter the Great. As the twentieth century draws to a close, however, on all six continents an ever-increasing number of persons know what eighteenth-century Frenchman wrote *Le Neveu de Rameau, Le Rêve de d'Alembert,* and *Jacques le fataliste.*

Throughout his life Diderot wished to be free, innovative, and creative. Posterity has become increasingly aware that his wish has been granted. In his writing as in his living Diderot was well aware of those realms that Jacques Barzun notes deal with "man in society, beginning with history and going on to literature and the arts, philosophy, and the essence of mind itself."[14]

Chapter Two

The Child Is Father of the Man

Denis Diderot, soon to turn forty-six, though a comparative unknown in contrast to Voltaire and Rousseau, already had some slight claim to fame when on 1 August 1759, he wrote to his beloved Sophie Volland in Paris. He was, at the time, visiting his native city of Langres in the heart of the French provinces, some one hundred and fifty miles south of the capital and less than fifty miles north of Dijon. "The inhabitants of this region," he told her, "are not at all lacking in wit, but they have too much vivacity, and are as fickle as weathervanes. . . . As for me, I am one of them, except that my years in Paris and hard work have taught me a lesson or two."[1]

These lines have caused some critics to take for granted the flexibility and, far worse, the inconstancy of his mind. This was a mistake, though, for he refused to consider truth to be either fixed or absolute; his tastes and his philosophy remained to the end remarkably stable. He was far from a weathercock, and his dialectical thought was methodical and hardly the plaything of the winds.

Early Steps

To reach Langres from Paris, the wayfarer of two hundred years ago took the horse-drawn stage along the dust-covered roads winding south and east to the edge of Lorraine and the headwaters of the Marne. Its ramparts and other architectural vestiges were—as they are today—clear enough indication that this had once been an ancient Roman city.

Despite its pagan origins, Langres was and remains, dotted with convents, churches, and seminaries. There the artisans and bourgeois could lead an active, bustling life, and knives, scissors, and surgical instruments—Diderot's father was a master cutler—are still, along with Denis Diderot himself, its most famous products.

Under the ancien régime Langres maintained a fierce loyalty toward God and king, and remained an effective bastion against all that it

14

considered alien to altar and throne. It never fell under the yoke of the English invader, totally rejected both the League and the Fronde, and, with a severity bordering on the ruthless, repudiated those other blood brothers, the Huguenots.

Montesquieu had reached the age of twenty-four, Voltaire, nineteen, Buffon, six, and Rousseau—who was to be his close friend and unrelenting enemy—was a little more than a year old when Denis Diderot was born in Langres, 5 October 1713. They were to be philosophes all, sharing the aims of the French Enlightenment, but often at variance as to how these aspirations were to be achieved. When Montesquieu died in 1755, Diderot was the only one from the *parti des philosophes* to attend his funeral.

Of the seven children born into the Diderot household, Denis was the oldest survivor. He always remained on excellent terms with his spinster sister, Denise, born in 1715, who, having developed a facial disfigurement, was obliged to wear artificial noses for the rest of her days. But Diderot is the one who set forth in retrospect these family relationships. In 1770, with death but several short years away, he wrote:

One of the things that has given me the most pleasure is the surly remark of a provincial a few years after I had lost my father. I was crossing a street in my native town when he seized me by the arm and said: "Monsieur Diderot you are good; but if you think you will ever be worthy of your father, you are mistaken." I don't know whether fathers are pleased to have children better than they, but I know I was glad to hear it said that my father was better than I. I believe and shall believe as long as I live that this provincial told the truth. My parents left behind an older son who is called Diderot the philosopher; that is me; a daughter who has remained unmarried, and a final child who became a clergyman. It's good stock. The priest is an odd person, but his trivial shortcomings are abundantly compensated for by boundless acts of charity which make him poor in the midst of plenty. I love my sister to distraction, less because she is my sister than because of my appreciation for what is outstanding. . . . Her good deeds remain unknown. Those of the abbé are of public knowledge.[2]

This passage, written in the mellowness of advancing years, is interesting perhaps more for what it does not say than for what it does. Diderot rarely spoke of his mother, eight years older than his father, who died in 1748 while Denis was seeking his fortune in Paris. There is no mention of his sister, Angélique, who, of her own accord, became an

Ursuline nun. She later went mad, and died at the age of twenty-eight. There is little here to suggest the lifelong discord between Denis and his brother, Didier, the canon, repeatedly shocked by the elder brother's bold disrespect for organized religion. Overtones of Diderot's reactions to the lives of Angélique and Didier will be apparent in Diderot's first great novel, *La Religieuse (The Nun)*.

That the three-year-old Denis should have been deeply disturbed upon witnessing the death of a human being at the hands of fellow creatures—a public execution that entertained the gathered crowds—is hardly astonishing. The fact remains that, throughout his life, Diderot deplored his own excess of feeling and, at the same time, man's inhumanity to man. Like many of his fellow philosophes, he was to foresee, at least dimly, the great revolution of 1789, but it is certain he would have rejected the unlooked-for carnage of the Reign of Terror of four years later.

Adolescence and toward Religion Bent

Diderot's elementary education in the form of the three R's undoubtedly took place under the paternal roof. In later years he will say that he learned arithmetic at home; the less complicated basics of reading and writing could have easily been taught by his father, his mother, or one of his uncles, all of whom had a particular interest in the future of this already promising child.

The Diderots, then, were a good, solid middle-class family, and one in which Denis's father and his father before him had brought the craft of cutlery to a high level. They were also pious, and Mme Diderot, Denis's mother, had a number of priests among her relatives. One of these was canon Vigneron, who carried out his clerical duties in the cathedral of Langres. He was getting along in years, and, following the tradition of the day, the good canon was anxious to choose a worthy heir to both his house and to his religious office. Father and uncle agreed that young Denis was admirably suited to inherit these advantageous legacies.

As far as his family was concerned, there was no longer any hesitation as to what course Denis's education should take. Already a most apt pupil, he was, upon the insistence of his parents, enrolled in the Jesuit College of Langres. He immediately demonstrated his superiority as a student and showed himself to be remarkably gifted in Latin and mathematics. It could well have been this period of his youth he was referring to when, the better to refute Helvétius's book, *De l'homme*, in 1773 he recalled an aspect of his early school years. Helvétius maintained in *De l'homme (On Man)*, as he already had in *De l'esprit (On the Mind)* some fifteen years before, that environment was everything, there being no such thing as an aptitude—inherited or inborn—for any human accomplishments. Contrary to Helvétius, Diderot refused to grant that environment explained all. For him, heredity too played its mysterious role as did the equally unfathomable gift of a distinctive talent. Looking back over the years, Diderot, then well into his sixties, had this to say about Helvétius's assertion that no one is born with genius or a particular talent:

Alas! the schools are so full of children so eager for praise, so studious, so determined! No matter how hard they work, torture themselves, occasionally bursting into tears because of their lack of progress, they do not move ahead any faster; while others next to them—flighty, fickle, inattentive, wayward, lazy.—excel without effort. I will never forget you, poor Garnier: your parents were poor, you would shut yourself up in the local churches, you would lower the lamp lighting our altars, the communion table would serve as your desk, you would ruin your eyes and your health all night long; but I would be in a deep sleep, and you never took away the place of honor either from me or from three or four others. (*AT,* 2:340)

But Denis already showed marked signs of independence, strongheadedness, and willful ways—traits that two other great philosophes, Voltaire and Rousseau, also first revealed while still in adolescence. Young Diderot's bit of occasional stubbornness, his lively mind, and his lifelong compulsion to be daringly outspoken brought reprimands from his superiors. This led him to tell his father in no uncertain terms that he had quite lost interest in studying for the priesthood. A disappointed father took Denis out of school and put him to work grinding knives and scissors in the family cutlery. Utterly bored with being an apprentice in the craft of making instruments, no matter how fine, Denis decided that academic study, even under the narrow and exacting tutelage of his Jesuit masters, was preferable by far to the equally confining but much more exasperating life of the workshop. So he returned to his studies and in August 1726—at the age of thirteen— was tonsured, called Monsieur l'Abbé, and donned the appropriate clerical garbs.

Two years later his uncle Vigneron fell ill and died. Notwithstanding his youth, Denis found himself indeed heir to the old canon's secular belongings and religious office. But the cathedral chapter immediately raised objections to taking this overly bright, somewhat difficult, and altogether too youthful abbé into the fold. Here again was another breaking point in his career, and Denis no longer wanted to be a canon. Perhaps, though, he could complete his studies and one day become a Jesuit priest. In this he received encouragement from a friend who was already a member of the order. The two of them had conceived a plan to flee Langres in the dead of night, their destination being a Jesuit seminary in Paris where Diderot could serve his ecclesiastical apprenticeship. Didier Diderot discovered his son's project in the nick of time. After careful family deliberations it was decided that Diderot *père* himself would take Denis to Paris. It was there and not in the bustling provincial town of Langres that his future would take shape.

And so the boy continued his studies at either the prestigious Collège de Louis-le-Grand under the Jesuits or the almost equally important Collège d'Harcourt under the Jansenists—or both. There he honed his wits on rhetoric and philosophy. He came to feel at home in Greek and Roman antiquity and took instruction in logic, physics, ethics, mathematics, and, of course, metaphysics, where Scholastic theology and Aristotelian philosophy were adroitly blended. Denis's precocity in his studies was everywhere apparent; in fact, he was considered *étincelant,* that is, "sparkling." In September 1732 he received the degree of master of arts at the University of Paris—the only philosophe among his compeers to do so.

With his studies concluded, what should he turn to next? He was nineteen, and now had to think of earning a living. He could, as his family suggested, take up a trade. Or, if he wished to continue his studies, there were the admirable professions of law and medicine.

Diderot, though, had not yet reached that stage in his intellectual development where he could discern the fascinations of medicine; that would come later. And the prospect of a career in law filled him with loathing. But his father insisted that he work for an attorney, Clément de Ris. For two years he endured what was for him nothing but legal drudgery; then, protesting that he had no desire to spend the rest of his life with his nose in the affairs of others, he abandoned this employment with no prospects in view.

Father Didier was not in the least disposed to support a son captivated by the heady life of France's capital and who, to all intents and purposes, had become as irresponsible as he was impractical. He was now quite on his own, not always certain where his next meal was coming from. His days of physical, moral, and intellectual bohemianism were at hand.

Chapter Three
The Intellectual Bohemian
Impoverishment and Obscurity

Then as now young men and, upon occasion, young women, born in the provinces and showing unusual promise in one way or another, gravitated to Paris. It was there they would find themselves as writers, artists, musicians, scientists, theologians, actors, and dancers, and even as gilded parasites—or fall by the wayside. Denis Diderot was one of these who answered the beckoning challenge of the nation's capital, perhaps the most dynamic, the most beautiful, and certainly the most resplendent cultural center of eighteenth-century Europe; it was, furthermore, a vast metropolis of about half a million inhabitants, ranking second in size only to London with a population of some 700,000. By comparison Langres, though a cathedral town, had, at the most, ten thousand souls.

Denis had hardly turned fifteen when, as a student, he was first dazzled by the splendors of Paris, its palaces and statues and parks, its chapels and churches, and the profusion of bridges, each with its own architecture, that joined one bank of the Seine with the other, as the river wound past Notre Dame through the heart of the city. The maze of narrow, intertwining streets teemed with humanity from all walks of life. The glittering coaches of the wealthy and titled splashed mud on scholars, clerics, hawkers of wares, shopgirls, on prostitutes and poets, as well as on criminals of all sorts who—like most Parisians—from day to day lived by their wits.

Enterprising though he was, Denis, with his allowance cut off, was now reduced to poverty. Forced to use any means at his disposal to eke out a livelihood, he changed lodgings when rent was overdue and concocted wild schemes for borrowing money. For some three months he was tutor in a well-to-do family but, unable to bear the confinement, let it be known he was available as a hack writer and even willing to write sermons. When possible, his mother, unbeknown to her obdurate husband, sent the family servant Hélène on foot along the endless road to Paris with provisions and whatever funds she could spare.

By 1740 young Diderot was very much a Parisian and well settled in his bohemian ways. There were long walks to take, plays to see, and actors and actresses to become acquainted with. There were hundreds of cafés with their coffee or lemonade to drink, with their journals to read, with the idlers and chess players to watch within and the passersby without. The bookshops scattered throughout the city afforded the opportunity for much browsing and an occasional purchase. Diderot frequented one in particular, leafing through the volumes and flirting unabashedly with the comely salesgirl who was later to become the wife of the painter Greuze. During all this time Diderot, still in his early twenties, lived in almost complete obscurity but managed surprisingly well to keep body and soul together.

The Collision of Two Ideals

In society as in physics, Newton's great law holds true: every action brings forth an equal and opposite action. In France, for centuries, altar and throne had been a dual symbol of stability. But as the reign of Louis XIV drew to a close, Bossuet, the most imposing prelate in the kingdom, thundered the warning that he foresaw the rise of a nefarious Cartesianism bent on undermining the authority and dignity of church and state. His remarks were prophetically true in that one of the chief philosophical procedures laid down by Descartes had been that of *le doute méthodique* (methodical doubt). To cast doubt on the prerogatives of these two imposing institutions of the ancien régime constituted a very real threat to the divine right of kings and other traditional ideals with which France's history was so profoundly imbued.

Certain signs of "methodical doubt" were already manifest in the writings of such early neo-Cartesians as Bayle and Fontenelle, two men who were to have no little influence on the years directly ahead—years later known as the French Enlightenment.

Although Enlightenment was a European ideal, cosmopolitan by nature and strongly averse to notions of nationalism and the fatherland, it stood for a definite revolution in the history of thought and had its clear expression in eighteenth-century France. On the one hand, it manifested itself through the popularization and dissemination of scientific ideas in literary form. On the other, it typified an all-pervasive philosophical and critical spirit that, while seeking new horizons, would limit the arbitrary powers of state and church.

Those in the forefront of the movement were generally referred to as philosophes, even though most of them shunned the construction and elaboration of philosophical systems. They believed that through the use of the experimental method in matters related to science and the free exercise of reason—God-given or not—in all things pertaining to man, human progress, though not necessarily inevitable, had become a distinct possibility. By mid-century, most of the philosophes were to be *encyclopédistes* as well; that is, contributors to the *Encyclopédie,* that stupendous intellectual and publishing enterprise of which one day Diderot—as the philosophe par excellence—would be the driving force.

The first generation of the Enlightenment in France, Voltaire and Montesquieu in particular, had grown up in the shadow of the skepticism of Bayle and Fontenelle, in the science and philosophy of Newton and Locke, and in the works of the great Greek and Roman classics. Montesquieu's boldly critical mind was constantly at work from the early brilliantly satirical *Lettres persanes (Persian Letters)* (1721) to that astounding product of a global mind, *L'Esprit des lois (The Spirit of the Laws)* (1748). The persistent and, in fact, final appeal in both works was to humanity.

A young Voltaire had caused the beau monde to double up with laughter at his unending witticisms and to applaud with enthusiasm his poetry and prose. Then in 1734 his lively, superbly written *Lettres philosophiques,* full of thinly concealed satirical intent directed against French institutions via praise of the English, burst upon an unsuspecting public. The slender volume, as a product of the Enlightenment, proved to be the first notable literary event of eighteenth-century France. It has been called the first bomb hurled against the old order, and, indeed, a warrant was issued for the author's arrest and the book was officially burned.

Voltaire was able to amass a fortune through financial speculation. Since his wealth gave him a novel position in letters, that of the independent writer, he did not have to rely for material survival either on the general public or on king, court, and pensions. Thus, with the passing years, his scintillating pen, his clear, incisive intelligence, and his international repute made him the titular head of that loosely knit group called *Le Parti des philosophes.*

With Voltaire's ascendancy a new generation of philosophes emerged on the scene. They were almost all born in the first or second decade of the 1700s, a coterie of young men, more often than not on the loose, sometimes protected by their title of abbé or secular ecclesiastic, but inevitably drawn to science, philosophy, and journalism, and eager to demolish all prejudices of the day. They were versatile, energetic, intellectually audacious, and numerous. This new generation, consisting of d'Alembert, Condillac, Rousseau, La Mettrie, Helvétius, Diderot, and a host of others, began to write seriously, seizing the attention of the public and the police by the middle of the century.

Diderot, who was to be called by the aging Voltaire another Socrates or Plato, actually earned in the course of his career the sobriquet *le philosophe*. It was a title he would bear to the end of his days with the same pride of accomplishment as Rousseau had in his title *Citoyen de Genève*. Yet, just as Rome was not built in a day, the distinction of being *Monsieur le philosophe* did not come to Diderot overnight.

In the ambience of intellectual bohemianism that marked the 1740s three young men especially were drawn to one another. They were Diderot, Jean-Jacques Rousseau, and the Abbé de Condillac. These three would gather for weekly dinners at the Hôtel du Panier fleuri where they reveled in one another's companionship and in the fervid exchange of ideas; moreover, projects for the future of each were trotted out and warmly discussed. Rousseau had not yet erupted upon the world with his impassioned *Discours sur les sciences et les arts (Discourse on the Sciences and Arts,* 1949). But Condillac would, with his *Essai sur les connaissances humaines (Essay on Human Knowledge,* 1746), soon be acknowledged as the representative of Lockean sensualism on the Continent and, with later works, finally come to be known as the philosophers' philosopher. During these first years of mental effervescence, Diderot was to have a strong influence on Rousseau's thought and even his style—as Jean-Jacques himself later admitted in *Les Confessions.* On the other hand, Condillac's influence on Diderot was to be particularly evident in the latter's spirited *Pensés philosophiques (Philosophical Thoughts,* 1746) and his daring *Lettre sur les aveugles (Letter on the Blind,* 1749), though Diderot's ready mind made this influence mutual. It could not have been otherwise for, among intimates, Diderot was recognized as an incessant fountain of words and ideas, dynamic, amusing, buoyant.

The Way Up

In 1741, at the age of twenty-eight, Diderot's eye had been caught and held by a girl with an exceedingly pretty face and a ravishing figure. Awareness of her existence emphasized the fact that his life should no doubt be more stable and that he could, perhaps, make more of an effort to earn a decent living, for the young libertine had, for the first time, fallen hopelessly in love. Antoinette Champion was three-and-a-half years older than he. By French bourgeois standards it was not a good match for Diderot. She was fatherless, scantily educated, and culturally dim; with her widowed mother, she ran a modest linen shop. Besides she had no dowry. Despite his impecunious circumstances, Diderot was several steps higher on the middle-class social ladder than this young woman in her early thirties who was destined to become his wife. Diderot had suddenly been converted into a very determined suitor for the hand of this presumably lower middle-class bit of femininity who would never be able to follow his demanding thoughts or share his soaring dreams but who might just possibly furnish the steadying influence he so sorely needed.

There is little to go on if we attempt to piece together the ten-year period in Paris following Diderot's decision to give up law.[1] We do know that his first published item was a frivolous poem in 1742 complimenting Baculard d'Arnaud for being irresistible to the fair sex. The genre was exceedingly popular at the time; in all probability young Diderot wrote and published a considerable number of verses of this sort along with equally anonymous dedications, prefaces, and snatches of literary criticism in the gazettes, journals, and miscellanies then flourishing throughout the city.

But any such publishing along with various odd jobs including private lessons in mathematics and sporadic ghostwriting combined to furnish nothing more than a pittance to live on. Diderot was, through sheer necessity, compelled to turn to something else. It was then that he came to public notice as a translator of English works filtering into France from across the Channel.

Of these, Temple Stanyon's *Grecian History* was the first. In the embarrassingly insipid letters[2] he was now dashing off to Antoinette, his "Tonton," his "Nanette," whom he also called—for reasons Freud would understand—his *maman* and his *chère mère,* there is no mention of the translation nor of the fact that he had met and made fast friends with a brilliant young player—none other than Rousseau—across the chessboards of the Café de la Régence.

The *Histoire de Grèce* was introduced to French readers in 1743. Its three volumes published by Briasson show Diderot to be a competent translator even though *Les Nouvelles Littéraires de Berlin* deplored his reluctance to depart from a conservative, overly literal approach. And yet, while Berlin complained of his lack of imagination and Paris of his negligence, a satisfied Briasson again recruited the budding translator with two others to begin work on Robert James's *Medicinal Dictionary*, which was encyclopedic both in length and in scope.[3]

This was a notable enterprise for a young writer on his way up in a world of philosophical and scientific inquiry.[4] Along with other sciences, the science of medicine was taking great strides forward both in England and on the Continent. James's multivolume compendium was in itself a protracted and exacting course in medical science for anyone attempting its translation. It must have had an impact on Diderot's future *Encyclopédie* both in form and content. And it might well have helped engender insights especially evident in such major posthumous works of Diderot as *Le Neveu de Rameau*, *Le Rêve de d'Alembert* (*D'Alembert's Dream*), and *Les Eléments de physiologie* (*The Elements of Physiology*). In any event, the six-volume translation, whose abbreviated title was *Dictionnaire universel de Médecine*, and which appeared in print between 1746 and 1748, did add lustre to a name that, though still associated with intellectual and social bohemianism, was slowly coming into its own.

Meanwhile, there were new developments in Diderot's career. He had long since abandoned the subterfuge—the better to frequent Mme Champion and her daughter—that he was in need of linen before embarking on studies for the priesthood at Saint-Sulpice. He was now on intimate terms with Antoinette. But for a young man to marry before the age of thirty in eighteenth-century France required a number of indispensible formalities, the most urgent of which was to obtain his father's consent. The law provided for disinheritance of a recalcitrant son.

It was agreed that Diderot should return to Langres to win parental approval. There under the family roof he wrote letters of encouragement to his fiancée. She learned that he was correcting proof for his translation of Stanyan and that both parents were impressed; obviously he had begun to lead a useful life in Paris. The future philosophe continued to make an excellent impression while biding his time. At last he solicited his father's permission to marry, but the elder Diderot flatly refused and on 1 February 1743 wrote a strong, eloquent letter to Mme Champion stating why his son and her daughter should not and could not be husband and wife. Denis defied parental authority and, in consequence, was put under lock and key in a monastery. Making good his escape, he was back in Paris and in Antoinette's arms by winter's end. At midnight on 6 November 1743 the couple was secretly married, but the family in Langres was not to learn this for several years. The father, again on good terms with what was to all appearances an obedient and industrious son who promised well for the future, had forgotten completely about disowning his eldest child.

The Fledgling Philosophe

To set up housekeeping with his Nanette, Diderot had to give constant thought to a livable income. Once married, the family would be expanding rapidly enough. Indeed, in August 1744 a daughter, the first of four children, was born; she lived less than a month. The trials of domesticity were already apparent.

With his *Histoire de Grèce* behind him and the translation of James's volumes lying well ahead, Diderot turned to the task directly at hand, of introducing to the French—but in his own way—the Earl of Shaftesbury's *Inquiry concerning Virtue and Merit*. The choice was significant for a number of reasons. Shaftesbury's ideas, in particular his system of ethics, having already appealed to such free spirits as Bolingbroke, Hutcheson, Pope, and Hume in England, and Voltaire and Montesquieu in France, were sure to appeal to second-generation philosophes like Diderot.

It was a decorous, poised philosophy based on reason and psychological experience, uncluttered by universals and the subtle distinctions of Scholasticism; furthermore, it was marked by religious tolerance. Its express purpose was to rectify contemporary speculation on human conduct through a functional analysis of virtue. But in the process it gave vent to a number of unorthodox ideas. These included the notion that if virtue has no meaning outside the social sphere, neither does good or evil. Similarly, no philosophical proposition or religious tenet is good or bad in itself. Belief in them is justified if they generate social action that is warranted by moral rectitude.

Such ideas, along with Shaftesbury's affirmation of the passions, his concept of the universe as a great whole, his doctrine that the useful is good, were, as Franco Venturi has noted, so many *centres d'enthousiasme* in nature, in art, and in man, that would appear time and again in Diderot's works.[5]

But Diderot modified Shaftesbury's *Inquiry* in various ways. He played down the English philosopher's optimism and theism, while rejecting his belief in the innateness of aesthetic notions. Even in terms of style, Diderot modified the *Inquiry*. Anxious to remain on peaceful terms with orthodox institutions, he carefully cloaked Shaftesbury's critiques of church and state in orientalism or in references to classical history, philosophy, and literature and, in general, reshaped the material into a more conservative product through the use of footnotes, dialogues, apostrophes, and questions.

In a sense, then, the *Essai* should neither be considered as an original work of Diderot's nor as a translation. Rather, it is a paraphrase, a product of Diderot's ability to seize upon an entire mode of thinking indigenous to his times and, through individual application, give it a new meaning. It is a method he often followed in writing. He knew how to adapt to his own ideas, sentences, whole developments belonging to others, and give them his very personal touch and often his own stamp of genius. We shall repeatedly see this approach in works to follow. In the present instance, the finished product bore the title *Principes de la philosophie morale, ou Essai de M. S*** sur le mérite et la vertu, avec Réflexions (Principles of Ethical Philosophy, or Essay of Mr. S. on Merit and Virtue with Reflections)*. The purported place and date of publication were Amsterdam, 1745, but the author's name did not appear, there being the danger that a treatise with stress on natural instead of religious morality might not sit well with the French authorities. The work was received with lively interest and widely read. By the age of thirty-two Diderot had taken a positive step into the field of philosophy; there would be no turning back. But another step, taken at the same time, was more personally irrevocable.

The dedicatory letter of the *Essai* was addressed to Diderot's younger brother, Didier-Pierre, who had genuinely felt the call to holy orders and, at that very time, was absorbed in studying for the priesthood in Paris. He was an ardently pious and provokingly intransigent young man. Consequently the *dédicace* "To My Brother" from a "philosopher pledging brotherly love," betrays an irony or a touch of mischief. Thus Denis, too, could adopt a tone of self-righteousness and here, in so doing, he proceeded to give an ill-concealed lesson in tolerance and understanding that, to be sure, fell on deaf ears.

Diderot when young had turned to the church hoping for an inheritance or for an extended education or—as in Paris—hoping to ward off hunger. The spiritual had little to do with any of these transient inclinations. Such was not the case with his brother, who was set on devoting his life to the Church Triumphant while Denis shifted to deism, then veered toward materialistic atheism. The two brothers had by 1745 developed the affinity of negative and positive forces—the one for and the other against the church, its teachings, and its dictates. Denis was to be continually outraged by his younger brother's single-minded ways of laying down the spiritual law, while the priest developed a bitter hostility to the older brother's free-ranging mind. Peace and understanding between them were henceforth to be wholly impossible. For the rest of their days the one would fervently and unflinchingly carry out his duties in the name of organized religion, while the other, believing that doubt was the beginning of wisdom, sought for truth by questioning and testing his own theories in all domains as well as the ideas and systems of his fellow men.

Chapter Four
Years of Commitment

Working and Loving

With the *Histoire de Grèce* Diderot had come into his own as a translator; with the adaptation of Shaftesbury's treatise on virtue he revealed himself to be a provocative writer and, perhaps, a potential philosopher as well. More offers to translate were forthcoming, but a new urgency was welling up in him; it was the desire to seek, if not to find, all the answers to the overwhelming questions of being and becoming.

His multifaceted, ever-fluctuating mind was thinking more and more in terms of philosophy, the theater, fiction, history, science, and also in terms of the reality and illusion of human existence. He wanted to get these ideas down on paper and into print so that he could share them with others who helped make up the contemporary scene. For the next decade or so all that he worked on was intended to have an immediate impact on the living. Publishing what he had written—whether an article, an essay, or a book, signed or not—was a commitment to his age. In a word, he was impatient to create an identity for himself and his contemporaries. He had become, as the French would say, *engagé.*

This impetus did not come solely from his ever-increasing interest in philosophy under its varied guises. There were other—some might say less elevated—factors that were at work as well—the love or infatuation for a woman, for instance. In his free translation of the *Inquiry* Diderot makes the point more clearly than Shaftesbury had done concerning those males who spurned the company of the opposite sex. He even goes so far as to associate *condemnation* and *tempérament dépravé* with any man—ecclesiastics and saints excepted—who is not drawn to women, or as he put it, to *le commerce des femmes* (*AT,* 1:29).

Throughout his life Diderot was brash, sensitive, intelligent, gifted, and in need of love. In one of his later, great works, the novel *Jacques le fataliste,* the distinction between *amour* (love) and *amourettes* (passing fancies) will be fully delineated. By the time of his courtship and clandestine marriage he had already had ample experience with these two aspects of love. How far and in what detail he was to carry his predilection for the *beau sexe* we can only guess, for, with the passing years, he became a man of many masks. By eighteenth-century standards, though, what indications we do have suggest that he did not push to an extreme any inclinations or advantages he may have had. That somewhere along the way he had become remarkably perceptive in feminine psychology is especially evident in the novels *La Religieuse* and the aforementioned *Jacques,* in some three or four scintillating short stories, and certainly in his delightful little essay on women appropriately entitled "Sur les femmes."

After several years of a frustrating and at times wretched marriage with its limiting existence, Diderot began looking for someone else, a woman with whom he could share some of the many ideas that were always racing through his mind—preferably one who would be a solace to him and who would have interests of her own that he could share as well. Such a woman he thought he had found in Mme de Puisieux, with her literary aspirations and a willingness to become the mistress of the brilliant and still young Denis. They may have met late in 1745 while he was cotranslator with her pedestrian husband, and he may have seemed just the covert yet talented collaborator she required for both the edifying works and the fictional romances she had in view.

In point of fact, at the most there were only four women toward whom he was to demonstrate with some steadfastness his ideal of a man in love: a loving, warmhearted, appreciative, virile being, offering and seeking both affectionate companionship and sexual fulfillment. His wife, despite her cultural shortcomings, her shrewish tongue, and her domestic practicality, was nevertheless to remain his companion to the end of his days. His debt to her was considerable, for she succeeded in keeping at least partially in line this husband who was at once impetuous, gregarious, imprudent, elemental, complex, and enormously gifted. Then there was the blonde, self-seeking, slightly unscrupulous Mme de Puisieux, to whom he was also indebted: her constant demands on his pocketbook forced him to compose with great speed, under considerable pressure, and for a quick sale one or two of his early works that might otherwise never have been written. There was also the charming, middle-aged widow, Mme de Maux, who remains a vague, even shadowy figure among eighteenth-century biographers. This turned out to be an abortive liaison that revealed to Diderot how ridiculous an engrossing infatuation could make an aging man, no matter how exceptional and accomplished he might be. Still, it was to give him a new awareness of passion and devotion; of the amalgam of sexuality and tender sensuality; in short, of love in all its complexity. This experience resulted in several absorbing dialogues and *contes* written late in life and revealing a still greater understanding of the broad spectrum of rational and emotional relationships between man and woman.

But ultimately only one woman was the object of an abiding, deeply felt love in any true sense of the term. To others, she was the stereotype forty-year-old spinster with glasses, when he met her in 1755. To him, however, Sophie Volland combined the best qualities of male and female. Out of this relationship that, in one form or another, lasted for a quarter of a century until her death shortly before his own, there came from Diderot's pen a correspondence that included some of the most intimate, some of the most eloquent, some of the most interesting letters written during a great age of letter writing. What her letters contained we shall unfortunately never know. But his pages to her give the feeling that this great love of Diderot's life turned him into the free spirit and the man of unassailable integrity he had earlier merely given the promise of becoming.

From the first days of their marriage, Mme Diderot held a firm grip on the family purse strings. The story goes that when her husband took his daily respite of an hour or two at the Café de la Régence for conversation and to watch the chess games, she would uncomplainingly dole out the six sous for his coffee. Mme Diderot's care in handling his scanty and unsteady earnings was a boon. Another child was on the way, expenses for food and lodging were a constant drain, and Diderot's desperation for regular wages, no matter how meager, was becoming more acute.

The possibility for such an income was in the offing, although the Diderot ménage was not yet aware of the fact. Plans were under way to launch a French translation of Ephraim Chambers's *Cyclopaedia, or Universal Dictionary of the Arts and Sciences* (1728). The government under Louis XV issued the necessary *privilège,* and in 1746 the editorship was given over to the Abbé Gua de Malves, with Diderot (still little more than a translator) and his friend d'Alembert (the illegitimate son of Mme de Tencin and soon to be one of the mathematical geniuses of the age) chosen to supervise the project.

The plan to translate Chambers's five volumes was now broadened to include additional and original articles. The printing and publishing house of Le Breton joined forces with three other large publishers to share the mounting expenses and added responsibility. The abbé, realizing his incompetence, withdrew, and the editorship was given to d'Alembert, particularly for the mathematical articles, and to Diderot for the rest. The Diderot household was now assured of an annual income of twelve hundred livres a year until further notice. These initial steps were to lead to the greatest publishing venture of the century, with much of the responsibility resting on Diderot's shoulders. Part of the credit for this change in Diderot's fortunes was due to his wife's clearheaded insistence on increased domestic and financial stability for the family.

Meanwhile Mme de Puisieux had insinuated herself into Diderot's emotional and intellectual life to the extent that she too looked for the financial benefits that might come from a nimble brain and an expert pen. Thus we are inclined to believe Mme de Vandeul's *Mémoires* when she says that her father wrote his first original work of any consequence— the *Pensées philosophiques*—over the weekend of Easter, 1746, which would fetch him fifty pieces of gold—a veritable windfall for Mme de Puisieux (*AT,* 1:xliii).

A Note of Modernity

If the unsigned *Pensées philosophiques* was composed with great speed, it was also written exceedingly well. Friend and foe alike attributed the work to some practiced hand—Voltaire, perhaps, or La Mettrie or even Condillac. The book was condemned by the Parlement of Paris in July 1746, and bundles of old papers were burned in its place by the chief executioner—a common practice when copies of the condemned book were not readily available. This gesture of civil and religious authority added to the popularity of the work already being widely and enthusiastically read.

If it had an attractive literary sheen, far more important was the fact that it was full of what were at the time dangerously engrossing ideas. Its very title, with the word *philosophiques* in it, like the same adjective in Voltaire's equally sensational *Lettres philosophiques,* was a promise of unorthodoxy to some and a warning of heterodoxy to others. In point of fact, the very first series of *pensées* was a rehabilitation of the passions: and all good Christians at that time knew that the passions do not direct the soul along the path to spiritual salvation. But typically, shockingly, and with a touch of anger, Diderot wrote in the first of his sixty-two *Pensées:*

We are constantly railing against the passions; to them we ascribe all of man's afflictions while forgetting that they are the source of all pleasures. . . . But what provokes me is that only their adverse side is considered. . . . And yet only passions and great passions can raise the soul to great things. Without them the sublime no longer exists either in morals or in creativity. (*AT,* 1:127)

Many of the issues discussed in the *Pensées philosophiques* may strike the present-day reader as merely intellectual commonplaces, and there are those who will say that the critical thinking therein is still all too often imprisoned in old-fashioned, even stale formats. Nevertheless, a note of modernity can be perceived in these *Pensées.* There is, for instance, the free-swinging form joining thought to substance with results that would not be uncongenial to the disciples of a modern critic like Roland Barthes.

Three main points can be extracted from the work. As we have seen, the first of these is a defense of the passions or, more exactly, an attempt to view biological and psychological man with greater understanding. The second is ostensibly a relentless attack against fanaticism, superstition, and religious dogma, but in reality, against any highly organized, stultifying force or forces. The third point, itself very much with us today, is that adherence to any faith, whether it is a personal or a group conviction, should pass through the necessary process of critical reasoning. There is a clear suggestion here, indeed modern in its implications, that for each individual as for each group, there is—between the rigid, unyielding principles of established institutions that have lost their usefulness and the unprincipled modes of individual or general anarchy—a vast middle area where true humanism can live and move and have its being.

Like those of us born in the twentieth century, Diderot found himself in a world where he was surrounded by people, books, and social, religious, and political movements, all claiming to have the answers to the general and particular problems of human existence. In his judgment, it was neither necessary nor expedient to strive to learn through some man-made organized ascendancy who we are, where we came from, why we were born, or how we are to achieve some measure of happiness in this life. It is up to the individual, however, to try to seek out the truth, and derive some satisfaction from finding sufficient meaning in the search itself. Diderot begins his twenty-ninth *pensée* by saying: "It should be insisted upon that I look for the truth, but not that I find it" (*AT*, 1:140). This maxim was to guide him throughout his life. In his search for truth the still youthful author of the *Pensées philosophiques* tells us that each individual has only one real guide. It is *la petite lumière* (glimmer) of his reason set in motion by the drive of his passions. Only in this way can we depend upon the accuracy of our own perceptions and feelings rather than upon the opinions of others, unless by chance these opinions strike a sympathetic chord and can also be verified by experience.

In this early work Diderot already shows the capacity to cut through jargon and sophistry—no matter what form they may take—and to test the validity of conflicting propositions by considering their practical consequences. Over the entire work there hovers a deep relevance to twentieth-century problems. Diderot insists upon intellectual and emotional self-reliance in the face of authority, whether it be authority grounded in past tradition or in the monolithic mass-thinking of the totalitarian approach. There is, then, throughout the pages of the *Pensées* the plea—sometimes hidden, sometimes overt—to preserve and even develop one's intellectual and emotional identity in the face of the authoritarian antagonist, whatever form he or it may take.

The work, despite its condemnation, was on the whole a circumspect little book, and the fifty-first *pensée* is even a profession of Catholicism. Still, the censor easily perceived the latent danger lurking in the book, and the *Addition* that appeared in the 1770 edition of the *Pensées* contains passages reminiscent of Voltaire at his most satirical. Each remark reveals certain of Diderot's notions pushed to their extreme conclusions. One of the more innocuous additions was "Lost in an immense forest at night, I have but a small light to show me the way. A stranger approaches me and says, 'My friend, blow out your candle in order to find your way.' This stranger is a theologian" (*AT*, 1:159). And another: "The Christian God is a father who prizes his apples but sets little value on his children" (*AT*, 1:160).

Such remarks would have been out of the question in the 1740s, a decade during which Diderot was in imminent danger of being reprehended for much less.

Philosophical and Literary Indiscretions

The translation and adaptation of Shaftesbury's treatise had not been overly compromising. But the reception by the Paris law courts of

Diderot's own *Pensées philosophiques* showed that, even in publishing them anonymously, he had been flirting with imprudence and even with danger. He was now pondering a new work full of indiscreet and, at times, impudent overtones. Obviously the author had reached the stage where he thought he could judge what would be suppressed by the censor and what would not. In consequence, *La Promenade du sceptique (The Skeptic's Walk)*, though completed by 1747, was held back and only appeared posthumously. This was just as well, for the budding philosophe, though not yet aware of the fact, was already in bad odor with both civil and ecclesiastical authority. In June 1747 a police lieutenant attached to the government mint, Perrault by name, denounced Diderot to the lieutenant-general of police, Berryer, as a wretch *(un misérable)* and "a very dangerous man who speaks of the mysteries of religion with a scorn that is conducive to the corruption of morals." This was shortly followed by a letter from the parish priest of Saint-Médard that went into greater detail concerning Diderot's intellectual, moral, and spiritual behavior *(Corr,* 1:53–54). Had the *Promenade du sceptique* been available, they would no doubt have argued that its contents bore them out.

La Promenade is a revealing minor work comprising a *Discours préliminaire* and three chapters cast in the form of an allegory, a genre in which Diderot did not excel. It has generally been held to be Diderot's last work composed under the direct influence of Shaftesbury. Such a conclusion requires some modification. An equally important fact has gone comparatively unnoticed: that the direct and indirect influence of the British philosopher George Berkeley (1685–1753) plays a considerable role, probably surpassing that of Shaftesbury, in the composition of *La Promenade*. In the *Discours préliminaire,* Cléobule-Diderot suggests that his own series of dialogues could be conceived in the manner of "Barclay" *(AT,* 1:185).[1]

Among the *philosophes* only Voltaire and Diderot had been aware before 1750 of Berkeley's charming dialogue, *Alciphron or the Minute Philosopher* (1732). Although in Diderot's *Promenade du sceptique* the name "Alciphron"—standing for "strong head" or "skeptic" in ancient Greek and in Berkeley—appears only once, *sceptique* dominates his title, and Alciphron's part is established at the outset. We are there told that "young Alciphron" offers his services as arbiter in the ensuing discussion on the worlds of revealed religion, of society, and of philosophy. These are precisely the topics around which the seven dialogues of Berkeley's *Alciphron* revolve.

Points of comparison between *La Promenade* and *Alciphron* could be multiplied showing that, both stylistically and in subject matter, Diderot tried to follow Berkeley more closely than the less inspiring Shaftesbury. The divergent viewpoints on theology are immediately obvious; still one can spell out the similarities in the initial rural setting, in the satirical portraits, in illustrations of points made, and even, now and then, in the very phraseology used.[2]

Cléobule speaks of the three paths—in reality the three modes of living—that lead us to our final resting place. Carefully scrutinizing the orthodox Christian, as well as the philosophical and the hedonistic modes of life, he has the path of thorns represented by religion; worldly sensual pleasure is found along the path of flowers. Both paths are unattractive— though the path of flowers less so—because they lead to extremes of bigotry and fanaticism, or to those of inconsistency, self-indulgence, and voluptuousness. But philosophy's path is the *allée des marroniers* (under the chestnut trees); only by joining those congregated under the chestnut trees—deists, atheists, skeptics, and idealists, including, in thin disguise, Shaftesbury and Berkeley—can one find relative peace and contentment. As we shall see, however, there will be times when the philosophers will wander into the path of flowers, and the pleasure seekers into the chestnut grove.

There would have been nothing edifying in such a book where the Sorbonne or the police were concerned. Diderot had written about three allegorical paths, but he himself was now walking on a narrowing road toward persecution from which there would be no way back.

The *allée des fleurs* of *La Promenade du sceptique* was less a place for strolling than a large garden where the five senses were indulged and sexual frivolity gave the upper hand to ladies as fickle as they were enticing. The theme of sexual love arising in these pages will become a leitmotiv in a number of Diderot's great works yet to be written: *La Religieuse, Le Neveu de Rameau, Le Rêve de d'Alembert, Le Supplément au voyage de Bougainville,* and, of course, certain of the *contes.*

Diderot was, at the age of thirty-five, little more than an apprentice in literary eroticism, but sufficiently captivated by the subject to be considered in the complete sense of the term *un philosophe libertin*— the apt title of part 2 of Jean Pommier's excellent little study, *Diderot avant Vincennes.*[3] Mme de Puisieux, ten years younger than Diderot's wife, had presumably questioned his assertion that with a suitable fictional device nothing was easier than to write a licentious novel in the manner of the then fashionable Crébillon *fils.*

In response to the challenges the *Bijoux indiscrets* (often translated into English as *The Indiscreet Toys*) came into being in a fortnight. Once again Diderot or the demanding Mme de Puisieux—or both— had pocket money, this time to the extent of fifty louis (*AT,* 1:xlii).

Writers of the French Enlightenment have frequently been depicted as moving into their later years deeply regretting their early literary sins. There is ample evidence that Montesquieu, with death drawing near and a Christian burial devoutly hoped for, expressed his profound sorrow that he had been reckless enough to write the *Lettres persanes* some thirty years before. Voltaire, author of *La Pucelle (The Maiden),* a burlesque poem on Joan of Arc that aroused the indignation of French patriots, declared in his correspondence that it was a sign of youth and that "never had a maiden so maddened an old man." Rousseau, in his *Confessions,* declared that all his misfortunes stemmed from his "First Discourse." Diderot is often quoted as having told his friend Naigeon that he would gladly lose a finger could he thereby cause *Les Bijoux*— this *"grande sottise"* (colossal stupidity)—to disappear forever. But it is difficult to take Diderot seriously, for about the time he made this declaration to Naigeon, he added three new chapters to his "novel."

It has been common practice to dismiss the fictional part of the book as tedious and stereotyped to an extreme. Diderot utilized a fantasy first introduced into the literature of the Middle Ages and employed in a narrative presumably by the Comte de Caylus as late as 1747; it consisted in having the private parts of the *beau sexe* speak out under given conditions.

In Diderot's tenuous plot Mongogul (Louis XV), a sultan in the Congo (France), bored with court life and uneasy about the fidelity of his favorite, Mirzoza (Mme de Pompadour), hopes to see this ennui and this gnawing doubt dissipated when a genie presents him with a magic ring. If the ring is directed toward a particular lady, it seals her mendacious lips while obliging the most intimate part of her body to talk with utter frankness.

This is the most frequently published but the least respected of Diderot's works, though not necessarily because of Thomas Carlyle's observation that it is "the beastliest of all dull novels, past, present and future."[4]

The opinion that, when the *Bijoux* was first composed, Diderot was walking "in the subterranean shades of Rascaldom," strikes the modern reader as excessive. The novel was doubtless liberally seasoned with ribaldry, but by no stretch of the imagination could it be considered erotic. Diderot was endowed with a gift for satire reminiscent both of Rabelais and of Jonathan Swift. And, as was so often the case in later works—the *Neveu de Rameau* immediately comes to mind—the satire in the *Bijoux* was multipronged. In fact, the objects of Diderot's barbs are almost inexhaustible as they present a collection of living tableaux, an animated portrait gallery, where contemporary customs, practices, and morals are paraded before the reader's eyes. Some of these vignettes are light and even frivolous, others are far more serious than first meets the eye. Still others are often interspersed with allegories both sober and farcical.

Essentially the novel is pornographic but with satirical intent. It reveals a well-educated, independent thinker of the rising bourgeoisie increasingly discontented with and antagonistic toward altar and throne. Louis XV, like his predecessors, ruled France according to the principle of the divine right of kings, and so received the all-out support of the church. In real life he was far more interested in reading the weekly reports especially prepared for him by the chief of Paris police on the moral indiscretions of members of the court and other notables, than in perusing administrative tracts on economics, sociology, education, international relations, taxes, and malfeasance.

As the sultan of Diderot's novel he remained quite true to form, less interested in ruling his country and showing concern for his subjects than in relieving boredom through titillating accounts of the adventures and sexual practices of the upper classes of his realm. The king's own sexual proclivities were already clearly marked by 1748, and Diderot strongly hints as much. It was not until 1755, however, that Louis procured the "Parc-aux-Cerfs," a small "pleasure dome" at Versailles where, with a sort of royal harem composed of carefully selected nymphets, he could find respite from his official love affairs. Under the aegis of Louis "The Well Beloved" scandalous reality far surpassed the fictional imaginations of Diderot's licentious novel.

The *Bijoux* is revolutionary in that it is a fairly early example of the relationship between pornography, obscenity, and even blasphemy on the one hand and the political and religious arm of society on the other. Such works multiplied greatly as the old regime drew to a close. In palmier days there had been basic agreement between the ruler and the governed predicated on the conviction that a harmonious relationship was advantageous to both parties. Once the ruled decided that the ruler

was no longer worthy of the authority vested in him, all signs of moral
turpitude on his part were underscored and even magnified. Throughout
the reign of Louis XV the government had alienated significant sections
of the population. These, in turn, criticized, sometimes with a con-
spiratorial smile, the king and his government. Intellectually the reign
of Louis XV was a period of ferment; politically it was an age of
intrigue, mismanagement, corruption, and indifference. The so-called
scatological aspects of Diderot's novel should not be too lightly dismissed;
they are a devastating attack on the established order and, more
specifically, they show a king far more interested in the boudoir than
in the council chamber.

On the other side of the coin, those chapters that for some readers
more or less justify the book's existence despite the explicit emphasis
on sex are few in number. Diderot himself calls chapter 29 "perhaps
the best and the least read of this story"; it is neither one nor the
other. It is a fanciful plea for experience or experimentation (both
meanings are in the French word *expérience*) to loom up like a growing
giant and cause the colonnades of mere hypotheses to crumble before
its advance. Diderot is taking early and elementary steps in the world
of the philosophy of science. But there is little that is new to the age
here except the allegorical presentation. More modern and more significant
is an appended chapter entitled "Des Voyageurs" dealing with an
experimental approach to the selection of couples so that married
happiness can be assured. These are pages that foreshadow present-day
studies both in technique and in subject matter. Modern, too, is the
often neglected penultimate chapter of the novel which, in its analysis
of platonic love, underlines the natural animality of man in unrelenting
conflict with what is often an artificial and misplaced spirituality.

Among several other chapters, the most challenging to today's reader
are the two on the location of the "soul." The conceit that the animating
spirit of each individual finally settles in a particular part of the body
is derived from Matthew Prior's Hudibrastic poem *Alma, or The Progress
of the Mind* (1718). *Alma* mocks Cartesianism and Descartes's metaphysical ideas on the spiritual by having the soul reside in the legs of
a dancer, in the stomach of the glutton, in the sexual organs of the
libertine, in the head of the serious philosopher, and the like. Diderot
appropriates the conceit and carries it to certain ultimate and startling
conclusions in such later works as the *Rêve de d'Alembert*. As handled
by Diderot it is, then, far more than an allegory satirizing metaphysics,
as some have thought.[5]

The novel appeared anonymously with the place of publication listed as Monomolapa (in reality, Paris). But within the year it was widely known that the up-and-coming philosophe was its author. Diderot had committed his first outrageous indiscretion; others would follow.

The influence of the *Arabian Nights* then in vogue throughout Europe was evident in *Les Bijoux*. Sultans holding court, genii displaying their magic, alien place names—all were part of Diderot's stock in trade and were essential to the plot of his first novel. *L'Oiseau blanc, conte bleu* was, in the same year (1748), another attempt of Diderot's to exploit this popular genre where allegory, wizardry, and the fantastic blended with hidden references to the contemporary French notables to form a bizarre tale.

Perhaps one day this banal story of a Japanese prince turned into a pigeon by a sorcerer, but again becoming the emperor's son when touched by the wand of the fairy "Truth," will unlock certain of Diderot's aesthetic and intellectual secrets that still remain hidden. This has happened with other of his works and, at times, magnificently. But, for the present at least, it appears unlikely that the tale of the White Bird has anything startlingly interesting to offer. One of Diderot's poorest literary attempts, it takes its place beside Montesquieu's *Le Temple de Gnide* among contemporary stories of flimsy fact and exotic fantasy. Among the philosophes only Voltaire, especially in his tale *Zadig*, could represent this philosophico literary genre in all its perfection. When the police learned that Diderot had written *L'Oiseau blanc*, they assumed that it would be a sequel to *Les Bijoux*, hence a dangerously scabrous work of political and social satire, and they tried to lay hands on the manuscript. It eluded them, however, and did not appear in print until 1798, some fifteen years after Diderot's death. It added nothing to his posthumous fame.

The year 1748 was an actively varied one for Diderot's mind and pen. The *Bijoux* reeked with the moral decay of king and court, but it also hinted at the possible scurrility of its author. To offset such criticism Diderot set to work on an entirely different sort of writing. The result was the *Mémoires sur differens sujets de mathématiques (Memoranda on Various Mathematical Subjects)*, in every respect inoffensive to police and public alike. Besides, the work was a clear enough indication that its author was sufficiently serious and learned to be the associated publishers' selection as director of the enormous and costly enterprise, the *Encyclopédie*.

The *Mémoires,* brought out in a deluxe edition, took up such questions as vibrating bodies and the science of sound, the realization of a complex, unconventional compass, the tension of cords, a novel type of organ, and the evaluation of atmospheric pressure on pendulums. The work, some two hundred and fifty pages in length, was a far cry from the episodes of the "indiscreet jewels." Furthermore, it served its purpose, for it was very favorably received and proved that Diderot was a mechanistically ingenious as well as a remarkably perceptive geometrician. Besides, he had an excellent grasp of earlier mathematical literature,[6] though his own role in mathematics has been sorely misunderstood.[7]

Like a number of his fellow philosophes Diderot was temporarily drawn to and showed a certain aptitude for mathematics. Isaac Newton, who enunciated laws of attraction that astounded all Europe, and who, together with Leibniz, invented calculus, continued to exert an influence on science over the whole Continent, though thirty years had now passed since his death. Diderot was to persist in writing on mathematics as late as 1761, although in a famous letter to Voltaire in 1759 he wrote: "The reign of mathematics is over. There has been a change of taste. The life sciences and literature are now in the forefront" (*Corr,* 1:38). This would soon be so not only for Diderot, but for Rousseau, Voltaire, and Buffon as well.

Caught in the Web

Although living the relatively inconspicuous life of a sturdy French bourgeois since his marriage in 1743, as early as the *Pensées philosophiques* Diderot had begun to think dangerously. It was a proclivity he would evidence to the end of his days. This would, in the eyes of church and state, be his fatal flaw. If, by 1749, he was well known to the police, none of his writings had as yet brought down the wrath of the authorities upon his head. But now he was engaged in a work that showed him to be a master of philosophical dialogue with its spirited give-and-take. It also showed that he could appropriate psychological concepts and scientific discoveries that were an important part of the contemporary European thought and, through his inquiring turn of mind, twist them into materialistic channels perilous to the salvation of the Christian reader's soul.

Several of Diderot's early philosophical works were concerned with the acquisition of knowledge and especially with the problem of communication. This is particularly true of what proved to be his notorious

Letter on the Blind that, complete with its ironic subtitle, reads in French: *Lettre sur les aveugles à l'usage de ceux qui voient.*

Since Descartes it has been intellectually fashionable to speculate on the cognitive value of the senses. William Molyneux, John Locke, and George Berkeley, British thinkers all, had indulged in much speculation on the acquisition of knowledge through sight or with the impediment of blindness. Furthermore, by 1728, the whole Continent knew of Dr. Cheselden's well-publicized account of his operation on a boy of fourteen for congenital cataract, an account that was undeniably dramatic, scientifically challenging, and full of human interest.

Cheselden's report and the problems of those born blind was what Diderot's probing, empirical mind yearned after rather than recent highly speculative studies such as those of his close friend Condillac, who in 1746 had endowed a statue with one sense at a time.

So far this would seem perfectly proper and gave no cause for alarm to traditionalists in politics, religion, or the sciences. But the man under surveillance was Diderot who, while believing in living conservatively, also believed in thinking boldly. It was impossible to foresee where his thoughts would carry him.

The philosophe's previous inquiries had led him to reach a definite materialism that would be all the more manifest in the *Lettre sur les aveugles,* a work that would also cover a wider field than anything he had written hitherto. In this new phase of his philosophical development Diderot posed difficult questions and sought satisfactory explanations for the theory of knowledge, the philosophy of nature, and even for the origin of the universe. Much that was to appear in the philosophy of his subsequent writings would be a development of the seminal ideas already taking shape in these pages. The *Lettre* pursues two general themes that are closely connected one with the other—perhaps at the express wish of the author—and that become hopelessly intertwined. The first of these is a study of those who are born blind and must rely on other senses, in particular that of touch, for an understanding of themselves and the world they live in. For the blind, seeing is *not* believing. Unencumbered by what is acquired through sight, a person deprived of vision since birth is, Diderot discovered, a good judge of symmetry. Furthermore, accustomed to his condition, a blind man— except for his curiosity regarding sight—would rather have longer arms or some other extended sense of touch than sight.

Diderot deplores the fact that reading through touch alone has yet to be conceived. After noting what a particular blind man had to offer on the psychology of the sightless he goes into a discussion of how the blind get ideas of figures, especially in the field of mathematics. A taut thread, for instance, gives the concept of a straight line. He then goes into detail about how a blind mathematician uses what we might call a crude pre-Braille system representing numbers to arrive at spectacularly new mathematical theories.

Even these aspects of the *Lettre* suggest that we have here the first truly scientific study of blindness. But the second theme goes still further as it examines the possible moral and metaphysical ideas of an individual born blind. Knowing no physical modesty, he is unable to understand why some parts of the body may be exposed to view while it is sinful to reveal others. Stealing, for obvious reasons, is a far more serious crime to one devoid of sight. Already Diderot is expressing his alarming views on the relativity of ethical and metaphysical notions, a most disturbing subject for the eighteenth-century establishment. But this is not all. A sightless person can easily remain untouched by the popular deistic argument of the day that the visible marvels of nature bear witness to the presence of a Divine Creator.

Diderot presents two case histories where psychological facts concerning the blind are brought to the surface. The first of these is based on the opportunity afforded him to question closely a certain blind man from the town of Puiseaux and thus learn a quantity of intimate details concerning the sightless, their reactions to themselves and to the world around them. The second case bears on Nicholas Saunderson (1682–1739), professor of mathematics and physics at the University of Cambridge who, despite being born blind, had had a remarkable career in his chosen field. In both cases Diderot, resorting to philosophical propaganda, speculates on whether the sightless, who do not have the same perceptions, ideas, and feelings as those who see, can nevertheless have the same moral standards and the same religion. He answers this to his own satisfaction—most dramatically and in his own way—by staging an eloquent and entirely imaginary deathbed scene where the dying Saunderson reveals his deep skepticism and a materialism bordering on atheism.

In an astounding flight of scientific imagination Diderot has Saunderson reject the concepts of order, purpose, and design in the universe while suggesting a theory of cosmological and biological evolution based on matter in constant movement. Through the blind mathematician Diderot is hinting that creatures on earth today are the survivors of eons of competition between predator and prey who have constantly struggled to adapt to the changing environment in an effort to win out over the varied forces of nature. The unsuccessful ones are already extinct. In this fictional account of Saunderson's dying words Diderot has found an artistically and dramatically compelling structure for his experimental vision of a world as it comes into being, runs its course, and, with time, exists no more. A small part of the passage addressed by Saunderson to the clergyman at his bedside is as follows:

The order [of the universe] is not yet so perfect that monstrous offspring do not appear now and then. It is my belief that, in the beginning, when matter in fermentation was fashioning life in the universe, blind creatures like myself were exceedingly common. But why should I not believe about worlds what I believe about animals? How many worlds, malformed and imperfect, were perhaps broken up only to be reborn and are constantly dispersing again in distant space which I cannot touch and you cannot see. . . . What is this world of ours? A complex entity subject to sudden changes which all indicate a tendency to destruction; a swift succession of beings which follow one another in quick succession, assert themselves and disappear. . . . The world is eternal for you, as you are eternal for the creature that lives only for an instant. Yet we shall all pass away without being able to adduce the real extent we filled in space, nor the precise time that we shall have lasted. Time, matter, space are perhaps nothing more than a point. (*AT*, 1:310–11)

The last part of the letter is taken up with the intriguing question posed a good half-century before by Molyneux: would a person born blind, but with his sight restored, be able to distinguish between a cube and a sphere without first resorting to the sense of touch? The question had already been answered philosophically by George Berkeley and medically by Dr. Cheselden. Diderot had little that was new to add to the subject.

The book as a whole, however, caused a considerable stir and, though it appeared anonymously, Diderot was soon accused of one more indiscretion and, indeed, a very serious one. His arrest was ordered on various accounts but chiefly for a book "on the blind." The Bastille being already filled, he was, on 24 July 1749, hurried off to solitary confinement in the fortress of Vincennes on the outskirts of Paris. This was a profoundly traumatic experience for Diderot. What would become of his family? What would be the fate of the *Encyclopédie* now on the point of being launched? Then there was his tendency to suffer from claustrophobia which many critics have failed to mention; and yet its

recognition opens up new vistas on the man and his work. He had
already experienced this dreadful feeling when incarcerated at his father's
orders in a monastery. He had brooded over a sister dying insane in
a convent at the age of twenty-eight. His own feelings were again acute
at Vincennes. Claustrophobia would continue to haunt the man and
his writings for the rest of his life, although it would have its most
intense literary expression in *La Religieuse* or *The Nun* conceived in the
early 1760s.

When under the persistent questioning of the police, Diderot finally
confessed to being author of the *Pensées,* the *Bijoux,* and especially the
Lettre sur les aveugles, and himself decried them as "excesses" of his
mind, his lot was made easier.

The Marquis du Châtelet, governor of Vincennes, allowed him to
stroll in the park surrounding the fortress, permitted him to receive
visitors, and to do a certain amount of writing. This last activity seems
to have been limited to composing petitions for his release and to
taking notes on Milton's *Paradise Lost* and the first three volumes of
Buffon's *Histoire naturelle.* Unfortunately the notes on these two works
appear to be lost forever.

Chief among his visitors were Madame Diderot and Jean-Jacques
Rousseau. In the *Confessions* Rousseau tells of his famous October visit
to Vincennes where he discussed with his imprisoned friend the possibility
of entering a prize contest offered by the Academy of Dijon on whether
the revival of the sciences and arts had contributed to purifying morals.
Following Diderot's advice Rousseau treated the negative aspects of the
inquiry, won the prize, and was catapulted to fame.

As the French say: *"A malheur quelque chose est bon"* ("It's an ill
wind that blows no good"). And it would have been an ill wind if
Diderot's unpleasant, even frightening, experience had blown him no
good. One evening profiting from his new freedom of movement he
left the prison and its park for a walk to the home of Mme de Puisieux.
There he discovered what he had been suspecting for some while, that
she was being quite unfaithful. And so he found himself rid of a
demanding mistress who had few if any saving graces. His imprisonment
had lasted for a little over three months—a period during which he
learned that he had profited from his incarceration in other ways as
well. He had become known as never before; furthermore, he was now
the acknowledged author of the *Letter on the Blind,* an essay that,
through its natural intelligence and scientific erudition, showed Diderot
as a man of sufficient intellectual discernment to carry on with much

more acceptable work, the *Encyclopédie* for instance. Shades of the prison house had not been forgotten, and Diderot resolved—at least for the time being—to commit himself to his age frankly and openly. He himself promised, and others hoped he would carry through, a moratorium on grave indiscretions, both philosophical and literary. In fact, he had no intention of again languishing, as Carlyle would have it, "in the Castle of Vincennes for heretical Metaphysics, and irreverence to the Strumpetocracy."

Building Blocks

The great Rameau's nephew, amateur musician, composer of sorts, parasite, sycophant, and would-be man-about-town, wrote for orchestra and actually had performed once or twice a composition entitled *L'Encyclopédie*. The musical score has long since been lost. At the time of performance, however, it was described as consisting of large blocks of music precariously piled up on top of one another, blocks that would finally come crashing down with a tempestuous roar of music.[8]

The *Encyclopédie* did indeed consist of great blocks—great blocks of knowledge, and for more than twenty years Diderot was to toil over this rising edifice of accumulated learning. But in spite of repeated threats, unrelenting censorship, suppression, and even the necessity of clandestine printing, the thirty-five-volume work did not meet the fate envisaged by Rameau's music and so ardently hoped for by the antiphilosophes.

The distinguished philosophy professor Sidney Hook once said that if a list were to be drawn up of the great intellectual events in human history, an undisputed place on it would be held by the publication of the *Encyclopédie, ou Dictionnaire raisonné des Sciences, des Arts et des Métiers (Encyclopedia, or Analytical Dictionary of the Sciences, Arts and Crafts)* whose chief editor, architect, draftsman, writer, and scapegoat was Diderot himself. Professor Hook goes on to say that "The Encyclopédie became synonymous with Enlightenment, and the beacons it lit still burn, sometimes only fitfully, in the free world."[9]

There had been a collective sigh of relief, particularly among the associated publishers, when Diderot was allowed to return to Paris. He immediately set to work putting in order his prospectus for the *Encyclopédie*. Though dated 1751, the document appeared the preceding year. In it Diderot assured subscribers that the *Encyclopédie* was much more ambitious than previous compilations. It intended to demonstrate

how the arts and sciences lent themselves to each other, thus offering
a general panorama of the efforts of the human mind in every way
and in all ages. Furthermore, it would popularize for the interested
layman the technical aspects of the mechanical arts and professions.
Hence the *Encyclopédie* would in itself constitute a library contributing
to the advance of human knowledge.

The first volume of the *Encyclopédie* appeared on 1 July 1751,
introduced by d'Alembert's *Discours préliminaire,* one of the great
documents of the Enlightenment. The *Discourse,* a product of d'A-
lembert's systematic mind, discussed the principles that were to guide
the unfolding of the multivolume compendium. Human knowledge
would be considered under three headings, history, philosphy, and the
fine arts, based as they were on the distinction of the three faculties
of the human mind: memory, reason, and imagination. In the second
part of the *Discourse,* utilizing what Diderot had already said about
the arts and crafts, d'Alembert proceeded to give a brilliantly sweeping
account of the progress of scientific knowledge mainly from the Ren-
aissance to 1750. In so doing, he paid homage to such great men of
science as Francis Bacon, Harvey, Newton, Descartes, Pascal, Hermann
Boerhaave, Locke, and Leibniz, as well as others who exemplified
humanity's deep attachment to erudition, literature, philosophy, and
science.

The philosophes and their friends were ecstatic over this first volume,
but cries immediately arose from the enemy camp. The Jesuits accused
the encyclopedists of plagiarism, and the charge was echoed and reechoed
that the first volume had not shown the respect to which church and
state were entitled. Later in the year Diderot's theories of sensationalism
were held to be implicated in the heretical Sorbonne thesis of Abbé de
Prades, himself an encyclopedist. Soon thereafter the King's Council
ordered the first two volumes of the *Encyclopédie* to be suppressed on
the grounds that they tended to destroy royal authority and to corrupt
morality while adding to the spread of irreligion and doubt. This decree
was tacitly revoked a few months later and the volumes appeared at
the rate of one a year until 1757 when they had reached the letter
G. By then the overall purpose of the work was clear. In his superb
article entitled "Encyclopédie" Diderot had already stated that the word
comes from the Greek meaning the "interrelation of all knowledge,"
and that: "In truth the aim of an encyclopedia is to collect all the
knowledge scattered over the face of the earth, to present its general
outlines and structure to the men with whom we live and to transmit

this to those who will come after us, so that the work of past centuries may be useful to the following centuries, that our children, by becoming more educated, may at the same time become more virtuous and happier, and that we may not die without having deserved well of the human race."[10]

Being assured of d'Alembert's support, especially important because of his reputation as a mathematician, Diderot then succeeded in gathering around him an impressive array of collaborators including among many, Montesquieu, Voltaire, Charles Duclos, Rousseau, Samuel Formey, d'Holbach, Morellet, André Théophile de Bordeu, Jacques de Vaucanson, and the indefatigable Chevalier de Jaucourt who, like Diderot, wrote hundreds of articles and supervised the work of an army of hack writers engaged in compilation.

The list of subscribers increased impressively and the fame of the *Encyclopédie* grew prodigiously. The enemy was far from asleep, however, and venomous polemics were repeatedly directed against the encyclopedists coming from the pens, satirical and otherwise, of such notorious antiphilosophes as Elie Fréron, Charles Palissot, and Jacob-Nicolas Moreau. Appearance of the seventh volume caused the subscription list to rise still higher, but it also contained d'Alembert's provocative article, "Genève," which, among other things, proposed that this thriving Swiss city would do well if it no longer banned legitimate theater within its walls. Rousseau, having already broken with Diderot, replied with his famous *Lettre à d'Alembert sur les spectacles* but with an enmity that had little to do with those factions hostile to the philosophes. Once again Rousseau was demonstrating his individuality. The year was 1758.

In the midst of his work, Diderot and his colleagues began to show—but with reasonable subtlety—the lack of respect for France's altar and throne that the traditionalists had already foreseen would be the case. Censorship became increasingly rigid, and only in obscure corners of the *Encyclopédie,* indicated by a complex series of cross-references, would hidden paragraphs emerge that represented the true spirit of the Enlightenment. But there were moments when the authorities caught up with Diderot and his enterprise.

D'Alembert defected—perhaps out of prudence and fear—preferring, as an alternative to constant harassment and, quite possibly, lodging at the government's expense in the Bastille, the distinctions and academic honors that were his due. By 1759 the parliament and the court had sat in judgment on various works, including Helvétius's *De l'esprit (On the Mind),* Voltaire's *Poème sur la loi naturelle,* and the *Encyclopédie* itself. Even Pope Clement XIII, on the other side of the mountains, wrote a pamphlet condemning the compendium, and the threat of excommunication loomed up for those bold enough to turn its pages. Voltaire gave advice and encouragement from the comfort and safety of the court of Frederick the Great, and even suggested that Diderot might be wise to continue his project in Germany.

In consequence, the team to carry out the task under Diderot's direction, though large, was an often-changing one. Some of the articles were anodyne; others were on subjects sensitive to the old regime, or deftly sprinkled with subversive ideas. Diderot came close to being imprisoned for a second time, but economics were involved. Profits for the publishers, though not for Diderot, were almost three hundred percent. The director was let off with a few stiff warnings and publication proceeded.

The variety of articles, ranging from "Asparagus" to "Eagle" to "Enjoyment" to "Fornication" to "Menace" to "Peace" to "Refugees" to "Torture," was enormous for the times. Studies in the late twentieth century are still attempting to ascertain which of the many articles Diderot composed entirely or in part, or rewrote from the articles of others. In the middle 1760s, still with only tacit government permission, Diderot, though otherwise pretty much withdrawn from an active part in the contemporary scene, through prodigious courage and perseverance, brought the work to a close, plates and all.

According to one authority, "Diderot was acutely aware of the imperfections of his *Encyclopedia,* its mistakes, omissions and infelicities of arrangement. He disarmed criticism by presenting it as a first attempt, to be superseded as soon as practicable by successors who would profit from his mistakes."[11]

If we try to sum up the results produced by the *Encyclopédie* we see three general consequences. The work organized human knowledge in a definitive manner for eighteenth-century readers (only in 1771 did the *Encyclopedia Britannica,* with its first three volumes, begin to attempt as much). The *Encyclopédie* under Diderot's inspired guidance bound closer together than would otherwise have been the case the great thinkers of the age. And finally it gave a certain unity, hitherto lacking, to the political, social, and religious doctrines of the day. There were more detailed results as well. For instance, in the *Encyclopédie's* pages "Providence" was replaced by "Nature," and man was relegated from the center of the universe to merely one manifestation of Nature to whose laws he must be accountable. Determinism with its insistence upon cause and effect had more influence than ever as a philosophical and sociological doctrine. Authority and tradition, especially in France, were rejected as never before; they were more and more frequently replaced by experience, experimentation, and evidence. The *Encyclopédie* was striving to establish facts; and when certain of these facts were once established, changes were inevitable. In matters of religion, for instance, traditional dogmas were discarded, and emphasis on the supernatural was greatly diminished and, at times, nonexistent. In politics opposition to the divine right of kings increased, along with such concomitant issues as the inexcusable privileges enjoyed by the nobility of the sword and robe and the dignitaries of the church.

The *Encyclopédie,* through its dispersal of knowledge and through its liberal philosophy, went far toward modifying the climate of opinion, first in France and then in the Western world. And, as Voltaire was to remark, it was to the son of a provincial master cutler, Denis Diderot, that the age was chiefly obliged for this revolution of the mind.

On Deafness and Other Matters

Diderot, with his ever-probing spirit, was not satisfied with devoting all his intellectual time and effort to the gigantic task of editing the first of the great modern encyclopedias. As he had with the *Lettre sur les aveugles,* he again wished to strike out on his own into some fresh field of inquiry. But following his months of imprisonment, he turned to the less precarious spheres of literature and art. His *Encyclopédie* article, "Beau" (1751), demonstrated his knowledge of what had been published both in France and in England on aesthetics. In the same year he brought forth what is today recognized as his extraordinarily original *Lettre sur les sourds et muets,* again with a slightly sardonic subtitle; this time, *A l'usage de ceux qui entendent et qui parlent.* Chronologically inserted between the more dangerous *Letter on the Blind* and the then-arresting *Pensées sur l'interpretation de la nature* of 1754, it long remained comparatively unnoticed. Today, it is additional proof that here was one of the most exciting minds in eighteenth-century Europe. As one critic has noted, Diderot's reflections on language and poetry, far more decisively than in the writings of his contemporaries, relinquish the realm of rhetoric and issue forth into that of general aesthetics then still in an embryonic stage.[12]

Published anonymously, it was—like the essay on the blind—concerned with problems of communication viewed from multiple perspectives. The *Lettre sur les sourds* ostensibly was written in answer to Abbé Batteux's unobjectionable and even rather useful little treatise on aesthetics, *Les Beaux-Arts reduits à un même principe*. In the 1960s and 1970s, it has been repeatedly pointed out that, with his peculiarly complex mind, Diderot was capable of assimilating and experiencing the most contrary intellectual perceptions and the most varied emotional states. An excellent illustration of how his mind worked is presented in this early scientific study on the deaf and dumb, where the art of communication by gesture and the relationship between gesture and language are examined. From the great actor who projects in gestures what he expresses in words, we are led to the deaf-mute who, standing before a color-organ, at last surmises that music is, like language, a means of communication.[13] He deduces this after having watched people's faces and expressions while music was being played outside his world of silence. There follows a discussion of the theory that the painter is capable of portraying but a single moment within which the past and the future should be suggested, whereas the poet is able to depict a moving toward simultaneity that is finally visual. The conclusion is drawn from this that some subjects are best described in one medium, some in another. Gotthold Ephraim Lessing, familiar with the *Letter on the Deaf and Dumb* in the year it first appeared, developed Diderot's aesthetic approach in his *Laokoon* in 1766, but the extent of Diderot's influence on the thinking of the German critic must be examined further before we can speak of direct and exclusive influence.

A poet, Diderot insists, is dealing with words, and words have both meaning and sound. The superior poet will then paint in sounds what he is expressing in meaning. Furthermore, poetry is the interweaving of hieroglyphs, that is, a series of pictures representing ideas. In this sense only the poet of genius succeeds in saying the unsayable as his lines aspire toward simultaneity rather than sequence.

Thus the reader, who has almost forgotten that he started out by reading a brief essay beginning with a discussion of grammatical inversions and moving to comments on the deaf and dumb, finds that he has arrived at a theory that leads directly to Baudelaire and the symbolists. It does so by means of fundamental principles that have not yet been fully explored.[14]

And so, for posterity, Diderot's little treatise is of particular interest, notwithstanding the scanty echoes it elicited in its own day. We should turn again to Paul Meyer's critical edition of the *Lettre* for what is a key statement to the work as a whole. He tells us:

Ever since Aristotle, theorists had considered the language of the poet as an integral part of rhetoric, whereas Diderot focused on aesthetics, which embraces all the arts, by availing himself of an argument that had recently figured in the Quarrel of the Ancients and the Moderns: The partisans of the former had maintained that grammatical inversion facilitates poetic creation, and for Diderot it became a matter of discovering the nature of poetry itself and what distinguishes it, not just from prose, but from the other arts generally. The choice of an epistemological problem—the origin and course of mental processes—as a point of departure for a study of linguistics and with the ultimate purpose of solving the problem of artistic creation, led to an investigation in which the brief work of 1751 marked only the first step.[15]

During the 1750s Diderot's sense of commitment to the age reached its fullest intensity. He had become involved in arts and letters, in philosophy and science, even in matters of religion, all the while showing an acute awareness of the general movement of ideas throughout the decade. In his perseverance where pledged interests were concerned he demonstrated a tenacity of purpose equaling the dedication of a Voltaire or a Rousseau, though, at the time, his efforts may have seemed somewhat less spectacular than theirs. He was, as the existentialists would have it, totally *engagé*.

In 1754, after four volumes of the *Encyclopédie* had appeared, Diderot brought out a collection of random reflections entitled *Pensées sur l'interprétation de la nature*. These *Thoughts on the Interpretation of Nature* derived title and initial inspiration from Francis Bacon. Both Bacon and Diderot, Herbert Dieckmann tells us, "were endowed with prodigious scientific imagination, in which the gift of exact observation and of realistic vision, the scientific spirit and the spirit of speculation, are strangely blended."[16] Diderot's book—less well written than his *Pensées philosophiques* and less successfully realized than the letters on the blind and on the deaf and dumb—was ridiculed for its presumed pomposity as indicated in the opening line of the exordium: "Young man, take and read."[17] Frederick the Great is supposed to have said that he would not bother with the book, since obviously it was not for men capable of sprouting beards. Still, in these pages urging acceptance of experimental science and envisaging the results that are possible from such an approach to the secrets of nature, Diderot may have done more toward giving expression to the spirit of modern scientific research than any other eighteenth-century man of letters.

There are fifty-eight *Pensées* in all, ending with a prayer to the Almighty in one version. The whole constitutes a somewhat disjointed but intellectually challenging essay, published anonymously and causing no unfavorable reactions from the authorities. Diderot was here involved, and very much so, in the philosophy of science. The *Interprétation de la nature* was, as Arthur Wilson calls it, "a tentative book,"[18] for it reached into new aspects of the methodology of science, asking questions and suggesting provisional solutions. Despite the loose nature of the presentation, we have here the expression of a spirit of fascinated but highly intelligent inquiry constantly at work. If the influence of Bacon is apparent, so is that of Buffon. For, like Buffon, Diderot is insisting upon the end of a great era in mathematical and physical sciences and the dawn of the age of biological or life sciences. The ideas of Pierre Louis Maupertuis and Louis Daubenton carried his speculation still further.

In *Pensée 12* he develops the idea of one animal as the prototype of all other animals. In previous works he had clearly hinted at the theory of biological and cosmological evolution; here he points toward the evolutionary ideas of transformism later developed by Jean Baptiste Lamarck and Darwin. Attempts by some present-day scholars to minimize and even deny this association have been made upon occasion, but the facts and the stages in Diderot's thought speak for themselves.[19]

In *Pensée 14* Diderot imagines the vast domain of the sciences as an enormous plot of ground composed of locations some of which are in the dark and others with light cast upon them. Our task should be, we are told, either to push back darkness encroaching on the lighted areas or to broaden the centers of light. The latter task, he concludes, is that of the creative genius; the former is for wisdom as it strives toward perfection.

In *Pensée 15* the reader is told that we have three principal methods at our disposal in the search for truth in the philosophy of science. There is observation, there is reflection, and there is experimentation. Observation collects facts, reflection combines them, and experimentation verifies the results at hand. To this he adds that creative geniuses are rare, so these three methods combined in one person are far from common.

Diderot reminds us in *Pensée 23* that he has been distinguishing two kinds of philosophy, the experimental and that based entirely on reason. Experimental philosophy is blindfolded and always walks gropingly, clutching at whatever comes within reach, and stumbling finally on something of inestimable value. Rational philosophy weighs various possibilities, passes judgment, and stops short. It says without fear of contradiction that light cannot be decomposed. Experimental philosophy listens, holds its tongue for centuries, then suddenly brings forth the prism, and light *is* decomposed.

At the outset *(Pensée 1)* Diderot had said he would let his thoughts follow one another as they came to mind, hoping they would reveal the course of his thinking. He may have been only partially successful in this, but it is nevertheless entirely possible that the *Thoughts on the Interpretation of Nature* of 1754 is the most important original work he was to publish during his lifetime.

The Play's the Thing

Throughout eighteenth-century France, even during the Revolution, the theater was easily the most popular form of entertainment for all classes. In the provinces, towns, no matter how small, could usually boast of at least one *salle de spectacle,* and the larger cities would often point with pride to several. Then there were the strolling companies, like that of the young Molière in the previous century, traveling in their large carts—little houses on wheels—the length and breadth of the country. Paris itself was, of course, dotted with an impressive variety of theaters, and the more successful plays were vigorously discussed in the coffeehouses and served as a rule as objects of criticism, both favorable and unfavorable, in the flourishing periodical press of the day.

Actors and audiences alike sought a continual variety in the dramatic offerings. As a result fables, maxims, legends, short stories, even snatches of history, furnished subject matter for writers and for a clamoring public. There were also revivals of Racine, Corneille, Philippe Quinault, and Molière, as well as eighteenth-century imitators of these leading playwrights of the reign of Louis XIV. The demand remained constant for new comedies, new tragedies, and novel dramatic spectacles of all sorts.

With age creeping up on him and with the last plates of the *Encyclopédie* finally off the press, Diderot, in the course of his *Réfutation du livre d'Helvétius intitulé L'Homme* (1773–74), wrote in retrospect: "Fate, but even more, life's necessities do with us what they will; who is more aware of this than I? That is why, for some thirty years, I have against my inclination, devoted myself to the *Encyclopédie,* while writing but two plays" *(AT,* 2:312).

Besides several abortive attempts in the form of dramatic sketches or adaptations from the English, there was to be a third play, considerably

later, *Est-il bon? Est-il méchant?* By today's standards as well as by
Baudelaire's, it was far more interesting than the first, which dealt with
a bastard son, or the second, about a father and his family. And yet
these two earliest pieces are now turned to with increasing frequency
because with their attendant essays each touches upon modes of dramatic
procedure radical two centuries ago and relevant today.

Diderot had a natural inclination for the theater and, as a young
man, had found it difficult to choose between the life of the stage and
his entirely different world of studies at the Sorbonne. During his
bohemian years in Paris he tells us in the *Lettre sur les sourds et muets,*
he knew many plays entirely by heart and sometimes during a performance he would stop up his ears in order to see whether the gestures
and the facial expressions of the actors corresponded to his recollection
of the lines. He early showed himself a master of dialogue, and for
the rest of his life it would be a favorite form not only for his
philosophical essays but also in his fiction, in his disquisitions on
aesthetics, and in his most blistering satire. Then too—and this is of
considerable importance—his original turn of mind—always looking for
new forms of expression—initiated novel dramatic techniques and theories
on evolution of dramatic art that he would have liked to put into
practice or, better still perhaps, would have gained satisfaction in seeing
successfully adopted by others. He was, in short, seeking larger dramatic
truths than those of the French classical theater that were repeatedly
reflected in the stale conventionalities of eighteenth-century imitations.
A new dramatic ideal seemed called for, drawn in part from English
precedents, partly from Nivelle de la Chaussée's *comédie larmoyante*
(tearful comedy), and partly from Diderot's own efforts to suggest and
perhaps foresee what the future held for dramatic literature. And third,
like Voltaire, he was persuaded that the theater could replace the pulpit
in setting men's minds straight about virtue and vice. The stage was
an admirable way to educate the public. It could, if properly utilized,
stir men's hearts and minds in the cause of enlightenment in much the
same fashion the liturgy aroused them in the service of organized religion.
Voltaire was in agreement with Diderot in this respect, and had written
a letter on 27 April 1761 to the Comte d'Argental saying: "I am not
at all unhappy to show little by little that the stage is older than the
pulpit, and that it is more effective."

Voltaire and Diderot, however, were never to be wholly in agreement
on reform in the French theater. The future patriarch of Ferney would
have found it intolerable to write anything approaching a bourgeois

tragedy with moral and sentimental elements served up with an admixture of joy and sorrow, laughter and tears. Here Voltaire—so often in the forefront of intellectual, social, and aesthetic movements—had fallen behind. In England and in France especially the importance of the middle class was becoming increasingly felt both in the novel and in the theater. It was now the city and not the court that dictated literary and, in particular, dramatic taste. This was a fact Diderot had seized upon without hesitation.

Still, both Voltaire and his younger brother-in-arms insisted upon the moral value of the theater and were well in advance of their time in showing consideration and respect for the acting profession. Voltaire's tributes to the superior actor were many, but his poem on the death of Adrienne Lecouvreur, *célèbre actrice,* was especially fitting in every way, and is as moving today as it was when written in 1730. Diderot's writings are strewn with anecdotes praising the superb talents of Lekain, of Mlle Clairon, or of the great David Garrick; and in the *Paradoxe sur le comédien,* realized between 1769 and 1778, he was to raise the exceptionally gifted actor or actress to the rank of genius for having a transcendentally clear awareness of the means of artistic expression.

Taking time out from the arduous labors and heavy responsibilities of the *Encyclopédie,* Diderot sought temporary release by turning whole-heartedly to matters theatrical. It was altogether natural that he should try his hand at playwriting. His first effort, *Le Fils naturel (The Illegitimate Son),* told of a young man, Dorval by name, born in bastardy, of excellent character but sensitive to his lot. He feels isolated, déclassé, a social outcast. The fair sex, however, is drawn to him because of his austerity and his moral rectitude. Following an inner struggle between love and conscience—as well as an instance of mistaken identity—he pledges troth to the right woman, and becomes a useful member of society.

Published in 1757, *Le Fils naturel* was, to Diderot's chagrin, produced only once—by a reluctant Comédie Française in 1771. This first play, which the novice playwright called a *comédie sérieuse,* was brought out under the same cover with a dialogue in three parts called *Entretiens sur le Fils naturel* or *Dorval et moi.* These dialogues in settings of natural scenery adroitly bring together many of his dramatic theories, which are also to some extent an explanation and defense of *Le Fils naturel* itself. He proposes that the action should be nearer to everyday experience than what is to be found in Corneille, Racine, or in the tragedies of Voltaire. The characters themselves should be realistically portrayed; that is, true to life. Both dramatic moments of silence and meaningful gestures should be indulged in to heighten spectator interest. For the same reason, there should be the judicious use of inarticulate cries. Another favorite concept of Diderot's is the replacement of *caractères,* to be found in traditional comedy (the miser, the hypocrite, the pedant, the prude), by *conditions* and professional idiosyncrasies (the father, the magistrate, the merchant, the soldier). These theories had considerable influence, especially in Germany where Lessing for one was much taken with them. Some came down directly from Diderot's dramatic concepts into the French theater of the nineteenth century while others filtered back into France from Germany. In the twentieth century the French playwright François de Curel said that his own dramatic ideas were much the same as Diderot's. There are those present-day writers for the stage who, in all truth, could make a similar deposition.

Le *Père de famille (The Father)* was published in 1758. This play too was to illustrate the *genre sérieux,* advocating middle-class heroes representing various social conditions or professions, and tendering problems drawn from real life. In this *drama* a father, affectionate and forbearing, has a son in love with a poor and virtuous orphan girl, as well as a daughter who loves an impoverished young man. The chief obstacle to requited love is the father's brother-in-law, a rich old codger, selfish, miserly, and gorged with social prejudice. After numerous vicissitudes, the father can at last give his blessing to his two children and those they wish to take in wedlock.

As a play Le *Père de famille* had most of the shortcomings already apparent in Le *Fils naturel.* As George Havens has pointed out, Diderot's tendency to proclaim a "propagandistic moral purpose" tended to "warp the drama" in his effort "to prove a thesis."[20] Both plays, besides being "preachy," lacked conviction in language, situation, and character portrayal. Le *Père de famille,* however, had a success in the theater that was denied its predecessor. It was first produced at the Comédie Française in 1761 and, to the author's gratification, was enthusiastically received in such large provincial cities as Toulouse, Marseilles, and Rouen, and even translated into English with the title *The Family Picture.* Moreover, following its inception, for a period of some eighty years, it was played in Paris 171 times.

Still, Diderot readily confessed that he did not have the dramatic genius of a Racine, but hoped, despite this, that his theories of the bourgeois drama would not be rejected. As matters turned out, in 1765 he was able to congratulate Michel-Jean Sedaine warmly for utilizing them successfully in *Le Philosophe sans le savoir*. Just as, along with his play *Le Fils naturel*, he had published a critical companion piece, so too he brought out with the 1758 edition of *Le Père de famille* a long essay called *Discours sur la poésie dramatique*. Here the word *poésie* of the title had less the meaning of "poetry" than that of artistic creation of a superior sort.

And so we find ourselves in the domain of aesthetics, which Joseph Joubert in his *Pensées* was to call "the literary conscience of the soul." The aesthetics of Diderot have often been studied in recent years, and one arresting work in which to ponder over them is his own *Discours sur la poésie dramatique* (*AT*, 4:301–94). As Arthur Wilson has observed, "This discourse on dramatic poetry is a full-flavored and self-revealing essay because Diderot injected into it a great deal of his own personality."[21] And, we could add, this personality might often give the air of being self-contradictory. The very title of his last and best play suggests as much, for we are invited to entertain the thoughts of whether Hardouin-Diderot is "good" or "bad."

Dr. Lenore R. Kreitman was among those who early saw the dilemma involved. In her article "Diderot's Aesthetic Paradox and Created Reality"[22] she extracts, often convincingly, the underlying element or paradox that runs through Diderot's concept of artistic existence and, indeed, his entire aesthetic. Diderot exalts sensitivity, emotion, and profound passion as distinguishing persons of great artistic capability. She is quite right in saying so, for the primary role of these three faculties, sensitivity and deep emotion as the impetus to artistic inspiration, is echoed throughout the discourse.

Nonetheless, paradoxically, only the lucid genius whose reason dominated his enthusiastic emotion is notably capable of artistic creation to any marked degree and of realizing the artistic expression of great emotion. Kreitman correctly points out Diderot's paradox of the truly great actor. He is one who creates a character on stage by exposing no personal character, by being presumably devoid of genuine feeling, by exercising rigid self-control, and by dispassionately and critically viewing himself as the spectator does. Kreitman sees Diderot's portrait of Rameau's nephew as emphasizing the paradox of artistic existence. In his enthusiastic frenzy the nephew is capable of the most remarkable musical pantomime. Once the frenzy subsides, however, he is left prostrate, incapable of the calm, lucid reflection required to re-create his instantaneous inspiration and embody his feelings in a permanent form. He remains merely a simple imitator, a buffoon. And Diderot's fictive reality, which acquires an authenticity as plausible as natural reality, is created by artistically tempering extraordinary reality and embellishing banal reality with small, carefully created details drawn from reality's norm. And so we see that Diderot's artistic mastery, evidenced by its verisimilitude, often results from artistic conventions that, at first glance, may seem highly contrived and unreal. In short, Kreitman—as have others in recent years—concludes that reality, unlike conventional realism, which often rings false, is so probable and credible that it seems as authentic as natural reality.

In this discourse divided into twenty-two chapters Diderot enlarges on his notions of what the bourgeois drama should be as each chapter proceeds to discuss some aspect of dramatic art. Toward the end of the essay there is the intriguing portrait of a certain Ariste. This Ariste depicts an idealized Diderot, the philosophe he would like to become a decade or so hence.

Diderot was already giving serious thought to the years ahead and wondering whether he had enough to offer in the way of talent and originality of mind to achieve the only immortality he aspired to—just appreciation from an understanding posterity. Furthermore, it was well that he should have thoughts of the future and what it might bring. He was fast reaching a crucial turning point in his life as changes of circumstances in one form or another came in fast succession. There was the growing feeling, soon turned into conviction, that his open commitment to the France in which he was living could not continue for long. The same year that *Le Père de famille* and the *Discours* appeared, Rousseau, long Diderot's closest friend, published an eloquent diatribe in his *Lettre à d'Alembert sur les spectacles* against the theater and all its appurtenances. This in itself was a very large straw in the wind. There had been the enemy from without; here was an enemy from within.

"Dégringolade" or a Touch of Disintegration

For the next several years a pervading mood hung over Diderot that might best be summed up in that onomatopoeic word *dégringolade* meaning, in French, a process of physical, mental, or moral collapse. Although he had suffered imprisonment in 1749 mainly for intellectual indiscretions, it was in the late 1750s that he was to undergo the most critical period of his life—one of infinite incident and endless uncertainty.

These were years filled with apprehension, disenchantment, despondency, and even a sense of betrayal. Sometimes it became a vague but absorbing melancholy as when he wrote his Sophie Volland that now his love would be brown in color, quite in keeping with his state of being (*Corr,* 3:108). Then there were times when he was more precise, as when he wrote Voltaire: "*Mon cher maître,* I am well past the age of forty; I am tired of all the chicanery. From morn to evening I cry out for peace, only peace, and there is scarcely a day I am not tempted to go and live unnoticed and die serene in the province from whence I came. What will it matter to me whether I was Voltaire or Diderot, and whether your three syllables or mine still exist?" (*Corr,* 2:39). These were dark words for one who depended solely on posterity for survival.

Early intimations of what lay ahead may already have been evident in his play of 1757, *Le Fils naturel,* which in no way was to enjoy the success he had wistfully hoped for. The piece contained a sentence to the effect that he who lives alone is *méchant* (perverse or spiteful). Rousseau who had been one of Diderot's closest friends for some fifteen years took the remark personally and found it highly offensive. But the two men, Jean-Jacques over-sensitive and quite possibly with incipient signs of paranoia, and Denis, well-meaning but blundering and sometimes intrusive in his attachments, had already begun to resort to mutual bickering. Rousseau was showing increased scorn for the ideals of his fellow *philosophes* and for the aims of the *parti des Encyclopédistes.* Diderot had in all friendship strongly advised Rousseau to stay away from Mme d'Houdetot with whom Jean-Jacques had become infatuated despite the fact that she was the officially recognized mistress of the Marquis de Saint-Lambert. In a letter to Rousseau late in 1757 Diderot even suggested that his friend might do well to serve as a traveling companion to his benefactress, Mme d'Epinay, who, because of ill health, felt obliged to consult Théodore Tronchin of Geneva, the most famous medical doctor on the Continent. Rousseau, furious, saw in Diderot's suggestion a plot to banish him to the city of his birth. Seizing the initiative, Jean-Jacques announced to the world at large in the preface to the *Lettre sur les spectacles* that his friendship for Diderot was no more. He did so with pathos and eloquence: "This work will be devoid of taste, circumspection, accuracy. In my solitude I have not been able to show it to anyone. I once had an Aristarchus, severe and judicious. I have him no longer, I no longer wish to have him; but I shall regret him always, and he is missing much more from my heart than from my writings."

In the same year Diderot—himself full of bitterness—set down on paper what one biographer has called a "catalogue of the Seven Rascalities."[23] In the *Correspondance littéraire* of 1795—long after Rousseau and his brotherly enemy had departed this earth,[23]—Jacob Meister published Diderot's private list of his grievances against Rousseau. In his role as editor Meister explained that Diderot kept the document in a secret corner of his desk and would refer to it whenever he wished to recall his former friend's "villainies." The *Tablettes,* as Diderot called them, were drawn up shortly after Rousseau's public and poorly received announcement in his *Letter on the Theater* that he was severing relations with this philosophe who for so long had been his closest companion. The list deals with events leading up to and causing the break, including Rousseau's "ingratitude" toward Mme d'Epinay, his attempt to seduce Mme d'Houdetot while Saint-Lambert was away with the army, and Diderot's unwitting revelation of the fact to Saint-Lambert, due to misleading information from Rousseau.[24]

It was also in 1758 that Helvétius, independently wealthy, philanthropically inclined, and a would-be protector of the philosophes, brought out *De l'esprit.* This treatise, *On the Mind,* underscored a utilitarian system of ethics and the all-embracing role of education and legislation in shaping the individual. He was completely won over by Locke's notion that, at birth, the mind resembles a blank sheet of paper ready for the imprint of sense impressions. According to Helvétius's philosophy the individual, born without character and unconcerned with good and evil, acquires everything, his virtues and vices, talents and prejudices, thus denying hereditary as well as innate faculties. Many of these same ideas, including the concept of the absolute and natural equality of man, were embroidered upon in the second of his two chief works, *De l'homme.* This book, *On Man,* was, in the name of prudence, published posthumously in 1772; it went even further than had *On the Mind* in striving to free morality from arbitrary metaphysical and religious forms.

De l'esprit immediately had great success, particularly among the pseudo-intellectuals of the period. But the author's educational theories ran counter to those of Rousseau. And others of the philosophic group strongly disagreed with the principles often so piquantly and enticingly set down by Helvétius. Voltaire's reaction has been summed up by an American biographer as follows: "I wholly disapprove of what you say—and will defend to the death your right to say it."[25] And Diderot in his *Réflexions sur le livre de l'Esprit and Réfutation . . . suivie de l'ouvrage d'Helvétius intitulé l'Homme* was to rectify some of Helvétius's more extreme ideas. The mind, Diderot claimed, has from the outset varying physiological propensities. Education, based as it is on experience, is of importance, but it has its limitations. The senations may indeed be the origin of judgment but do not embody the faculty of judgment. Moreover, since experiences cannot be identical even in the same environment, neither moral nor intellectual equality can be expected among individuals.

If the philosophes, many of whom were also contributors to Diderot's *Encyclopédie,* did not for the most part readily agree with Helvétius's theories, neither did they always agree with one another. Reactions to *On the Mind* revealed that there were real differences of opinion within the party. The fact is interesting, for those in the enemy camp chose Helvétius's *De l'esprit* as the book that combined between its covers all the poisons available in the works of the philosophes themselves.

Latent resentment against the philosophic group exploded when the fanatic, Robert-François Damiens, slightly wounded Louis XV in an assassination attempt. The advocate general of France, Omer Joly de Fleury, went so far as to declare before the Parlement of Paris that a conspiracy was in the making, and that the chief tenets of Helvétius's work were simply the principles and deplorable consequences of many previously published books, in particular, Diderot's *Encyclopedia.*

Reactionary circles insisted that lax censorship had been allowing subversive ideas against both altar and throne to be published in various progressive works, including *De l'esprit* and especially the *Encyclopédie.* In 1757 such charges as these unleashed a whole series of satirical attacks in pamphlet form against the leaders of the philosophical movement. Scriveners like Charles Palissot, Jacob-Nicolas Moreau, and Abraham de Chaumeix were particularly effective in presenting aggressive plaquettes and tracts that heaped ridicule on those who were recognized members of the encyclopedist camp. D'Alembert, though coeditor of the *Encyclopedia,* was more or less spared, since, in addition to being recognized as a mathematician of consequence, he was fortunate enough to have influential friends in high places. Diderot, though, was but an upstart and a mere cutler's son. Accordingly, it was he who was the target of the most telling satire and the sharpest invective often mixed with accusations of plagiarism in his plays and in certain of his *Encyclopedia* articles.

In considering Diderot as he saw the 1750s draw to a close and a new decade upon him, we may not be able to reconstruct a well-ordered system of events leading to a change in the man as he saw himself and the world. A change, nevertheless, did occur. All about him, as we have noted, a whole set of changes both spiritual and material were taking place more or less at the same time. The increasing predominance of the bourgeoisie, the advances in science, technology, and what we might call industrialization, were all important in a general way to Diderot the philosophe, the *encyclopédiste*, the critic, and the creative writer. But there were more personal events, more intimate changes that impressed him then and perhaps left their marks for the rest of his life. There was the agonizing break with Rousseau, shortly followed by d'Alembert stepping down from the coeditorship of the *Encyclopédie*. There was the feeling of profound personal loss in the death of a father whom Diderot had so deeply loved and esteemed. And only three months before on 6 February 1759, the *Encyclopédie* was condemned by both the Parlement of Paris and the King's Council. This body declared by royal decree that "the advantages to be gained from such a work regarding progress in the arts and sciences, can never atone for the irrevocable damage it has caused so far as morality and religion are concerned," (*AT,* 13:118). Words of advice and reassurance from the safety of distance were scant comfort to a beleaguered Diderot, the object of continuing and proliferating attacks of malevolent satire directed against him over the very head of Lamoignon de Malesherbes, the straightforward and high-minded magistrate in charge of regulating the book trade in France. The most vicious of these attacks had been carefully prepared by Charles Palissot, who fancied himself the eighteenth-century Molière. Hilde Freud, in her book *Palissot and "Les Philosophes,"* relates the sequence of events as follows:

All in all the recent happenings were an excellent omen for the forces of reaction; their attacks were having the wished-for effects, and victory seemed almost within grasp. By withdrawing as co-editor of the *Encyclopédie,* d'A-lembert showed that he had no intention whatsoever of being burnt at the stake, figuratively or literally, for the cause. Voltaire's counsel and encouragement from the relative security of the Swiss border gave the impression of following Rabelais' dictum of willingness to go "jusqu'au feu exclusivement." Of the three, Diderot alone was to suffer from the flames of ridicule and slander in the auto-da-fé that Palissot was preparing. This particular auto-da-fé was to be attended by a large number of the Parisian theatregoing public and was to be known under the title of *Les Philosophes.*[26]

During the late 1740s and throughout the 1750s, Diderot, despite censorship, derision, even imprisonment and threats of further censorship, continued, through the printed word, to deepen his commitment to the thinking man of his day. By 1760, except for those publishers who wished to carry on the *Encyclopedia* clandestinely, the staunch loyalty of a few *encyclopédistes* like the Chevalier Louis Jaucourt, and a scattering of devoted comrades-in-arms—Friedrich Melchior Grimm and the Baron d'Holbach, for instance—Diderot was surrounded by a ring of hostility that viewed him with fear and disdain. The years that lay ahead would demand courage, fortitude, and, no doubt, resilience. He would have to adopt a new outlook, new objectives, and find renewed faith in himself while, at the same time, determining a fresh perspective on his place in the world of eighteenth-century Europe. The time for reassessment had come.

Chapter Five
For Self and Posterity

New Directions

Diderot has long been pictured as one who wrote with great speed and, at times, with undeniable brilliance, making little or no effort to correct, revise, and ponder over what he had written before it became frozen in printer's ink. This is the impression his daughter left in the *Mémoires* and it has been repeated countless times since. There is no doubt that Diderot was an extraordinary conversationalist who could bring to life a large drawingroom or a packed stagecoach. His words poured forth in a never-ending stream as he related anecdotes, summarized his own writings or those of others, discussed the current scene, or outlined plots for short stories, novels, and plays with remarkable ease. Such monologues—Voltaire is supposed to have said that it was impossible to carry on a dialogue with Diderot—were a delight to all within range of his voice. There is also little doubt that much of his writing during the 1750s had a spontaneity and, at times, an alarming facility about it, and certain articles of his that were already appearing in the *Encyclopedia* revealed talents of a skilled journalist rather than those of either a dedicated man of letters or an original thinker.

But by 1760, the springtide of his exuberance and his impulsive individuality had ebbed, leaving a man edging the fifties. This was without question the most critical period in Diderot's life. Voltaire's *Candide,* a product of 1759, had been translated into many languages and was acclaimed throughout Europe for its sparkling wit and needlelike satire. Here was the leading cosmopolitan Frenchman of the day and France's greatest living writer. And Rousseau, who once had had so much in common with a younger Diderot, had for several years been acknowledging his own widespread fame which, in essay form, had stemmed from his anti-Enlightenment thesis that the advance of civilization had caused man to lose his inherent sense of virtue. By 1761 he had embellished the thesis in a sensational love story, the epistolary novel *La Nouvelle Héloise.* Its success was immediate and prodigious.

But Diderot knew he still lingered in the shadows as a creative writer. The realization that, compared to Voltaire and Rousseau, he had made little impact either on the world of ideas or that of belles lettres, gave him pause. It is hardly surprising that he should be troubled by such preoccupations for, throughout his life and writings, the creative impulse was one of those subjects to which he would most frequently return. Constantly alert to its manifestation in others, equally often he wondered about his own creative potential. In the early 1760s, with national fame such as election to any of the French academies and nationwide esteem in general denied him, with little indication of warm acceptance of his work even among his closest contemporaries, he began to reflect more and more seriously on other possible sources of recognition and understanding. More aware than ever that he was no longer young, striving to assess what talent he had and wondering whether the tyranny of genius would forever elude him, he became singularly preoccupied with serious self-questioning. He had reached the point where he felt driven to take stock of himself and of the world around him.

Appreciation of whatever talents he had could, conceivably, find response in three ways. The first of these would be through himself. In following a compulsive urge to write for his own satisfaction, he could freely set down on paper his most original, his most tantalizing, and his most daring thoughts, thoughts which, remaining in manuscript form, would cause him no harassment from the traditional authorities. Then there was the possibility of passing his thoughts, notions, and vivacity of mind on to interested parties beyond the restrictive borders of France. And, finally, though the ultimate target might for the time being be less apparent, it nevertheless lay ahead, unknown and unpredictable—the opinion of posterity.

Of Salons and Such

It was a time of tenuous relationships, even in friendship and love. Diderot's wife was bitter over his attachment for Sophie Volland. Sophie, unmarried and over forty, was, it seems, unsure and at times unhappy about the philosophe's intentions and his regard for her. Besides, published correspondence of Diderot suggests that his lively imagination was plagued by the suspicion that he had a formidable rival for the affections of his Sophie in none other than one of her two married sisters. Lesbianism was for Diderot, as some modern critics might have it, *une hantise.*

Following what appeared to be little less than outright desertion on the part of most of his male friends, there remained only Baron Grimm in whom he felt he could have implicit trust. Diderot and Grimm had been brought together by Rousseau in 1750, at a time when Rousseau was an intimate friend and admirer of both. German-born and some ten years younger than Diderot, Grimm had an excellent knowledge of French language and literature, and proved to be a competent critic as well. It was Grimm who could offer Diderot during this period of withdrawal from the French scene the opportunity to express himself at regular intervals through the written word.

In 1753 Grimm had inherited from the Abbé Raynal a private newsletter the purpose of which was to give confidential political, social, and cultural information concerning France to subscribers in high places outside the country. Diderot, an intelligent connoisseur who knew all the great artists of the period, often dropped into their studios in order to understand their problems and techniques. There are, in fact, those who credit Diderot with the invention of modern French art criticism as a literary genre. Beginning in 1759 he wrote a series of nine articles on the Paris "Salons" (biennial exhibitions of painting and sculpture) for Grimm's *Correspondance littéraire,* copies of which were prepared by professional scribes and sent out in manuscript form to various corners of the Continent. Neither Diderot's *Salons* (from 1759 to 1781, with none for 1773, 1777, or 1779), nor his other pieces inserted in the newsletter saw the published light of day until Grimm's now famous *Correspondance* appeared in print well after the death of both.

Perhaps the first point to be emphasized concerning Diderot's *Salons* is that they were addressed to foreigners who themselves did not have the opportunity of viewing the objects of his criticism. His first aim, then, was to make the readers see the paintings described; this technique itself he raised to a high art. But the main problem in discussing Diderot as an art critic is posed by his general way of working.

The brief letter to Grimm in September 1761, referring to the exposition of that year, is cavalier in tone—possibly because Diderot was not sure of himself in the field of art criticism. Still, it is informative in that it gives an indication of his overall procedure:

Here, my friend, you will find the ideas that passed through my mind at the sight of the paintings on display this year at the "Salon." I have jotted them down without attempting to sort or write them out. Some will be good, others bad. Sometimes you will consider me too severe; sometimes too lenient. Doubtless I shall criticize where you would approve; I shall forgive where you might censure; you will continue to be exacting where I shall be satisfied. No matter. My only concern is to spare you a little time you could use to better advantage even if it were to be spent among your ducks and turkeys (that is, "at your country place"). (*Corr*, 3:309)

Diderot speaks of "jotting down ideas." He called one of his more important essays on art *Pensées détachées sur la peinture*.[1] Detached thoughts on art appear, in fact, in most of his major works. He was so absorbed by the concept of pictorial art that his novels, his short stories, his theater, and even his letters are full of animated tableaux, of paintings brought to life. This tendency has led some critics to the conviction that it was through pictures that he was in the habit of composing. This was only partly true; with the passage of time and the experience it brought, Diderot tended to develop characters that went far beyond the living tableau; each took on a personal individuality and a psychological meaning belonging to itself alone.

Diderot's art criticism is often too literary or too moralistic for the twentieth-century professional and even amateur art critic. He is nevertheless frequently so fascinating in his anecdotes, in his moralizing interpretations of a particular picture, or in the literary sweep of his pen (when, for example, he describes a canvas with moonlight reflected on the ocean waves, the dark, racing clouds overhead, and a ship in distress) that any serious amateur could scarcely fail to find him interesting. Even though much of Jean-Baptiste Greuze's work is characterized by false sentiment and sensuality, Diderot is captivated by his moralistic and symbolic paintings, such as that of a girl weeping over the death of her pet bird (representing remorse and a broken engagement) or the canvas entitled *La Cruche cassée* ("The Broken Pitcher," symbolizing lost virtue).

If Diderot finds in Greuze certain traits—even those strongly appealing to sensuality—that are grounds for lofty moral reflections, he can in a quite different key moralize on the licentiousness of François Boucher and his disciples. Diderot finds Boucher's art flawless, but superficial, a waste of exceptional talent on the explicit gallantries of nymphs, gods, and goddesses—mere boudoir paintings to satisfy the jaded tastes of the aristocracy under the ancien régime. For a moralizing Diderot, Boucher has only too obviously prostituted his gifts in the service of a debauched clientele totally indifferent to aesthetic or ethical truth. Writing in the *Salon of 1761* in a typical moment of pique, he says of Boucher: "This man picks up his brush only to show me breasts and buttocks. I am delighted to see them but I cannot bear having them pointed out to me" (*AT,* 11:189).

This is the discursive criticism of an eighteenth-century authority on art who, acknowledging that pagan mythology offered more voluptuous forms and scenes for contemporary canvases than did other sources of inspiration, is also the solid bourgeois of the day insisting that all of this savoring of the artificially sybaritic has nothing to do with the natural events of life. Boucher was, in Diderot's judgment, endowed with all the gifts of a great artist except that of veracity.

Jean-Baptiste Chardin was something else again. Like Diderot, he was a rising and prominent member of the third estate. And, like Diderot, he was fascinated by and often sought graphic inspiration in the realities of daily existence—the sights, colors, forms, activities of the world in which he lived. Diderot's admiration for Chardin was wholehearted and justified as he recognized with sure taste the painter's exceptional technical skill and his ability to perceive in nature what lay hidden for others. Speaking of Chardin's understanding of colors and reflections, Diderot has this to say in his *Salon of 1763:* "It is not white, red, black with which you daub your palette, it is the very essence of things; it is the air and light you pick up on the end of your brush and put on the canvas." (*AT,* 10:195) It is also in the *Salon of 1763* that Diderot describes Chardin's picture of a gutted stingray, "The subject," we are told, "is revolting, but it is the very flesh of the fish, it is its skin, its blood. . . . Such magic surpasses our understanding. Thick layers of color are applied one on the other, those underneath showing through what is above." Then Diderot, always with the apt anecdote, adds this: "I've been told that Greuze taking the stairs up to the Salon and noticing hanging there the painting of Chardin I have just described, looked at it, and passed on muffling a deep sigh. Such praise is more to the point and better than mine." (*AT,* 10:195).

There is nothing systematic about these *Salons.* They are by turn sprightly, generous, caustic, yielding, seasoned with chatty anecdotes and, at times, arresting insights. They often strike the reader as lively, even brilliant, conversations, the kind in which Diderot was usually the leading participant. Such a disordered approach has long disconcerted and even provoked staid, methodical art critics, especially if they themselves have had a somewhat heavy touch. How could a man like Diderot be taken seriously as a connoisseur of art? But undeniably there are the flashes of insight. Diderot believed that art should not be judged solely on its technical aspects. He felt that other considerations should be taken into account—the subject matter in general, the delineation of character, the psychological shadings. All of these, we are told, a man of letters can weigh as well as and perhaps even better than the artist himself. Then too, Diderot had delved into the aesthetics of art prior to the *Salons*—especially in his treatise deriving from Shaftesbury, his *Encyclopedia* article "Beau," and his noteworthy *Lettre sur les sourds et muets*—and at least two studies written in conjunction with the *Salons* themselves show a high degree of competence in the field of art criticism. The first is his *Essais sur la peinture* (completed in 1766), which is the end product of his experience in professional criticism. The second is the *Pensées sur la peinture, la sculpture, l'architecture et la poésie,* a forceful aftereffect of his visits to the great galleries of Holland, Germany, and Russia, and his reading of Christian von Hagedorn. This was Diderot's last significant contribution to art criticism, composed during the mid-1770s and, seemingly, continually revised up to the time of his death. Both the *Essais* and the *Pensées* were available in Grimm's *Correspondance* but were published posthumously.

There is a touch of irony in this. Not only can a good case be made for the assumption that Diderot was France's first modern art critic, it could also be said that he was, under the old regime, the leading art critic of the third estate whose influence was to extend well beyond the coming revolution.[2] At the same time, it was he whose judgments on paintings and sculpture had already set the standards of an affluent aristocracy in other countries than his own, an aristocracy only too willing to purchase what his aesthetic fantasy and his search for artistic sincerity and truth had suggested.

Diderot was perfectly aware of the difficulty of his task. In a letter to Grimm he wrote:

For a person to describe a *Salon* to my liking and yours, do you know, my friend, what he should have? All sorts of taste, the capacity to fall under every charming spell, a mind susceptible to a great number of enthusiasms, a colorful style that falls in with a variety of paintbrushes; to be able to be great or voluptuous with Deshays, simple and sincere with Chardin, refined like Vernet, as touching as Greuze; but tell me where such a Vertumnus [the Roman god of change] can be found. We should perhaps have to go to the shores of Lake Geneva" [that is, to Voltaire]. (*AT,* 10:160)

But Diderot was being coy or overly modest. It was he, not Voltaire, who, in the world of eighteenth-century art criticism, was endowed with the gifts of Vertumnus.

Jean Seznec, in his expertly edited volumes of the *Salons* has made
scattered references to Diderot as an art critic who, in his day, had
been one of the clandestine apostles of the philosophe's critical talents
and a member in high standing of a more or less invisible little religion
sowing its seed for an appreciative posterity.[3]

"As an art critic," Gita May reminds us, "Diderot is undoubtedly
at his best when he gives free play to his aesthetic sensibilities without
allowing ideological preoccupations to interfere unduly with his direct
response to a painting." And she adds, "His enthusiasm knew no
bounds when he found himself in the presence of a composition that
revealed originality of vision reinforced by mastery of execution."[4]

Veiled Collusion

Preparation of the *Salons* and his very genuine interest in the fine
arts took up some of Diderot's time and energies now that he felt no
longer explicitly committed to a fickle French public, intolerant authority,
and to the great city of Paris that, despite its past grandeur, was
showing an ever-expanding corruption quite out of joint with the ideals
of a philosophe. He would often spend time in the country with Grimm
at one or another of the estates of Mme d'Epinay, where there was a
pleasant rural simplicity in the surrounding woods and fields. Mme
d'Epinay, a gracious hostess, supplied the setting for a few well-chosen
guests who could appreciate good music and enjoy scintillating conversation under an always hospitable roof.

Another congenial ambience for Diderot was furnished by the Baron
d'Holbach either in his sumptuous town house—called by a select group
of encyclopedists "The Synagogue"—or at his mother-in-law's chateau
that, as Diderot has shown in letters to Sophie, was for him a sojourn
of intellectual and gustatory delight where the waking hours of all were
filled with gaiety, mischief, compatibility, and a pervasively refreshing
sense of freedom. Everything under the sun was discussed, and everyone
talked excitedly and unrestrainedly of music, history, politics, the theater,
astronomy, physics, agriculture, and morality. The women of the d'Holbach household prattled charmingly and, now and then, carried on in
mild ribaldry. They and a few welcome foreigners (Horace Walpole,
David Hume, and the Abbé Galiani were, at one time or another, the
baron's guests) gave variety to the scene. The uninvited slurringly referred
to d'Holbach as the "maître d'hôtel" of the encyclopedists, and Diderot
dined well, in fact too well (tender passages in his letters to Sophie

are often interspersed with his digestive problems) in the midst of unbridled conviviality. All this afforded much needed interludes—short-lived escapes—from the weight of the now-clandestine *Encyclopédie,* from an ever-nagging wife, and from the relentless attacks of his enemies. And Diderot performed well. Speaking of one of the baron's dinners, "It is there," the Abbé Morellet tells us, "that I heard . . . Diderot converse on questions of philosophy, art, or literature, and by his richness of expression, fluency, and inspired presence, hold our attention at great length.[5]

D'Holbach was much more than a wealthy and generous house steward for an intimate circle of friends among whom Diderot held forth with such dazzling animation. The baron wrote scientific articles on metallurgy for the *Encyclopédie* but was constantly composing under various names and pseudonyms an impressive number of books that were unrelenting attacks on the world of Christianity in his day. His atheism was so militant in these works that it was decried by Voltaire, and those who knew what he was up to gave him the title of "the personal enemy of God."

To Diderot's closest friends, it may be supposed that his future never looked doubtful. He was too interested in life, he was too intellectually alert, and he was too good company for himself or others for it to appear that his life would end in failure. But what form would his destiny take from now on?

The death of Denis's father in 1759 was a profoundly depressing experience, for, as is evidenced throughout the son's writings, there was an abiding love and esteem for the old cutler who had been a good father in every sense of the word. The masterly short story entitled *L'Entretien d'un père avec ses enfants,* written years later, is an excellent illustration of the headstrong, brilliant son's deep respect and devotion for a father who was, from the point of view of character and temperament, so different from his intellectually wayward offspring. The father's dying words had been "Live in unity." The specific reference was to the ideological abyss that, for years, had separated the philosophe and the younger brother, Didier, who was totally immersed in the work of the church. In his father's memory and for the sake of possible harmony, Denis promised the devout brother that never again would he publish a word against religion. This fitted in well enough with his determination to sever all commitments to his age and to write for future generations only. If, during the years ahead, Diderot published little or nothing against formal religion, he nevertheless wrote for himself, perhaps for a few intimates, and for posterity, attacking organized religion as such sometimes covertly, sometimes openly, in novels, philosophical dialogues, essays, and even poems. These were works that would not see the light of day during his brother's lifetime any more than during his own. Carol Blum has neatly summed up the decade directly following the father's death:

It was during those years between 1759 and 1772 that Diderot produced the works that future generations were to hail as his masterpieces. *La Religieuse, Le Neveu de Rameau, Le Rêve de d'Alembert, Jacques le fataliste* were written in the privacy of his study, intended with few exceptions for Diderot alone, and free from the exigency of presenting an ideal philosopher who would at once impress the public and offer the author a model whom he could call himself. If, as Diderot remarks in the *Neveu de Rameau,* his thoughts were his harlots, he had decided to enjoy their company unhampered by the petticoats of polite society. The promise to Didier marked the end of an era in Diderot's life and the beginning of a long and painful period of turning inward.[6]

In 1760 Diderot, full of vitality and intellectually coherent as usual, began *La Religieuse,* his first bona-fide novel with a well-defined plot (actually a plot within a plot) as well as clearly delineated characterizations. Both the *Bijoux indiscrets* and the disingenuous *Oiseau blanc*— composed twelve years before—were, by comparison, pitiful attempts at fiction, whatever other merits they may have possessed. Though an articulate and zealous priest under the empire charged *La Religieuse* with being partly responsible for bringing on the French Revolution, the novel was not published until 1796; at approximately the same time it appeared before a somewhat scandalized British reading public translated as *The Nun.* Still, eighteenth-century Europe had for years been regaled or shocked by accounts both fictional and authentic of social and religious practices, some less edifying than others, in convents and monasteries in various Christian countries, especially France. Of this flood of convent-oriented literature, Diderot's pathetic story of Mlle Simonin, Sister Suzanne, stands out far above and beyond the others. There are a number of reasons for this, and they might quite suitably be introduced by a general statement, to wit: through ingenious admixture of truth and fiction, psychology and aesthetics, the author has portrayed social and conventual life in France under the ancien régime in the form of a complex narrative, a narrative within a narrative, in which he attempts to transcend the reality of life itself.

The inner story of *La Religieuse* is of a beautiful, talented, unfortunate girl (she herself—or rather, Diderot—tells us as much) who, against her will, is forced to take the veil. Imprisoned within the walls of several convents on the outskirts of Paris, she undergoes a succession of painful vicissitudes that are related in the first person as memoirs. Finally managing to escape her cloistered existence, she briefly ekes out a precarious living in the cesspool that was Paris and, having hardly reached womanhood, dies.

The overall plot or framework in which the story of Sister Suzanne is contained is a mystification. This should not come as too much of a surprise since Diderot, like Swift and Voltaire, was one of the eighteenth-century past masters of the hoax, literary or otherwise. In January 1760, in conjunction with Grimm and Mme d'Epinay, he conceived a plot to bring back to Paris the elderly and charming Marquis de Croismare who, having retired to his chateau in Normandy with his daughter, was greatly missed by his friends. He was a kindly man, an art and music lover of the first order and, though a good Christian, was held to be a fellow philosophe because he was able to converse spiritedly and intelligently with out-and-out atheists like themselves. They had been finding his absence of some fifteen months intolerable.

A letter was concocted as coming from a recently escaped nun to which the marquis replied without hesitation. From this resulted a correspondence of several months with a lady in Versailles as the indispensible "letter drop." The ruse was unsuccessful, for the marquis—instead of returning to Paris—insisted that the unfortunate Mlle Simonin take the *diligence* to Normandy where his chateau would afford her the hospitality and care of which she was obviously so desperately in need. Following a flurry of letters—genuine on the marquis' part and counterfeit on the part of the little band of conspirators—there was nothing left to do but to bring sickness and death to the poor, suffering, and imaginary girl.

Some years later the marquis discovered the hoax that had been played on him and laughed as heartily at his own expense as did his prankster friends. But this exchange of letters, some true, others false, immediately kindled Diderot's creative imagination, and he was soon plunged into writing the memoirs of his nonexistent nun, weeping over them while so doing. They were memoirs addressed to none other than the good marquis.

Perhaps these pseudo memoirs were a fortunate and even necessary distraction. Diderot had suffered but had been recently absolved from

charges of plagiarism regarding the plates of the *Encyclopédie;* this in
itself proved to be an ordeal. Then, on 2 May 1760, the first performance
of Palissot's *Les Philosophes* was warmly applauded by curiosity seekers,
gossip mongers, and members of the antiphilosophe camp. Though
Rousseau, Helvétius, and Jean François Marmontel were among those
ridiculed in this impudent comedy, the play's chief scamp and malefactor
was Diderot, depicted under the name of Dortidius. He was only too
well aware of the comedy's existence, and Goethe may have been right
in saying that it served as an initial impulse for Diderot's *Neveu de
Rameau,* one of the most vitriolic satires of the age, begun the following
year but turned to again and again for careful revision over long stretches
of time.

The main lines for the plot of *La Religieuse* were entirely plausible
in that they followed closely the actual case of a nun, Sister Marguerite
Delamarre, member of a wealthy, middle-class family, who was obliged
to take the veil at the age of eighteen. She repeatedly brought before
the law courts of Paris the plea to be freed from her religious vows.
In May 1758, however, she lost her suit once and for all. She died
as a nun and in a convent many years later; the Revolutionary authorities
offered to release her but by then it was too late for freedom.[7]

Diderot's tale was, therefore, a plotted novel based upon a factual
case. But it was much more. There are, in effect, many other components
to *La Religieuse,* some more important than others, but all worthy of
consideration. For instance, Samuel Richardson was by now well known
on the Continent; he was a writer who impressed Diderot greatly, as
the Richardsonian discussions in Diderot's correspondence between 1760
and 1762 indicate. The story of Suzanne was Diderot's novel in the
manner of the British writer especially inspired by the anguished life
and tragic death of Richardson's Clarissa Harlowe. In both instances
there is the moving story in epistolary or memorial form in which a
gifted, most attractive young woman is victimized in a world that
represents at once realism, illusion, morality, immoralism, and pathos.

There are, as well, in Diderot's tale of convent life intimations of
the Gothic novel to come, a genre to be realized a few years hence by
Horace Walpole, Ann Radcliffe, and others. But Gothic elements were
also apparent in earlier works across the Channel, in some of the poetry
of Alexander Pope, in that of Edward Young, of Joseph Warton, and
perhaps especially in the poetry of Thomas Warton the younger, as
noted by Kenneth Clark in *The Gothic Quest.*

Whether Diderot, who read English with ease, was familiar with this British poetry emphasizing moods of reverie and abandonment, the sensitivity of melancholia, the cold, dark corridors in stone, the Gothic vaults, and other reminders of the beckoning graveyard, or whether he merely sensed all this as being in the air at the time, we do not know.

But Diderot's charged atmosphere and monastic settings in *The Nun* had often more than a passing resemblance to those of the castles later to be created by British writers of fiction. Both Diderot and they, whether devising the topographical and atmospheric properties of a convent or a castle were, at the same time, dealing with the structure of the mind, the winding corridors of consciousness. With Diderot, and later with Walpole, the fiction involved was written with wondrous psychological energy. Most important of all, perhaps, Diderot and the British novelists in his wake, were dealing with subterranean impulses of the human psyche. It is an aspect of Diderot's novel that deserves further study.

So do certain strong personal preoccupations of Diderot. One of these is claustrophobia. Claustrophobia is among the more common phobias. It would seem to correspond to primitive fears of being trapped by some force or power in a situation from which there is no escape. *La Religieuse*, it goes without saying, is shot through with this apprehension, Suzanne Simonin being the principal victim of a living entombment. Agonizing experiences from Diderot's own past, confinement in a monastery at his father's behest and incarceration in the donjon at Vincennes, conspire to lend a strong personal touch to the atmosphere of the novel. Moreover, evidence of autobiographical claustrophobia can be found in other works of Diderot, including his correspondence.

The litany of madness in various guises also runs through the works of Diderot. Sometimes it manifests itself in unbridled passion for another person, sometimes it is depicted as an endless dream, at other times it takes the form of hysteria or delirium; it is, upon occasion, closely linked to the phenomenon of genius. In all this, like Julien La Mettrie, the miscreant of the philosophic school, the most notorious materialist of the day and author of *L'Homme machine*, Diderot held that the mind could affect the body, and the body the mind. Moreover, Diderot, like La Mettrie, who was a medical doctor, believed that man, the machine, or the animal, is so complicated that we can never hope to discover his essence nor even all the springs that control human behavior.

As we have already seen, Diderot's sister, Angélique, by her own choice an Ursuline nun, died insane in her convent well before the age of thirty. Diderot's daughter was later to confide to Meister that "It is the fate of this sister that gave my father the idea of the novel, *La Religieuse*."

One present-day critic has declared that "For Diderot the two most important sources of madness are seclusion and deprivation of sexual love."[8] Man is, in Diderot's view, a social being, and the dangers of solitude, of sequestration, are everywhere apparent in *La Religieuse*. In one instance they take the following form: "Man is born for society; separate him, isolate him, his ideas will disintegrate, his character will become deformed, a thousand absurd notions will well up in him; extravagant thoughts will take root in his mind like brambles in uncultivated soil" (*AT,* 5:119).

Among other allusions to madness—and there are many—Diderot takes up step by step the growing dementia of one of the mothers superior. She begins by lying long hours in bed, indulging in erotic reverie, and in fondling herself. She then feels sexually drawn to the younger members of her convent. Particularly attracted to Sister Suzanne but unable to seduce her, she becomes tormented to the breaking point. She is finally overwhelmed by inexplicable guilt, sinks into a profound nervous depression, and dies. The theme of madness could have derived specifically from Diderot's own sister, insane in her mid-twenties, and that of lesbianism from his insistent suspicion of abnormal relations between his beloved Sophie and her enticing sister. Besides all this, though, there is a coherent message in the novel: it is that no human being should be forced to live a life for which he or she is in no way suited.

There are those who believe that an unresolved novel is like an unresolved chord in music. In fiction the denouement should pick up the loose ends and tie everything together by establishing the raison d'être of the story. But in his convoluted novel Diderot provides two conclusions, one for the inner story, the other for the outer story, which is the whole structure, including what Diderot himself called the *Préface-Annexe*.

The plot of the inner story, that of Suzanne illegitimately born into a middle-class family and obliged to take the veil, comes full circle. She has left an unappreciative, blemished social milieu in eighteenth-century Paris and is confined to one convent after another. At last an escapee, she again finds herself in the world of the throbbing city, now not even protected by the walls of a religious institution, and where vice in its diverse forms far exceeds that of her conventual life. If this inner story is a scalding satire of monastic life, it is equally, but in less detail, the satire of a socially corrupt Paris under the old regime. That too is a subject to which Diderot will often return.

But the novel has, especially on aesthetic and psychological grounds, much more to offer. The original edition of *La Religieuse* already presented the reader with the document entitled *La Préface-Annexe* that comprised letters, pseudoletters, and explanations demonstrating that the tale of Suzanne Simonin was a long-drawn-out prank. Early critics protested against the *Préface-Annexe,* finding it an uncalled for account of collusion and detrimental to the part of the work we have been referring to as the inner plot or story. This inner plot was admired and appreciated from the beginning as arresting and even brilliant fiction based on fact or half fact and revealing Diderot as a storyteller par excellence. That this tale of a nun's plight was effectively executed, sometimes profound in its psychological insights and at times deeply touching, has been recognized to the present day. Yet only with Herbert Dieckmann's research and subsequent evaluation in the 1950s has it become evident that here was a creative work far more complex than had been previously suspected. Professor Dieckmann convincingly proved that, in later years, Diderot carefully revised what we have called "the outer plot"—in reality the *Préface-Annexe*—and even transformed it into an integral part of the novel. The Dieckmann conclusion becomes inescapable:

The *Préface-Annexe* can no longer be considered as a document which gives the biographical and historical background of *La Religieuse,* the "true story" behind the "fiction" of the novel, and it certainly is not a scaffolding which Diderot ought to have removed according to Devaines and Naigeon, as well as other critics who echo these arguments or elaborate on them. The *Préface-Annexe* is part of the novel, it is as much invention and fable as the novel itself. Diderot subjected it to the same "literary" revision to which he subjected *La Religieuse* and the more he revised it in style and content, the more he transformed it into a work of art. . . . To be sure, the preface still gives the immediate occasion for the novel, its origin in a trick played on a real person. But soon the trick became part of the overall invention and, as Diderot combined part of the correspondence with the novel and modified the original text, the line could no longer be drawn between the "real" story and the work of art.[9]

Viewed as such, the novel takes on a new dimension and foreshadows some of the most challenging of twentieth-century fictional techniques.

Despite this touch of the modern, Diderot found it a moment to think of the recent past as well. In 1761 Samuel Richardson was no more, and the author of *La Religieuse,* moved by deep feeling, wrote a short but important essay in praise and in memory of the English master of the epistolary novel.

Around the *Eloge de Richardson*

Moral criteria have not been fashionable in aesthetics for a long time. The classical triumvirate of truth, beauty, and good has been reduced by at least one, and the other two have formed strange relationships. Diderot's attempt to establish the meliorist credentials of the novel in the *Eloge de Richardson*[10] may therefore strike us as dangerously quaint. And indeed the effusions of sentiment, the virtue-happiness cliché, the *utile dulce* motif, and, above all, Diderot's self-complacent posturing make for some uncomfortable comments. But a supercilious approach to the *Eloge* would be as unenlightened as the traditional Diderot scholar's condescension toward Richardson's art itself.[11] For it is by his appreciation of Richardson as a consummate artist that Diderot makes a unique contribution. As usual, it has taken posterity two centuries to catch up.[12]

In the *Eloge* Diderot flatly states his preference for Richardson's *Clarissa* (*AT,* 5:226). When he plunges into that novel in detail, there emerges an exquisite comprehension of the English author's complexity, his exploitation of paradox and ambiguity, his stylistic range, his verve and audacity, and, above all, his artistic tact and mastery. Though they alternate with some of Diderot's less appealing effusions, these critical passages themselves contain none of the posing and posturing that we find objectionable. This does not mean that they are nonpersonal, purely "objective." Quite the contrary. Lacking the self-conscious sense of audience conveyed by Diderot's emotive proclamations, they seemed directly linked to deep and genuine personal involvement. The motive is clearly revealed at the end of the *Eloge:* "I am moving toward the end of my days without trying anything that can also recommend me to posterity."

By 1761 Diderot's long-nurtured artistic aspirations had not achieved their lofty goals. The dramas of the 1750s, in which he had sought to apply the intimate techniques of the Richardsonian novel to the perspective of the stage, had not taken the public by storm. In 1760, pilloried by Palissot, he had immersed himself in the Croismare hoax.

But this long-delayed adventure into the realm of the new novel was neither in form nor in content capable of release to the general public. Diderot had only his own tears, the accolades of his immediate circle, and the shadow-audience of posterity on which to base his hopes. Not very definitive testimony all told. And it was precisely at this point, we recall, that his former friend, Jean-Jacques, burst into 1761 with *La Nouvelle Héloïse*, a Richardsonian novel—and conquered the world.

All of this must have presented a bitter challenge to Diderot. He undoubtedly kept turning, or returning to Richardson in an earnest attempt to form himself upon the master. In fact he says as much: "Several times I began reading *Clarissa* to give shape to my writing; each time I forgot my plan to do so by the twentieth page" (*AT*, 5:221). His exasperation rings absolutely true. His awe before this immense technique is desperately sincere. His inability to maintain craftsmanlike objectivity is proof to him of the master's power (and the apprentice's impotence). "Richardson's genius has stifled what little I had" (*AT*, 5:227).

As with so much of Diderot's criticism, then, the praise of Richardson comes from within, from anguished experience, from frustrated emulation. The warmth is not mere reflection. In this multifaceted and uneven manifesto the public and the private Diderot make contact by proclamation: the clarion *Eloge* was born of the same ambitious malaise that spawned the first draft of the clandestine *Neveu de Rameau*. This latter work, open to so many interpretations and called in turn a satire, a novel, a philosophical dialogue, has, since Goethe, been admired as a satire of the first water and, generally speaking, an unquestioned masterpiece by knowledgeable readers.

Rameau's Nephew: The Springs of Human Action

What to many critics appears an unquestioned masterpiece—and some consider it Diderot's greatest—has often left the casual reader either bewildered or apathetic. *Le Neveu de Rameau* has been called "that endlessly faceted enigma," and, in its complexity, it seems to touch on more aspects of Diderot's thought than any other single work. This may be the reason that the *Neveu* has been dipped into time and again for intellectual interpretation and artistic appreciation in a variety of efforts to discover its true significance.

In a swiftly moving dialogue that gives at once the impression of deep seriousness and playful levity, we see the philosophical probity of

a self-questioning Diderot pitted against the ready expediency of Rameau's brilliantly erratic nephew[13] who was at that moment facing the
obstinate fact of his artistic, social, and moral collapse. *Moi* and *Lui,*
these are the interlocutors of a debate where much of the truth may
well lie in the tensions of a subtly sustained dialectic that, at first
glance, would seem to be little more than vacillation or even contradiction
on the part of the author himself.

By drawing both epigraph and inspiration from Horace's satire of a
fellow who for inconsistency knew no peer, Diderot has indicated that
the *Neveu de Rameau* is, among other things, a portrait. In the
unprincipled nephew recently ejected from his parasitic existence in the
salon of the wealthy Bertin and Mlle Hus, his actress "hostess," Diderot
has presented us with an arresting figure in all the palpitating realism
of his physical and moral being. This vivid characterization suggests a
transition between the technique of portrayal already employed in novels
by Pierre Carlet de Chamblain de Marivaux and the Abbé Prévost and
those techniques to be used later by Honoré de Balzac and Gustave
Flaubert. More broadly viewed, the portrait produces in the apparent
looseness of its structure the impression of a segment of the river of
life, a glimpse of predatory and morally corrupting evils of eighteenth-
century Parisian society, with its financiers, art patrons, and bohemians.
Once again we are reminded of literary devices that will be common
among succeeding generations of writers.

Impetus was doubtless given to the composition of the dialogue by
repeated assaults on the *Encyclopédie* by its enemies. Palissot, in particular,
had written, as we have seen, his polemical play *Les Philosophes,* which
was a venomous attack on Diderot as philosopher, playwright, and
moralist. This would seem to explain in no small measure the bitterly
personal invective of *Le Neveu.* Its virulence is directed against the
society of such men of wealth as Bertin, who not only gave wholehearted
support to the adversaries of the *Encyclopédie,* but even worse, utilized
his fabulous riches to support men of letters, actresses, and playwrights
who were usually devoid not only of genius but even of talent.

In this respect the *Neveu de Rameau* is a personal satire in what is
now the more or less accepted sense of the term—a writing whose
specific aim is to inveigh against particular persons or groups and their
social, intellectual, and moral idiosyncrasies. And indeed Diderot's own
title for the dialogue was *Satyre 2*[de.] But what *Satire I: Sur les caractères
et les mots de caractère, de profession, etc.* already indicates, is borne out
in the *Neveu*—that Diderot had given the word *satire* not only the

French meaning, but also that of the Latin *satura,* in which freedom of form and subject matter were mingled with traditional moral problems. The conception of satire as a more comprehensive form of the genre than that accepted by most of his contemporaries allowed Diderot free rein to indulge in a mixed and, to all appearances, rambling composition dealing with a variety of human activities, feelings, and opinions. Hence the interlacement of the different themes that compose the perplexing but no less fascinating intricacies of *Rameau's Nephew,* a work which, nevertheless, preserves an artistic and intellectual unity that Goethe had been quick to recognize when, in 1805, he translated it from a copy presented him by Frederick Schiller of a St. Petersburg manuscript, and entitled it *Rameaus Neffe.*

Among those themes that critics have often marked for special attention is what they hold to be an illustration of the dichotomy in Diderot's character. Such an interpretation assumes the dialogue between *Moi* and *Lui* to be nothing less than a prolonged dialectic where Diderot's two natures, represented by idealism and materialistic realism, moral responsibility and fatalistic determinism, clash in unremitting conflict only to move on to an insoluble dilemma. It has even been intimated that the basic theme of the work is scarcely more than a pre-Freudian collision between the id and the ego. Others have drawn attention to the possible confusion in Diderot's mind between ethical and aesthetic values, which is brought into focus by the sudden shifts from moral considerations to merits of Italian and French opera, Giovanni Battista Pergolesi and Duni as opposed to Jean Baptiste Lulli and the great Jean Philippe Rameau. This, though exemplifying one phase of the "Querelle des Bouffons," also opens up new paths for the most modern aesthetic theories—one critic has even been persuaded that the *Neveu* is fundamentally a study of music. Most scholars mention, at least in passing, evidence of Diderot's philosophical, artistic, sociological, and neurobiological preoccupations that will, upon occasion, be treated in greater detail in his later works. These elements are already given a certain emphasis in the question of talent and genius that rises to the surface as the satire unfolds. More specifically, we see and to some extent understand why the nephew, though gifted with unusual power of expression, is unable to embody his musical talents in a form that has either permanence or validity. The theme becomes most clearly manifest and reaches its crescendo in the final remarkable scene of musical pantomime where the reader is witness to a moment of such mad, unconstrained inspiration that the subject's gifts defy disciplined expression. This phenomenon will be given renewed emphasis some years later in the *Paradoxe sur le comédien*.

Scholarship has convincingly shown that the *Neveu de Rameau* is a unified product of the year 1761, the essential elements of which have remained unchanged; this in spite of interpolations and minor revisions extending to 1775. For obvious reasons Diderot could not publish this dialogue during his lifetime—Palissot and Mlle Hus, in fact, long survived him—nor was it ever mentioned by any of his contemporaries. Indeed, it is evident that he wrote it for his own satisfaction and for posterity, from whom he expected recognition and, quite possibly, immortality. The first French edition, in 1821, was retranslated from the German. Other French copies were to appear sporadically for publication throughout the nineteenth century, but the text that caused so much sensation was Diderot's autograph manuscript, found by the bibliophile, Georges Monval, on the quais of Paris and now in possession of the Morgan Library in New York City.

Complex though it may be as it reflects the variety of Diderot's interests, the satire nevertheless reveals in striking fashion the author's consciousness encompassing a great number of individual centers, each linked to the next, and their totality offering a glimpse of the universal. Carlyle was able to say a century ago that the *Neveu* represented something "perennially poetic," "a sulphurous Erebus," "holding of the infinite."[14]

While this is certainly so, equally true is Jean Fabre's remark that the work achieves its unity, not through any given thesis, but through a presence, that of Rameau the nephew, the *Lui* of the dialogue.[15]

It would be impossible to treat in detail the various problems that are taken up in the *Neveu,* each slowly turned in the light of Diderot's mind, before he concludes with a conception that is not simple, that he does not wish to be homogeneous, and the synthesis of which he often leaves to the reader. Among other problems, though, it has been noted that the question of talent and genius is central to the dialogue.[16] As the conversation progresses, it becomes evident that the theme of talent and genius is being filtered through two temperaments, examined on two planes, even though, as some would maintain, the characters of the satire are but divergent manifestations of Diderot himself. Reduced to its simplest terms, the *Neveu* appears as a series of discussions between a retrograde artist, who is cursed with an illustrious family name, and a philosopher of considerable intellectual prominence. As a study in character, the dialogue is first and foremost the portrait of a fellow who is both eccentric and inconsistent. We have been warned of this in the Horatian epigraph that introduces the work: "Born under the malignant influence of change."[17]

Like Montaigne, Diderot was ever intrigued by man's nature, "diverse and undulating," and as late as the *Eléments de physiologie* he persisted in his view that "The most constant of humans is he who changes the least" (*AT, 9*:423). Thus, as the dialogue unfolds, we see the nephew moved in turn by pride and self-contempt, hope and dejection, faith in what he has already accomplished creatively but acceptance of its insignificance, and first satisfaction, then depression, in recognizing that the mark of genius is not upon him. So, too, we see him catering to his innate hedonism, while regretting it with his instinct as an artist. Nor in any way does Diderot seem to violate the dictum in Horace's *Ars poetica*: ". . . let the first impression be preserved to the end, and let his nature be consistent."

Like Jean Fabre, June Siegel sees the *Neveu de Rameau* as unified, not by a thesis, but by a presence, that of *Lui*. More specifically, she tells us that in the nephew as depicted by Diderot we encounter irrepressible force, violent urge, and a certain frenetic hypersensitivity. He, like Richardson's Lovelace, she adds, "emanates mainly from inner imperatives whose very repression, explosive, propels them beyond their contemporaries, the finely-developed figures of Marivaux and the jaunty creations of Fielding." How does this energy manifest itself? Professor June Siegel asks, and answers her own question as follows:

First of all, in a fantastic volability of language and gesture—mind and matter in accelerated motion. Much has been written about the extraordinary musico-gestural rhapsodies in *Rameau's Nephew*. The work itself is not just a dialogue. Its pattern is more complex: an interplay of audacious disputation and inspired miming. Diderot's fascination with supra-verbal expressivity of all kinds is well known. It derives from the materialist's somatic orientation, from primitivistic longings of the age, and from deep temperamental pro-clivities of his own. It is the "gut" factor which makes Diderot's theorizing on the subject more than theoretical. In the *Neveu* we have not simply an application but literally an incarnation of Diderot's ideas, welling up from something deeper than words or even images. There is a kinesthetic urgency about *Lui*. Theory, put to action, has acquired the vivid complexity of life.[18]

Scholarship devoted to the *Neveu de Rameau* has been so prolific during the third quarter of this century, it has presented so much new information on the structural aspects of the dialogue and so many different theories concerning the work's meaning or meanings, that one finds it well-nigh impossible to keep abreast of the advances made.

L. W. Tancock, in the introduction to his translated edition of *The Nephew,* expresses the problem as follows: "Behind this very readable conversation, with the frolics and outrageous opinions of an exuberant personality, who is a great comic creation of Rabelaisian proportions, there is an extremely complicated and difficult work which raises questions not yet all clearly answered by the researches and criticisms of generations of scholars. One man's guess is almost as good as another's."[19] The picture is complicated by the fact that Diderot, like many of his fellow philosophes, had a genius for synthesis assimilating the ideas of thinkers both ancient and modern, giving a new slant to these ideas, and finally fusing them into novel and challenging forms.

Among the various interpretations of the *Neveu,* one especially seems to have made appreciable progress toward revealing, beneath the tangled threads of the satire, a truly coherent pattern. In *Diderot the Satirist*[20] Donal O'Gorman has opened a fruitful line of inquiry by demonstrating the importance for Diderot's thought of an influence heretofore almost entirely neglected: that of ancient Greece. This is not to deny the role of Palissot's recent comedy, *Les Philosophes* (already discussed), in providing the immediate impetus toward the creation of the *Neveu;* but Professor O'Gorman calls our attention also to a brief text from *De l'esprit,* published by Helvétius in 1758 and reviewed by his friend Diderot shortly after its appearance, that could have inspired the Encyclopedist to construct his dialogue on two levels, one modern and the other ancient. Indeed, Helvétius's words can be construed as a direct commission to write such a work, for he suggests the portrayal of two opposed types of mentality for the purposes of satirizing contemporary French society: the spirit of the present age (censorious, mocking, malicious) and the spirit of Greece (high-minded, pensive, serene). One is tempted to see a corresponding design in the perverse cynicism of Diderot's *Lui* and the lofty intellectualism of *Moi.*

This key passage from Helvétius—the first of its kind to come to light—implies the existence in the dialogue of a double-tiered structure that Professor O'Gorman proceeds to explore. He insists that although both interlocutors were modeled to a large extent upon living personages (Jean-François Rameau [*Lui*] and Diderot himself [*Moi*]), they were conceived also in terms of analogous characters or situations known to ancient literature, whereby they were endowed with universal significance. Thus, the celebrated quarrel over French and Italian opera, which furnishes the artistic background for the dialogue, evokes a famous historical parallel: the dispute concerning Dorian and Phrygian music so well known to Plato, and the related mythical contest in which the sun god Apollo, having enchanted the Muses with the rational harmonies of his lyre, is judged the winner over a satyr-musician named Marsyas who was renowned for the wild, impassioned strains of his flute. Professor O'Gorman finds convincing textual evidence that Diderot consciously used this classical commonplace as an allegorical substructure. Then, stressing the moral and intellectual connotations traditionally given to music, he infers that Diderot intended to oppose not only two musical styles, but also two life-styles—those we call today "Apollonian" and "Dionysian." (Earlier critics had described the *Neveu* in these terms without attempting to justify their use of concepts first formulated by Nietzsche almost a century after Diderot's death.) And he concludes that *Lui,* like Marsyas, is destined by the author to lose out against his opponent, *Moi.* If the debate appears on the surface to end in a stalemate, it is not, then, because Diderot has refused to take a stand. The Marsyas-Apollo myth contains, in concealed form, the author's true sentiments, and thus plays an essential role in the mystification of the reader.

Having examined the basic metaphor on which the meaning of the satire may be said to depend, Professor O'Gorman goes on, with the help of texts from antiquity that were familiar to Diderot, to draw a number of conclusions that it is possible only to enumerate here: the *Neveu de Rameau* can be read as a modern satyr-play, composed according to the norms of that ancient genre and replete with its particular spirit; the dialogue is, in this tradition, a mock-serious verbal contest between an ironic Socrates (*Moi*) who represents philosophy or enlightenment, and an instinctual energumen (*Lui*) who incarnates Dionysian enthusiasm; the language employed by the interlocutors closely follows the instructions given by Horace in the *Ars poetica* to those who would write satyr-plays; the Dionysian life-style, totally alien to the Enlightenment ethic, was perhaps best exemplified in the eighteenth century by Diderot's archenemy, Jean-Jacques Rousseau, so that *Lui* may be seen as a caricature of Rousseau at least to the extent that, more consistent than the Genevan, he ruthlessly draws the ultimate logical consequences from his Rousseauist principles; and finally, the moral and aesthetic significance of the dialogue appears immensely enriched by the vast resonances of Plato's theories of music, education, and imitation.

The O'Gorman book, with its fascinating insights and its wealth of documentation, will prove challenging to future scholars, even though all the author's statements and conjectures may not find universal acceptance. It shows incontrovertibly that, in the *Neveu,* we have one of the greatest satires of modern times. From beginning to end, in the most general as well as in the most specific sense of the term, the *Neveu de Rameau* remains a satire. And through the infinite variety of his satirical means, Diderot has manifested a profound and sympathetic comprehension of the complexities of human character, the wellsprings of human laughter, and the manifold ironies of the human condition.

Considerations for Self and Posterity

No evidence exists that Diderot ever mentioned orally or in writing even to his closest friends that he intended to compose, was composing, or had composed a work entitled the *Second Satire* or *Rameau's Nephew.* He did, in letters, touch upon certain other of his works such as *La Religieuse, Le Rêve de d'Alembert,* and *Jacques le fataliste,* none of which would, like *Le Neveu,* see the printed light of day until some date in the distant future. Perhaps he was unable, for one reason or another, to put them into final form for publication during these years of comparative withdrawal from the contemporary scene. More likely, though, he wrote them for the personal, intellectual, artistic, and emotional satisfaction they gave him. Most likely of all, he wrote them because he was convinced they would be published and read with understanding and appreciation by future generations. Besides, for the most part—by eighteenth-century standards—they were antireligious in spirit, subversive in tone, and shocking in substance. In consequence, they would never—and Diderot was fully aware of the fact—have been allowed to appear in print under the ancien régime, that is, until well after his death. These works, then, were written for the self, sometimes for a small parcel of friends as well, and surely for posterity.

But the sculptor and quondam associate of Diderot, Etienne-Maurice Falconet, was of a quite different turn of mind; an artist of great talent, he wanted his work to be appreciated while he was still alive, he wished to hear the plaudits from his contemporaries and to receive tangible recompense from those capable of appreciating his artistic genius.

In 1765 a friendly discussion arose between Diderot and Falconet, which was to turn into a controversy by correspondence that was suppressed by Diderot, mysteriously published in part in the nineteenth century, and would not appear in full until 1958 and 1959 in two strangely different versions.

The question between them was, "Whether the consideration of posterity was responsible for doing the noblest deeds and producing the best works."[21] With Diderot taking the affirmative and Falconet the negative, they ranged far and wide over the fields of art and philosophy. Falconet, eager for fame in his own lifetime, for renown not only as a sculptor but also as a man of letters, a philosophe, and a match for Diderot, prepared manuscripts for publication and pressed Diderot for his approval. Diderot demurred, anxious for his future fame, for immortality. To Falconet he had purposely written "in a style that was terse, arid, and abstract."[22] For posterity he wanted to rewrite the letters rhetorically as "a formal discourse with all the nobility of style, all the enthusiasm, and all the logic I believe I have."[23] At a rumor that Falconet had published the original letters, Diderot exclaimed, "I shall never forgive you for having so little respect for the pride of your friend. Woe betide you if you gain the upper hand in this dispute. You have to fashion better statues than I, but I have to turn out a better literary effort than you."[24]

Diderot never wrote the discourse. After his death his son-in-law, M. de Vandeul, faithful to Diderot's design, changed the structure as well as the style of the correspondence, adding sections, transposing passages. But he failed to complete the well-nigh impossible project of reconciling the spontaneity of the original letters with the formality of a studied discourse. In 1831 some of Diderot's letters, secretly copied from a Falconet version that had been sent to Catherine II in Russia, were published in Paris with the dramatic claim that the dying Diderot had left them to Grimm. Their mysterious source unrevealed, these and other letters of Diderot from Falconet's papers were published by Assézat and Tourneux in 1876 but without Falconet's letters. It was not until Diderot's *Fonds Vandeul* was discovered and Falconet's versions were transferred to the Bibliothèque Nationale in the 1950s that full editions became possible of at least two very different versions of the one correspondence.

Ironically, it was preserved for posterity largely through Falconet's disregard of posterity: he had collected all the letters and prepared the basic manuscripts for his own time. And in these letters posterity now discovers a Diderot trying to keep from posterity what he feared might tarnish his future glory.[25]

But by 1765, the year of the beginning of the controversy with Falconet, Diderot had intimations of immortality in a decidedly tangible way. It was then that Catherine the Great of Russia, perhaps through a gesture that would redound to her own honor and sense of generosity, perhaps because she had acquired a genuine admiration for Diderot—as she had for Buffon—bought his library for fifteen thousand livres. Moreover, he was to be curator of the library as long as he lived, with a pension of three hundred pistoles a year. The fifteen thousand livres could be more or less equated with five thousand uninflated American dollars, and the three hundred pistoles were roughly equivalent to three thousand dollars a year. The fifteen thousand livres could be more or less equated with five thousand uninflated American dollars, and the three hundred pistoles were roughly equivalent to three thousand dollars a year. All told, this was a tidy sum, for the buying power of such an amount far exceeded that of the dollar in the second half of the twentieth century.

Diderot was later to receive further indications of Catherine's interest and largesse. But, at the time, the purchase of his personal library by one of the great crowned heads of Europe—while his French enemies, like a pack of jackals, continued to snap at his heels—had to be a good omen for a man hoping for the recognition of a grateful posterity.

Life Is Not a Dream

Given the opportunity, Diderot would talk to anyone or about anything. And when he could not talk he would write. One of the results of this writing is a correspondence that, along with the letters of Voltaire and of Rousseau, comprises some of the most varied, the most informative, the most scintillating epistolary intercourse of eighteenth-century Europe. It is fitting that in a letter to Sophie—when he was unable to talk with her, he would write—he should discuss the nature of conversation as such, saying that, though it might at times seem senseless, erratic, extravagant, and even mad, nevertheless it always had a certain logic or order, hidden though it might be. "Conversation is," he wrote, "a strange thing . . . ; see the circuitous paths we have traveled; the delirious dreams of a patient are not more meandering. And yet, since there is nothing unconnected either in the head of a man who dreams or in that of one who is mad, everything in conversation is also connected; but at times it is difficult indeed to recognize the imperceptible links which have joined together so many incongruous ideas.''[26]

Le Rêve de d'Alembert is about a delirious dreamer babbling in his sleep; hence the title. It is also a series of brilliant conversations, an extraordinary amalgam ranging from biology and medicine, through teratology and other forms of transformism, poetic and scientific visions, matter always in constant movement, artistic and moral sensibility. Behind all this we can see a mental drive not afraid to confront the seeming abyss between the qualitative and the quantitative, between inorganic and organic matter, and between the idealistic monism of Plato and the materialistic monism of Diderot. More concisely, the trilogy or the triptych called *Le Rêve de d'Alembert (D'Alembert's Dream)* or simply the *Rêve*, is a series of eloquent, dramatic dialogues, each bolder than the preceding one, presenting insights into moral, social, thinking man and the world of matter of which he is an integral part. The word "triptych," much in use of late to characterize the work, is apt in that it is an altarpiece to Diderot's deterministic materialism, with the two side panels illuminating each other as well as the central panel, and the central panel in turn adding to a more complete understanding of the side panels.

The work has also been likened to a play in three acts.[27] If so, the first act, entitled the *Entretien entre d'Alembert et Diderot*, has as its setting Diderot's lodgings or a nearby café. When the curtain goes up we find ourselves listening to an argument, or at least a discussion. Diderot has obviously been debating along materialistic, hence atheistic, lines. D'Alembert, a skeptic, believes that a wholly materialistic explanation of the Godhead, of the universe, or of man's soul—all three are possibilities here[28]—raises as many questions as it answers. The ensuing discussion, with Diderot leading the way and d'Alembert—under the pressure of his opponent's Socratic questionings, inadvertently helping—tries to get around the various difficulties that a completely materialistic outlook poses. The origins of life, the creation of new forms of life, and, in particular, animal reproduction, may, finally, be explained if all matter is shown to be sensitive in varying degrees, and if so-called inorganic matter can be assimilated with organic matter through physical and not spiritual processes. The first act would then end with Diderot's warning to d'Alembert that he will dream about these matters when night comes.

Act 2, with its title *D'Alembert's Dream*, revolves around the dream proper. Mlle de Lespinasse has been up the entire night nursing a sick, in fact delirious, d'Alembert who had returned home the evening before in a greatly disturbed state. The famous Dr. Bordeu, an acquaintance of Diderot's and a personal friend of the d'Alembert-de Lespinasse ménage, is called in. D'Alembert remains sleeping fitfully behind a screen. With the help of notes she has jotted down, Mlle de Lespinasse tries to give an account of his nocturnal raving. Bordeu, sounding like the Diderot of the first act, anticipates much of what Mlle de Lespinasse has to report; through illustrations and analogies he gives unity to d'Alembert's seemingly disjointed rantings, and arrives at conclusions that, for Mlle de Lespinasse, are both startling and plausible.

Act 2 is the longest and the most substantial of the three parts of this highly intellectual little comedy. A tentative theory of evolution is offered, when animal mechanism, with its breakdowns and its mutations, is discussed. Here, foreshadowing Lamarck, Bordeu-Diderot concludes that organs produce needs and, reciprocally, needs produce organs. As in the first part with its image of the vibrating harpsichord to demonstrate involuntary memory, so in the middle part, there are striking illustrations where the human body is likened to a spider and its web, the web being the nervous system extending to the farthest reaches of the body, and the spider representing the nerve center in the brain; and the illustration of the swarm of bees to explain the passage from contiguity to continuity in organic matter. With all this there is a great deal of speculation about monsters, freaks of nature, Siamese twins, and much more. Occasionally the conversation between Bordeu and Mlle de Lespinasse is interrupted by d'Alembert, now carrying on in his sleep, now awake and querulous. Bordeu must visit other patients, but Mlle de Lespinasse invites him to return for lunch. Thus we are prepared for the third act.

The curtain rises on Act 3 shortly after lunch. We now have the *Suite du Rêve* which, Diderot wrote in a letter to Sophie, "would make my sweetheart's hair stand on end" (*Corr,* 9:140). "Sweetheart," however, stood for Sophie's sister, so hard to pin down by Diderot or anyone else. With a touch of the frivolous and a few lewd overtones, Diderot, in the guise of Dr. Bordeu, pushes still further certain of the biological implications in the discussion taking place that morning. The subject of crossbreeding—very much in the air during the eighteenth century— and other, more advanced biological experiments, is further explored. Of still greater importance, perhaps, is the reexamination of a number of moral and psychological issues. Here, the doctor proposes that some physical acts may have nothing to do with morality. In the *Suite,* or

Conclusion, we are in the midst of some, though not all, of Diderot's views on sexuality. Morality is, he claims, a social concept, and if the act does no harm to the individual, or any other human being, or to society in general, no question about its validity need be raised. In these final pages Bordeu-Diderot will acknowledge that men have always attributed a great deal of importance to the act of generation. And he thinks they are right to do so, but he demonstrates throughout his writing his dissatisfaction with both their civil and their religious laws on the matter. Here too, Diderot shows himself to be noticeably modern in his views.

During his lifetime Diderot made it a practice to say little or nothing about his great posthumously published works. *Le Rêve,* however, is a happy exception. In September 1769 Diderot was more or less alone in Paris and hard at work on his dialogue. Especially in his letters of the second and eleventh of the month, written to an absent Sophie Volland, we have a good idea of the conception and rapid progress of *The Dream.* Diderot had abandoned the notion of having a discussion among three people arising from the ancient Greek savants, Democritus (who held that matter in motion created the universe), Hippocrates (father of medicine), and Leucippus (advocate of the atomist theory), for he would have felt too severely hemmed in by the narrow limits of their philosophy. Instead he chose three eighteenth-century contemporaries, all of whom he knew on a more or less intimate basis—so intimate, in fact, that d'Alembert and Julie de Lespinasse, upon reading the manuscript, found it too personal for comfort, and demanded that it be burned. One of their objections could be something of a surprise for today's readers, for the work implies they were living together in a platonic relationship, which, if generally known, might have made this couple, each born illegitimate, the laughingstock of a highly sophisticated eighteenth-century. Fortunately, Diderot, though burning the manuscript as promised, had prudently made a copy.

Thus we find Diderot, like Plato long before him in ancient Athens, representing contemporary personalities and setting; the dialogues reflect the social character and intellectual life of eighteenth-century Paris and ancient Athens respectively.

So Diderot's three characters in his dialogue are historical personages, each well chosen to express his or her own ideas and bring out those of the other two. We see d'Alembert true to life—capable of faithful attachment, honest, intellectually independent, but lacking the capacity for feeling and imagination. The first third of *Le Rêve,* the *Entretien,* is essentially an encounter of d'Alembert's tightly rationalistic system with Diderot's freely synthesizing, expansive naturalism that easily has the upper hand in lyrical expression as well as in originality. In fact, it has been frequently repeated that some of the greatest poetry of the French eighteenth century lies in certain prose passages both in *Le Rêve de d'Alembert* and *Le Neveu de Rameau*.

The character of Mlle de Lespinasse personifies that intuitive, synthetic mode of thought often identified with the *beau sexe*—sudden analogies and spontaneous comparisons. Here we have, as elsewhere in Diderot, woman's role as the counterpart of man's.[29] She is capable of bringing out the best in him, sometimes with the sublimation of the erotic instinct. In his letters to Sophie Diderot would now and then tell his mistress of her powers of inspiration. Still, the relationship here depicted indicates another of the author's preoccupations—the association of mental activity and erotic feeling where the two unite in an overall understanding of man and the universe.

For instance, we should note the setting of the central dialogue. It is the bedside of d'Alembert which suggests a background for allusions to the earthy aspect of the relationship between the sexes in general. D'Alembert's relationship may, in effect, well have been platonic. And yet we have the mathematician dreaming of his Julie, that is, Mlle de Lespinasse, with the dream ending in an erotic climax that is closely linked to the cosmic vision occasioned by his delirium. This latter includes the association of rhythm of the reproductive act and the flux of living, palpitating forms in the universe—inevitable for one who is of Diderot's makeup. And over all, man is portrayed as requiring the receptivity of woman to bring forth his creative abilities. Julie de Lespinasse, then, is a highly important, indeed indispensable character in the dialogue.

Dr. Bordeu, as an advocate of the eighteenth-century Hippocratic revival, has a distinguished place in the history of medicine. His approach to illness was based on respect for the working of nature, which was envisioned as a general creative force particularized in the individual. In short, each illness was a special case, and treatment was regarded as lending a hand to the natural processes. A similarity of orientation toward the problem of life between Diderot and Bordeu makes plain why the latter was chosen as one of the leading personages of the dialogue. His direction of scientific knowledge toward a deeper understanding of organic processes coincided with Diderot's own efforts to find an experimental basis for his antimechanical materialism.

Of the many aspects of this complex and extraordinary three-part dialogue—Arthur Wilson says that in its philosophical sweep and imaginative power, *Le Rêve de d'Alembert* is Diderot's greatest work of all[30]; we might touch upon one or two.

The *Suite* of *Le Rêve* shows Diderot in a characteristic posture as one who, in his mind, likes to live on both sides of the looking glass. These few pages in themselves might also have justified Heinrich Meister's conclusion that Diderot's ideas were more powerful than the man himself and, in their force, swept him off his feet. Here we have the philosophe proposing bold new concepts that, for his day, would have projected the imagination onto yet uncharted seas of sexuality. What he has to say here is self-evident or at least perfectly understandable to the twentieth-century reader and therefore need not occupy us further.

But from the many fruitful ideas in Diderot's preliminary conversation with d'Alembert, we might briefly consider this discussion of the neutral mechanism of the phenomenon of memory. Memory, Diderot explains, is the ability of the nervous system to retain and record sense impressions. In fact, this is the only source of the organism's consciousness of itself; and the slow unfolding of the happenings of existence, registered in the memory, gives us an awareness of the continuity of our being, that is to say, of self-consciousness and personal identity. Almost immediately, Diderot's naturalistic approach leads him to modern conclusions in psychology and aesthetics.

Considering the quality that the mind strives to attribute or deny to a particular object, Diderot is obliged to employ a limited number of words—the precise terminology now in use was not yet available—to describe what he believes is taking place. In the following passage, for instance, he appears to be using "fibers" to represent nerve centers. He tells d'Alembert that at times he has been led to compare the "fibers" of our organs to sensitive vibrating strings that oscillate and resound long after they have been plucked. "It is this vibration, this kind of unavoidable resonance which keeps the object present while the mind goes on to contemplate any of the object's qualities it so desires." But he adds:

Vibrating strings have still another trait, that of making other strings vibrate; and this is how the first idea recalls a second, the two of them a third, these three a fourth, and so on, so that there is no end to the ideas aroused and joined together in the mind of the philosopher as he ponders and communicates with himself in silence and darkness. This instrument is capable of astounding leaps, and an idea called up will sometimes set vibrating a harmonic at an inconceivable interval. If this phenomenon can be noted between resonant strings that are inert and separate, why should it not take place between points that are alive and connected, between continuous and sensitive fibers. (*AT,* 2:113).

The "astonishing leaps" Diderot refers to, followed by his comparison between man and the sensitively responsive harpsichord (*AT,* 2:114) show him attempting to give psychology in general and the faculty of memory in particular a firm, physiological basis that will be broadened still further in the nineteenth and twentieth centuries. The sympathetic vibration of strings at unexpected intervals—and aesthetically speaking, the creation of original metaphors, as well as the apprehension of unguessed relationships—is the result of a rich accumulation of delicate and varied experiences. Diderot is here offering us conceptions of conscious and unconscious or voluntary and involuntary memory. We are in a realm of psychology that is close to certain fundamental theories of Freud and the modern psychoanalysts. Aesthetically speaking, especially with the stress on involuntary memory, Marcel Proust comes immediately to mind.

What Diderot is suggesting is that memory is a storehouse from which remembered sensations—ideas in the Lockean sense—are, on the one hand, consciously chosen for comparison. But on the other hand, the storehouse of images and impressions secretly lodged in the darkness of nerve centers can spring forth in an unpredictable and often inexplicable manner and unite with present ideas to form the metaphors of poets and the hypotheses of scientists. It is not always clear here or elsewhere how Diderot distinguishes memory from imagination, nor is it easy to trace his steps in the creation of an image. But his conjectures that we have just touched upon are profound and they imply most of what modern investigation holds essential to a valid explanation of the imaginative processes.[31]

Before turning, by way of conclusion, to two passages central to *Le Rêve* proper, we should perhaps inquire into why the title itself, as well as the middle part of the dialogue revolves around the dream device. In a highly informative study Aram Vartanian has this to say about Diderot's use of the device: "In general what suited the dream to Diderot's purpose is that it permitted, on the one hand, a phenomenological transposition of everyday reality, while, on the other, it invested this transposition with a sort of *prima facie* psychological evidence that gave it a semblance of philosophical truth."[32] In short, the phenomenology of the dream is a process through which the seemingly incomprehensible becomes meaningful and in which wild conjecture can be used in a way that is at once speculative and legitimate. Vartanian's philosophical exegesis casts considerable light into the dark crevasses of *Le Rêve*.

At the same time, justification for the dream device can also be found on a less intellectual level. It is a device as ancient as Homer and Plato, both of whom recognized certain psychological values of the dream. The unpredictable leaps and twists of a dream were always— or at least ever since the *Bijoux indiscrets*—of interest to Diderot. In *Le Rêve* the author will succeed in finding a scientific formula to express the psychophysical reality of dreaming.

Moreover, here is a device whereby, with a touch of irony, Diderot can put some of his most original and brilliant ideas in the mouth of d'Alembert who, in real life, is the stolid, even though exceptional, mathematician, the often unimaginative writer, the flat skeptic. Then there is Diderot's fascination with the psychosomatic—in the present instance an opportunity to demonstrate the physiological origin of dreams: the autostimulation of the whole nervous system, the phenomenon of sensations, and movements calling up other sensations and movements. Even the style represents the dream state, for there are short, interrupted sentences, random repetitions, agitated gestures on the part of the sleeper, ending in a release of sexual tension during sleep that suggests the ebb and flow of all life, the cosmos in universal flux. Throughout, there is the interplay of the conscious and the unconscious with no laws to follow other than those that hold together the whole past experience of the dreamer. As a result, the one impossible dream is that the dreamer is someone other than himself. But in all this dreaming the somnolent and sometimes delirious d'Alembert unwittingly helps Diderot realize his own deepest and most extravagant thoughts. And so it is as a dream that Diderot presents his philosophy, a dream that, with the passage of time and the approval of posterity, might indeed be called prophetic.

The two passages fundamental to an understanding of the nature of Diderot's dynamic materialism follow hard, one upon the other. They represent the only time that d'Alembert is dreaming out loud; the rest is a recorded dream that Mlle de Lespinasse has jotted down. These passages are, moreover, at the very center of the piece (*AT*, 2:137, 138–40). And there seems little doubt that Diderot wanted it so. They are the nucleus of the triptych in the way the spider in Diderot's metaphor or image is in the center of the web. Everything leads up to these two utterances of the dreaming d'Alembert, and later, everything derives from them. They are the most complete expression we have of Diderot's materialistic philosophy.

In his first outburst d'Alembert says:

Why am I what I am? Because I had to be. Here, yes, but elsewhere? . . . If a distance of a few thousand leagues can alter my species, what will be the effect of an interval of many thousand times the world's diameter? And if all is in perpetual flux—as the spectacle of the universe shows me to be the case—what may not be produced here and elsewhere by several million years of variations? (*AT,* 2:137)

Then after speculating on whether thinking and feeling exist on the planet Saturn—and an exchange of reactions by Dr. Bordeu and Mlle de Lespinasse—d'Alembert continues:

So I am what I am because it was inevitable. Change the whole and you are obliged to change me. But the whole is forever changing. . . . Man is simply a common product, the monster is a product that is out of the ordinary, but both are equally natural, equally inevitable, equally part of the universe and the general order of things. And what is remarkable about that? All life is constantly intermingling, and so, in consequence, are all species . . . all nature is in a perpetual state of flux. Every animal is more or less man, every mineral more or less plant, every plant is more or less animal. In nature, all boundaries overlap. . . . Everything is more or less one thing or another. . . . Is there in all of nature one atom precisely like another? . . . Don't you agree that everything is interconnected and there can be no missing link in the chain? What do you mean, then, with your individuals? There are none, no, there are none. There is but one great individual, and that is the whole. . . . Consider the entire mass, and if your imagination is too limited to take it all in, consider your own origin and your final state. Oh Architas, you who measured the globe, what are you now? A handful of dust. . . . What is being? The sum of a certain number of tendencies. Can I be anything more than a tendency? . . . No, I am moving toward a certain end. And species? Species are merely tendencies moving toward an end peculiar to them. . . . And life itself? A series of actions and reactions. When alive, I act and react as a mass . . . dead, I act and react as separate particles. . . . Then I do not die? . . . No, certainly in that sense I do not die, neither I nor anything else. . . . To be born, to live, and to die is only to change forms. . . . And what does any form matter more than any other? . . . Each form has the happiness and the misfortune indigenous to it. From the elephant down to the flea . . . from the flea down to the living and feeling molecule—the origin of everything—there is not a mote in all of nature that does not suffer pain and enjoy pleasure. (*AT*, 2:138–40)

In the years directly preceding *D'Alembert's Dream* there had been spectacular advances in scientific knowledge on various fronts. It was also an age when there was, through increasingly adroit use of microscope and telescope, a keen awareness of the infinitely small and the infinitely large, along with an awakening realization of vast expanses of time. More specifically, this realization included the duration of time that the study of the earth was beginning to reveal. Like Maupertuis, Buffon, and others, Diderot was struck by the fact that change was ceaselessly at work under the apparent fixity of forms.

By 1769 Diderot was well prepared to develop an original philosophy of science, a monistic theory that, upon occasion, has been characterized as naturalistic humanism and vitalized materialism going far beyond the mechanistic theories of such writers as the Roman poet Lucretius and the French physician La Mettrie.

A materialist and a materialistic determinist, Diderot holds closely, but in his own way, to the laws of cause and effect that are at the heart of his ethics. The basic principles of his code of morals are to be found most handily in *Le Rêve*. Willpower and freedom of action (free will) are for Diderot Bordeu meaningless terms. They are for a dreaming man the same as they are for a man who is awake. In both instances, they are the latest impulse of desire or aversion, the most recent accretion to the accumulations from birth to the present moment (*AT*, 2:175). An act of will, we are told, is always induced by some inside or outside stimulus, whether by the impression of the moment or by some recollection of the past, or by some passion or by some project for the future.

The only other thing to be said about freedom of action is that it is the most recent thing done of each one of us, and is the unavoidable result of one single cause—ourselves. The conclusion to all this is that, so far as morality is concerned, virtue, the most sacred idea in all nations, must be transformed into the concept of doing good, its opposite into that of doing harm. One is either well or poorly endowed by nature, and each of us is carried along on the general current leading one individual to deserved recognition and another to ignominy (*AT*,

2:176). Rewards and punishments have their place, for they can be methods of correcting the modifiable person we call evil and encouraging the one we call good.

But in his ethics Diderot makes a clear distinction between determinism and fatalism. The lower animals are constantly prey to their ever-demanding senses. In man, the self, the brain with its attributes of imagination and memory, intervenes between the stimuli from without and the act itself.

We have already spoken of Diderot's materialistic monism; this monism can be viewed as Plato's idealistic monism in reverse. There is, then, no reason for surprise in finding many similarities in their thought. Like energy and matter, their interpretations may well represent different phases of the same mystery. In *Le Rêve*—first available in print only in the third decade of the nineteenth century—Diderot revealed himself to be a brilliantly imaginative thinker, a master of the dialogue in what George Havens has called "one of its most convincing examples,"[33] and a writer whom posterity would, in due course, be forced to acknowledge as one of the greatest of the French Enlightenment.

During the 1760s three of Diderot's most ambitious and most challenging works had been set aside with a view toward presenting them to future and, no doubt, more appreciative generations. Both *La Religieuse* and *Le Neveu* continued to be worked on—though in total secrecy—during the following decade. But *Le Rêve* seems to have reached the nineteenth century in much the same form it had come tumbling out of his head in 1769. It had long been taking shape in his mind, however, partly drawn from certain of his previous writings—*La Lettre sur les aveugles* and the *Pensées sur l'interprétation de la nature,* for example—but also from innumerable conversations he had long been engaged in with fellow-*philosophes* on the human animal and the universe in which he lived and died.

In the midst of all his other preoccupations Diderot frequented the Louvre hour after hour, day after day, month after month, and toiled over the *Salon of 1767,* another of his works written not for his French contemporaries but for small clusters of discriminating readers in other countries. His mind and body grew heavy with fatigue, but the *Salon* was not to be ready in time for the *Correspondance Littéraire* of an impatient and even annoyed Fréderick Grimm. Despite his protestations to the contrary, however, the finished product was certainly as rich and varied, as judicious and rampantly wild, as imaginative and original as any of those previously written. In fact, it turned out to be the greatest *Salon* of all!

The 1760s also saw Diderot bringing to a close another work; it was one from which he hoped his own age as well as posterity would benefit—the *Encyclopédie*, which had barely weathered so many storms. In 1764 he had learned to his deep chagrin that, without his knowledge, the publisher Le Breton had, in Diderot's judgment, shamelessly mutilated certain articles in the last ten volumes of the text. His anger was at once indicative of his courage and his seemingly incurable imprudence. If Le Breton had not effected some of the changes, Diderot would again have incurred the wrath of the government and, quite possibly, would once more have found prison walls closing in about him. As it was, French officialdom still did not approve of these final volumes, but decided to allow their distribution abroad and in the provinces, though not in Paris or Versailles. They bore an imprimatur in the name of a bookseller in Neuchâtel, Switzerland.

Through a twist of irony, it was Le Breton, the scrupulous, self-appointed censor, who was arrested and, for a spell, imprisoned in the Bastille; he had after all been rash enough to send without permission of the authorities several copies of the *Encyclopédie's* last volumes to Versailles, where the king held court. By 1772, the remaining two volumes of the plates were also published but, by then, neither Diderot nor Le Breton had any part in the enterprise. For both, the first great modern encyclopedia was finally a thing of the past.

On more than one occasion Diderot had confessed that the formidable and often ungrateful task of his vast editorial achievement might leave him broken in body and spirit. In his famous letter to Grimm which introduces the *Salon de 1765* he wrote: "My head is weary. The burden I have borne for twenty years has bent me almost double, and I have little hope of again sitting up straight" (*AT*, 10:237). The perpetual warfare waged over the *Encyclopédie* for so many years had taught Diderot a great deal. He now expected less, far less from life and his fellowmen. And it was perhaps normal that he was no longer sure that the political and social changes for which the philosophes still hoped and for which they continued to fight would ever be realized.

Yet Diderot was by now reasonably certain that not only the completed *Encyclopédie*, but also the three works, *La Religieuse*, *Le Neveu*, and *Le Rêve*, which would appear some while after his death in all their lustre, would assure him of recognition that he desired far more than a seat among the forty immortals of the French Academy—the recognition of an appreciative posterity. He had written his own epitaph in the last sentence of *Le Neveu:* "Rira bien qui rira le dernier" ("He who laughs last laughs best") (*AT,* 5:488).

Chapter Six
The Aging Stoic

With the 1770s now upon him Diderot was more aware than ever of the ineluctable passage of time. He was moving into a new period of his life. With the early part of the decade his originality of mind, his creative powers, did not change perceptibly. Arresting and even outstanding works still came from an active pen. Moreover, he was—up to a point—coming into his own; he was finally the object of international recognition, although not on the scale enjoyed by Voltaire, Rousseau, and Buffon.

There were moments when his writing had a touch of the acerbic, especially when he saw persistent signs of incomprehension, intolerance, and injustice on the part of governmental and religious authority. He had, nevertheless, become more mellow with the years, sometimes playing unconsciously but superbly the role of the somewhat guileless elder statesman of letters as well as that of the amiable and aging stoic.

Essays on an Old Dressing Gown, on Women, and on Agnosticism and Carnal Sin

Diderot's long narratives, scattered shorter stories, and letters are liberally sprinkled with a great variety of tales and anecdotes. They also contain delightful little psychological or philosophical essays that, when removed from the main text, stand on their own without the slightest difficulty. But, in addition, a number of individual essays are conceived quite independently of more ambitious works. Three, written during the later part of Diderot's life, are considered minor classics because of their charm, their piquancy, and the wisp of nostalgia that, almost imperceptibly, hangs over them.

The first of these is *Regrets sur ma vieille robe de chambre*. Late in the 1760s Grimm, with a foreign prince in tow, unexpectedly dropped into Diderot's home in the rue Taranne for a friendly visit. Equally unexpectedly, Grimm found that his friend, having abandoned his old *robe de chambre*, was ready to receive guests in an elegant, even ostentatious dressing gown. Grimm playfully chided the philosophe on his newly acquired taste for luxury. In return, Diderot wrote a few pages of contrition in which he deplored his folly in casting off the old dressing gown that had so well fitted his body, his habits, and his moods. He readily confessed that the splendid dressing gown he had been wearing had brought other changes: the picture he had commissioned Vernet to paint, and items of furniture supplied by Mme Geoffrin—a bronze and gold clock, a sumptuous armchair, and other objects. As for the old dressing gown: "Why did I not keep it? It was made for me, and I for it." He now realized, he said, that there was a danger in the acquisition of wealth, that poverty could give one a sense of freedom and riches a feeling of intellectual and material constraint (*AT,* 4:5–12). There was, he added, a boundary beyond which he would not go; there was a limit to the changes he was willing to make. The remark is significant. Diderot, like Montesquieu, Voltaire, and even Rousseau, wanted a change in the political and social status quo of France, but none would go so far as to advocate a violent and wrenching break. The guillotine-minded radicals would still have to wait their turn in the wings.

Diderot's fictional characters as well as his correspondence reveal that he had far more than a passing interest in what was for him at once the stronger and the weaker sex. If he found women indispensible to his appreciation of life, he also felt he had much to offer them either individually or en masse, and on diverse levels. Moreover, he was convinced he could explain them to themselves and to others, for he prided himself on a warmth of understanding and an admiration for the feminine psyche uncommon in a member of his own sex.

In 1772, with the appearance of Antoine-Léonard Thomas's *Essay on the Character, Morals and Mind of Women in Different Centuries,* Diderot found an appropriate occasion, as he entered his sixtieth year, both to take issue with Thomas and to express his own ideas briefly and exclusively on a most intriguing subject. He did so in Grimm's *Correspondance Littéraire* later in the same year (*AT,* 2:251–62). He titles the piece simply *Sur les femmes.*

At the outset of his essay Diderot chides Thomas for his objectivity, his cool logic, and his lack of feeling. "When writing about women," Diderot tells Thomas as well as men in general, "we must dip our pens in the rainbow and dry the ink with the dust of butterfly wings." To this he adds: "The symbol for women as a whole is that of the Apocalypse, on whose forehead is written the word 'Mystery.' " All this is well and good, but Diderot does not let matters rest there. Women more clearly represent extremes than do men. On the one hand, they may faint upon seeing a mouse or a spider, but they can also stand up against the greatest horrors of human existence. There is a marked discrepancy between the violence of their impulses and the softness of their features. They are a constant source of astonishment to the opposite sex, for they are "as Beautiful as Klopstock's seraphim and as terrible as Milton's angels."

In a less poetic vein, he notes that they can be relentless in love and ruthless in hate. Then, with an explicitness rare in his time, he tackles the question of female sexual arousal, thereby anticipating some of the controversies and conjectures of present-day sexologists.

To psychology and physiology he adds some rather advanced sociological considerations. Taking heed of woman's lot in eighteenth-century Europe, he notes that civil laws are generally as harsh on her as the laws of nature. In fact, he observed, historically women have been treated like imbecilic adolescents even in the most civilized societies, and blames many of their shortcomings less on some innate defect than on the unrestrained harassments they must bear from men.

As the essay itself suggests, Diderot was motivated not only by his reaction to Thomas's book but by personal preoccupations involving women. With his sixtieth birthday in sight, he found himself rejected in a late-blooming romance with the coquettishly attractive Mme de Maux. Sophie Volland, now little more than a gently devoted, rapidly aging friend, was no balm for the philosophical ego. On the other hand, as *père de famille* he could rejoice that the engagement of his sole surviving daughter, Angélique—who had always been dear to his heart—was now under way and, within the year, she would be married to Caroillon de Vandeul. A problem, however, seems to have arisen in the form of Bemetzrieder, Angélique's harpsichord teacher. Bemetzrieder had long enjoyed the family's warm hospitality. Diderot had even helped him write his *Leçons de clavecin et principes d'harmonie*, published in 1771. Yet all at once he became *persona non grata* in the Diderot household. Could Angélique's music teacher have unexpectedly made unwelcome advances to his pupil? We can only conjecture, but such an event might have impelled Diderot to insert the following, often-quoted admonition into his essay:

What is [Diderot wrote] the meaning of that declaration so lightly made, so capriciously interpreted, "I love you"? Its true meaning is: "If you would only sacrifice your innocence and your morals to my desires, lose your self-esteem and the respect of others, move in society with eyes downcast, at least until you have become sufficiently accustomed to wantonness to acquire the brazen conduct that accompanies it, abandon all thought of a respected place in society, cause your parents to die of grief, and give me a moment of pleasure, I shall be much obliged. (*AT,* 2:261)

This is a reprise, slightly embellished and with perhaps a new urgency, of observations Diderot had made to Angélique some years before, in a conversation intended to acquaint his adolescent daughter with the facts of life. He had been rather pleased with this admittedly charming bit of rhetoric, but in its new setting it seems a touch of condescension, or at least convention. Indeed, as advanced as Diderot's approach was, traces of condescension can be felt throughout the essay. Still, Diderot makes a sustained effort in these pages to give some idea of the remarkable assets and unusual traits of the feminine mind and heart. *Sur les femmes* is also important in that it throws added light on the psychologically complex women who people his world of fiction. It would be difficult for any woman to take issue with the concluding sentence of *On Women:* "When they have genius, I believe its imprint is more original in them than it is in us."

The third of the three little essays was written two years later, in 1774, as Diderot was returning from Russia. Like the other two, it is marked by grace, charm, feeling, wit, and urbanity. The form this time is a lively dialogue in which the freethinking Italian poet Tomasso Crudeli (read: "Diderot") discusses with a lady, presumably Mme de Broglie—an attractive woman, a virtuous wife, and a pious mother—the question of religion and morality. The work is entitled *Entretien d'un philosophe avec la maréchale de*** and, in translation, has been called *Conversation with a Christian Lady.*[1]

The causerie opens with Mme la Maréchale voicing her astonishment that Crudeli, devoid of religious sentiment, should have moral principles as stringent as those of a believer. He replies somewhat mischievously that there is no reason why a religious man, if he is also honest by nature, should not be as high-principled as he, an agnostic. The lady freely admits that she fully expects to be rewarded in the hereafter for the virtuous life she is now leading on earth. Furthermore, if she were not convinced that the Supreme Being would mete out rewards and punishments for her immortal soul, she might be sorely tempted to indulge her appetites to a greater extent. Crudeli-Diderot finds that, generally speaking, believers are inconsistent in that they are guided more by their passions than by their faith. But he admits his own inconsistency in that he clings to an idealistic code that runs counter both to his reason and to his desires. He believes he knows how to be virtuous, but he has his doubts as to why he should be virtuous either under the anarchy of nature or in a society where vice is too often prevalent.

In the discussion Diderot returns to a parable he has used before of the young Mexican floating on a raft and lulled to sleep by the roll of the ocean. He is washed ashore in some distant land where he is welcomed by a venerable old man, the ruler of a vast empire. The moral is that, if there is a supreme being, He will be gently firm, completely understanding, and ready to forgive the young Mexican, or anyone else, for not having believed in His existence.

As Lester Crocker has remarked, this piece is light, gay, and Gallic while dealing with serious subjects.[2] Furthermore, it could be taken as a model of scintillating conversation in the refined salons of eighteenth-century Paris where sophisticated people often blessed with a sympathetic tolerance for their own weaknesses or those of others derived exquisite satisfaction in dealing with ideas sometimes modish, sometimes subtle, and often both. Like the *Regrets sur ma vieille robe de chambre* and *Sur les femmes,* the *Entretiens* is a tribute to a society whose speculative verve is tempered by a fine sense of human reality.

Two Moralizing Tales

A journalist of the day relates how he and a group of fellow passengers were about to take the post chaise on a long, jolting trip from Paris to a town in the provinces. Suddenly to his great pleasure the journalist noticed Diderot among the wayfarers. This was luck indeed! What had promised to be a tedious journey became a lark as, through the hours, Diderot regaled the other travelers. He outlined a play he had in mind, taking the role of each character in turn. He related stories and anecdotes real and imagined which he interspersed with a lively banter fresh from the Parisian scene they had that morning left behind. One and all were oblivious to the heat and the dust of the road until their destination had been reached.

Often salons in eighteenth-century France were so arranged that the chairs and sofas were placed against the walls. Whoever was holding forth at the moment had to speak loudly, interestingly, and wittily if he wanted to keep his audience. Rousseau, dour and introverted by nature, though scintillating in a limited tête-à-tête, was ill equipped to cope with the demands of a salon. By contrast, Voltaire and Diderot, with their sense of drama, their verbal facility, and their ready wit, frequently held center stage. Whether talking or writing, they were known as exceptional raconteurs. For better or worse, Diderot's gift showed up early in the *Bijoux indiscrets*. It was amply confirmed in his correspondence and in the cosmopolitan intimacy of d'Holbach's renowned circle, among others. He himself, in a letter to Sophie, told of a soirée in which he appeared to those gathered there extraordinary, inspired, divine. We have no reason to doubt his word.

In Diderot's writings it is difficult to isolate the short story per se from among the brilliant narratives that function as moving parts of larger works, not to mention the innumerable superbly related anecdotes that crop up everywhere. Many of the happenings in *La Religieuse* and *Le Neveu* might be called stories in themselves, although they fit perfectly into the overall pattern of each work. It has been said that some eighteen or twenty tales of one sort or another enter into the novel, *Jacques le fataliste*. From the moment of its appearance to the present, however, the episode of Mme de La Pommeraye has been hailed, first by the Germans, then by others, as one of the great short stories of the century.

Among the kinds of short stories that found favor in eighteenth-century France was the moral tale, of which Marmontel's *Contes moraux*— a collection of insubstantial stories told agreeably and with moral intent— was considered an outstanding example. In the early 1770s Diderot himself wrote two tales that, by their titles alone, suggest their kinship with this genre. The first, *Entretien d'un père avec ses enfants, ou le Danger de se mettre au-dessus des lois,* could be translated as *Conversation of a Father with His Children, or the Danger of Setting Oneself above the Law.* The other was simply *Les Deux Amis de Bourbonne,* or *The Two Friends from Bourbonne,* in which friendship is carried to its outer limits.

The tales are significant for several reasons, not the least of which is the very fact of their publication. The philosophe had for some time been acquainted with poems of Salomon Gessner of Zurich that had been translated into French. In 1771, when a volume of Gessner's pastoral poetry was scheduled to appear soon in France, Diderot suggested that the two *contes* be included. As a result of this symbiosis, 1772 saw the first of Diderot's tales since those in the *Bijoux indiscrets* and the only short stories published by him during his lifetime.

The venture was fruitful in many ways. First, it gave him the opportunity to see his work in print and observe public reaction. The reception was reassuring. The stories caused considerable stir by their assertive style, their originality of theme, their superb characterization, and their pertinence to the eighteenth-century scene. Diderot clearly had something of note to add to current concepts of the short story, and he was now aware of the fact. And posterity concurs. As might be expected, his tales suggested moral reflections far more challenging than those of the conventional *conte moral* of the day. And certainly they evinced an aesthetic realism and a psychological finesse far in advance of what Marmontel and other contemporaries had to offer.

The tales have a number of points in common. Each grew out of trips taken late in the summer of 1770 and appeared in the Gessner volume some two years thereafter. The first of these trips was to Langres. Diderot had been negotiating his daughter's engagement to Caroillon de Vandeul. He had wanted to involve what was left of his family (his sister and the abbé brother) in the transaction. One of the motives behind this desire was to convince his brother of his sincere fraternal affection, and thus achieve a reconciliation. The abbé remained inflexible, however, refusing the philosophe's advances on religious grounds.

Yet the visit to Langres evoked fond recollections, for this is what he wrote at the time: "I am unable to express my feelings. I would like to weep. O my father and mother, it must be a tender memory of you that is stirring within me" (*AT,* 17:335).

It is more than likely that, in *The Conversation of a Father with His Children,* Diderot was harking back to an actual family incident that took place during an earlier visit to Langres, probably in 1754. One evening, Diderot's father, seated in his armchair, had told the following story. As executor of the estate of a priest, and about to distribute the curate's sizable holdings evenly among the relatives, he had at the last moment come across a strongbox. To his surprise and pain he found among other dog-eared papers an old will, still legal, leaving the priest's estate to a prosperous and flinthearted relative, thus neglecting family members equally close but steeped in poverty. Old Didier Diderot's first impulse had been to burn the manifestly unfair will without leaving anyone the wiser. But, urged on by a God-fearing priest, he had finally decided to uphold the letter of the law and reveal the contents of the will.

Other anecdotes or incidents were then brought up illustrating the abyss that so often separates legal justice from natural justice. Diderot's father declared that his own peace of mind depended on obeying the laws of church and state. But the *conte* ends as he wishes his son, Denis, goodnight, and whispers in his ear: "I would not be too displeased if the city had one or two citizens like you, but I would find it uninhabitable if all the rest had similar views" (*AT*, 5:308).

Family relations, however, had no hand in Diderot's trip to Bourbonne-les-Bains in August of 1770. Some believe that infatuation for the delectable Mme de Prunevaux had brought him to this slightly dreary watering place. It appears more likely that the philosophe's infatuation was directed toward Mme de Maux, Mme de Prunevaux's mother, and the poor man's last (and perhaps most frustrating) romantic attachment. It was a time, however, when friendship even more than love was the modish theme for long and short fiction.

Mme de Maux and her daughter had received from Paris a copy of Saint-Lambert's *Les Deux Amis, conte iroquois,* an improbable and wretchedly composed tale of friendship and enmity among American Indians. As though to give Saint-Lambert a lesson in fictional verisimilitude, Diderot fabricated a story told with moving simplicity and arresting psychological detail. It concerned the friendship of Felix and Olivier caught up in a series of violent, colorful, and pathetic episodes in the region of the Haute Marne. These two devoted friends are, because of demanding laws and their impoverished state, led to commit crimes for which death is the sole reward. The tale was extensively revised for the Gessner volume. Upon publication it caused a sensation, partly because of the injustice toward the lower classes it exposed, partly because of the political and social anarchy it hinted at, partly because of the strong feeling of fictional realism it evoked. Some idea of its enduring quality is indicated in Goethe's remark that Diderot's "children of nature," Felix and Olivier, had been ennobled by the author's creative gifts, and that his courageous "poachers and smugglers were very much to our liking" (*AT*, 5:264).

The tragic account of the profound friendship between Felix and Olivier has a ring of truth about it that reveals Diderot as past master in the art of the short story. A postscript to *Les Deux Amis* has been turned to time and again for its explanation of how the realistic tale can foster belief on the reader's part. There are those who say it has little to do with Diderot's aesthetics. Whether or not this is so, it stands high among theories on short-story writing. It reads in part:

An example borrowed from another art will perhaps make my point clearer. A painter depicts a head on canvas. All the features are strong, noble, and regular; the result is perfection itself, something altogether rare. Taking it in, I am moved by respect, wonder, and dismay. I look for the model in nature, and do not find it; by comparison everything is deficient, small, and pitiful; we have here an ideal head; I feel it, I tell myself as much. But if the artist lets me notice a slight scar, a wart on the temple, an imperceptible cut on the lip, it is no longer an ideal head but a portrait. A pit from smallpox in the corner of an eye or close to the nose, and this woman's face is no longer that of Venus; it is the portrait of one of my neighbors. And so I shall tell our writers trying to write realistic tales: Your portraits are no doubt splendid; but the wart on the temple, the cut on the lip, the smallpox scar close to the nose, which would make them authentic, are all missing. (*AT,* 5:277)

Of Love Dispossessed: The Three Codes

Though Voltaire was, like most men, vulnerable to the opposite sex, he had little use for the fiction of the day. He found it almost entirely preoccupied with the vicissitudes of love, hardly a subject for the philosophical mind to linger over. For him Rousseau's famous novel of star-crossed lovers, *La Nouvelle Héloïse,* was a revolting absurdity from beginning to end. Diderot, though not taken with Rousseau's fiction, had always been deeply impressed with the phenomenon of love, its power, its unpredictability, its manifestations, its role as the guiding creative principle of the universe, and its influence—now brutal, now fair to middling, now exquisitely refined—on human relations.

In the early 1770s Diderot's journey through life was about to enter its final decade. His only surviving child, Angélique, would from now on be lost to him through matrimony; Sophie Volland was in poor health and his letters to her were increasingly in the tone of "my good friend," which implied that a temperate fondness had replaced love. Quite different were his feelings for the enticing Mme de Maux, former mistress of his deceased friend Damilaville. We do not know how deep this last infatuation of Diderot went. But all these circumstances made him more fully aware of the advancing years and sharpened his interest in the intricate and dimly understood psychology of love. It was a moment when Diderot turned to erotogenesis and other manifestations of love with even greater power and urgency than in *La Religieuse* and *Sur les femmes.* And thus evolved three works that, by his own confession, should be considered as interrelated. They were *Ceci n'est pas un conte* (*This Is Not Just a Story*), *Mme de La Carlière*, whose alternate title, presumably added by Naigeon, might be translated as *On the Inconsistency of Public Judgment on Our Personal Actions,* and the considerably longer *Supplément au Voyage de Bougainville.* All three use the dialogue form extensively; this heightens the realistic tone of each. And, in the two tales especially, Diderot gives an added dimension to the dialogue form by having the author, as raconteur, enter into lively discussion with the reader-interlocutor.

Time after time, during the eighteenth century, philosophes and others depicted Paris as a great city steeped in a physical, moral, and spiritual miasma, where civil and religious law did little to improve matters. To counter crass reality, there was the compensating image, the centuries-old device turned to by imaginative peoples in song and story dreaming of distant Arcadias, remote terrestrial paradises, where the myth of the golden age might be preserved. In that lost garden, valley, or island of time life would have been fuller, richer, more free, and simple.

The idea, shaped by circumstance or reason, threaded its way through the Enlightenment in one form or another. Among the scores of examples were the two utopias of Fénelon's *Télémaque,* the primitive golden age of the noble savage on the banks of the Baetis in Spain, and Salentum on the isle of Crete where sumptuary laws and a strictly regulated class society held in check the relaxed morals and easy vices of effete civilization. In the twelfth chapter of the *Lettres persanes* Montesquieu depicted a new race of troglodytes whose happiness was assured by virtuous living. In Rousseau's *La Nouvelle Héloïse* the simple pleasures and innocent joys of country life at Clarens, shared by master and servant alike, are extolled. The Eldorado of Voltaire's *Candide* is a never-never land of perfection, an absurdly vapid utopia in which we altogether human mortals cannot expect to find gladness or contentment. Now, through outside circumstances it was Diderot's turn—late in life—to dream of a utopia on his own terms.

Louis-Antoine de Bougainville, navigator, explorer, and soldier par excellence, who had led an expedition to the South Pacific, published an account of his trip in the *Voyage autour du monde* in 1771. The book was an immediate success. Diderot's *Supplément au Voyage de Bougainville,* completed the following year, was circulated in manuscript form until its publication in 1796. An English version of the long subtitle, *Dialogue between A and B on the Trouble with Attaching*

Irrelevant Notions to Certain Physical Actions, gives promise of a piquancy that is only half met in discussions of sexual relations.

For in this work, the specific pornographic overtones that color certain pages of the *Bijoux indiscrets* and *La Religieuse* are lacking. In offering a philosophic comment on Bougainville's work, Diderot had seized the opportunity to expound his belief that civilization had in many respects too narrowly confined man's natural instincts. In praising the lot of the noble savage of Tahiti, he was not recommending a return to nature but rather a modification of certain unnatural laws and artificial restraints in French society. As the dialogue draws to a close, A says to B. "Go through the history of the ages, of nations both ancient and modern, and you will find man in the grip of three codes, the natural code, the civil code, and the religious code, and forced to transgress these codes in turn, for they are never in agreement: and so it happens, as Orou surmised about ours, no country exists where there is a natural man, a citizen, or a man of piety" (*AT,* 2:241–42). It is in the light of the three codes that the following passage should be read. The chaplain of the Bougainville expedition finds himself confronted by a predicament running counter to his moral code, to all he had been taught in France. During his first night as guest of Orou, a Tahitian family man, he is on the point of going to bed alone as usual. Orou, who had withdrawn, now reappeared with his wife and daughters, all naked, and said: "Here is my wife, here are my daughters; choose the one you prefer, but if you wish to consider my feelings, select the youngest, she has not yet had a child" (*AT,* 2:220) The chaplain protests that his religion, his holy orders, his morals, and his sense of decency forbid him to do so. Orou's daughter, Thia, adds her pleas to those of her father, and the priest finally accedes while moaning, "But my religion, but my good name!"

As this passage indicates, Diderot—in the *Supplément* at least—does not stress sex for its own sake as a natural function. Like so many other thinkers of the eighteenth century, he was under the misapprehension that Europe was in the throes of depopulation. Women on his imaginary Tahiti who are barren but insist upon engaging in sex are outcasts. The grand old man, *le vieillard* of the *Supplément,* in an eloquent burst of outrage, castigates the Europeans who come to the island with their vices and their disease-ridden bodies in search of nothing but sexual gratification from the still uncorrupt maidens. Propagation in Diderot's fancy-wrought utopia, and not sexual freedom, is presented as foremost in the desire and need for human fulfillment.

The three texts, the *Supplément* and the two *contes,* form an ensemble; Diderot subtly suggests as much at the end of the *Supplément* and makes the point in two letters to Grimm (*Corr,* 12:131, 144). Editors until recently, however, have broken up this triptych, publishing the two short stories along with Diderot's fiction, while relegating the *Supplément* to his philosophical works.

One of the two main themes linking the three pieces is that of love dispossessed in one way or another. At the beginning of *Ceci n'est pas un conte* the narrator lays this theme down obliquely by admitting to *le lecteur* that he is merely repeating something known throughout eternity, namely, that "man and woman are two very malicious creatures" (*AT,* 5, 312). This particular tale, which Diderot calls a very poor tale or no tale at all, contains two stories.

In the first, the woman (Mme Reymer) is motivated by greed, hypocrisy, and unscrupulousness, but her desires are too obvious to be considered devious. An admiring male (Tanié) sees through her, but his love—without blinding him—gives him excruciating pain, and, as a result, he dies of raging fever. The first of this pair of stories may be fiction but the second is based on fact, for Diderot personally knew Mlle de La Chaux whose loving devotion and self-sacrifice were brutally rejected by a surly, acerbic, ugly little scientist (Gardeil) who had grown weary of her. In both instances, however, the underlying notion exists that there is a contradiction between the inclination for permanence and constancy among members of the opposite sex on the one hand, and on the other the fleeting nature of love between two people.

The following *conte, Mme de La Carlière,* preoccupied with the same idea, opens with a discussion of the weather. The author utilizes it to symbolize the change in all things, and especially the unpredictability of swirling nature around man and woman, which parallels their own instability of heart. This leitmotiv of the fickleness of nature symbolizing the instability of human emotions will open the *Supplément* as well.

But of Diderot's poignantly charged short stories, *Mme de La Carlière* is probably the most implausible and hence the least gripping. Here, in exploiting the theme of love dispossessed, the author carries his attacks against the civil and religious codes with their strong social implications to conclusions that skirt the incredible. It is as though he would like to see whether a *drame bourgeois* in the Diderot manner would work better as a *conte* than on the stage.

A beautiful, young widow, Mme de La Carlière, in hesitantly taking a second husband, M. Desroches, makes him swear before the tribunal of God, and equally important, before a tribunal of their mutual friends, his undying faithfulness. At the same time, she threatens dire consequences should he break his pledge. After two years of an idyllic married life, M. Desroches, through kindness for a friend, becomes enmeshed in an intrigue that requires an exchange of letters with a woman from out of his past. Mme Desroches, upon discovering the correspondence, refuses to listen to explanations from her husband, and leaves with her son, who dies (as do her brother and mother). Society blames Desroches for these misfortunes. As a final blow, his wife, having resumed the name of de La Carlière, dies in church while attending mass.

In *Ceci n'est pas un conte* and *Mme de La Carlière*—with the characters moving about on the Parisian scene—there are no cries of joy, only those of rage and frustration. Here are stories that unfold under the artificial civil and religious codes with the imperious code of nature hidden but ever present. The theme of the three conflicting codes that can tear an individual to pieces is implicit in *Ceci n'est pas un conte*. It is brought out into the open full of haunting vibrations and brooding darkness in *Mme de La Carlière*.

How different is Diderot's depiction of an island in the South Pacific. His Tahiti is luminous and joyful; one senses the bright sunshine, the warm, soft nights, and the inviting cool of the cabins. This imagined Tahiti represents the airiness of individual and even collective freedom where the inhabitants follow only the dictates of the code of nature.

In the *Supplément* Orou is Diderot acting out a utopian fantasy, a persona some of whose principles run counter to his own eighteenth-century bourgeois interests and those of his beloved daughter, Angélique. Critics have occasionally reproached him for not having reached hard-and-fast conclusions, but the work is not only paradoxical, it is also full of speculation on civilization, primitivism, religion, laws, customs, and, perhaps as much as anything else, on sexual freedom and restraint. He goes beyond dogmatism and skepticism, either of which could lead to inaction. He does not doubt the power of reasoning or that of experimentation. But he is skeptical of reasoning or experimentation alone. The constructive role of skepticism in the *Supplément*—as in several other of his later works—is to infuse a negative element into man's thinking that might otherwise consist of dogmatic absolutes. By admitting that nothing is completely false or entirely true, Diderot's dialectical doubt obliges the mind to bring thesis and antithesis face to face and to hope for a possible synthesis.

In the two tales, in the *Supplément,* and still later in *Jacques le fataliste* and certain chapters of the *Essai sur les règnes de Claude et de Néron,* Diderot reveals himself as a master observer of the socio-psychological aspects of love. We see his desire to bring to the surface the internal conflicts of both undercivilized and overcivilized man. In his persistent concern with the subject Diderot anticipated Freud even more than is commonly assumed. There is a touch of the Freudian in almost all he wrote—including his correspondence. Freudian too was Diderot's conviction that at the more complex levels of society both aggressive and erotic energies, inexorably directed inward, can lead to an agonizing civil war in society itself and among the individuals who comprise it. By bringing man's instincts of sex and aggression into the open light of reason, these conflicts might be reduced if not dispelled. But Diderot, like Freud, knew that there was no simple solution; any solution, in fact, would be slow and difficult.

Although warmhearted, lovable, and temperamentally susceptible, our philosophe shows himself to be in the two tales and in the *Supplément,* as well as elsewhere, a remarkable sexologist if not a very subtle analyst of the psychology of love in the French tradition. The more delicate operations of romantic feeling do not escape his lens. There is in Diderot a brilliant link between brain and gonads that seems impatient of slow detours through the heart. Diderot, too, may be, to a certain extent, "of love dispossessed."

Of Art and Paradox: The Time of Illusion

Early in his career as a writer (*Pensées philosophiques,* 1746) Diderot saw the passions as the main source of sublimity in literature, art, and life itself. This outlook continued to find expression in his enthusiasm for the more sentimental paintings of Greuze, and in plays such as his own *Père de famille* (1757). It more or less reached its culmination in the *Eloge de Richardson* (1761), after which the passions lost their privileged place.

Morally unprincipled, a helpless prey to his appetites, and lacking in artistic discipline, the *Lui* of *Rameau's Nephew* (1761, passim) is an antihero grossly incapable of following his distinguished uncle in the world of music. By 1767 Bordeu-Diderot, in *Le Rêve,* will ask: "What is a person of feeling?" and will answer his own question:

One who is abandoned to the mercy of his diaphragm. . . . If a great man has had the misfortune to be born with this natural inclination he will ceaselessly try to lessen it, to master it, to have control over what he does. . . . It is then he will be able to contain himself in the midst of grave dangers; he will think coolly and collectedly. Nothing that is useful to him will escape his attention; . . . At the age of forty-five he will be a great king, a great minister of state, a great politician, a great artist, especially a great actor, a great poet, a great musician, a great doctor. . . . Those whose emotions prevail or who are mad are on the stage. He is among the spectators; it is he who is the sage. (*AT*, 2:171)

If Diderot had formerly supposed the passions to be the very content of life, he now began to reconsider his position. He was both older and wiser, and "the sage" was an expression that kept cropping up in his writing on the ideal model. In the mid-1760s he was already applying these new and broader views to the theater and in particular to the art of acting. And throughout the following decade he would insist, time and again and in various places, that irrepressible sensibility and unbridled enthusiasm will always be an insurmountable handicap, especially for the poet, the artist, the orator, and the actor hoping to achieve greatness.

His sundry discussions on drama—especially the *Entretiens sur le Fils naturel* (1757) and the *Discours sur la poésie dramatique* (1758)—had already made an important addition to the dramatic theories of the day. There was, for instance, the insistence that neoclassical tragedy with its outmoded decorum should yield to an intermediate form between poetic tragedy and classical comedy. The subject of this new drama would be drawn from everyday, middle-class life. Moreover, this life could be best depicted as a matter of social status, or what Diderot termed "conditions." There would be the condition of the judge, the soldier, the father, or the merchant, for example, which would be substituted for the *caractères* of traditional comedy with its misers, its prudes, its hypocrites, and its pedants, among others. This new theater would not hesitate to utilize pantomime, tableaux, and other aids for both the playwright and the actor. And finally, since Diderot—like Voltaire—believed the pulpit had lost its authority as a moral guide, the need of the theater as a moral civilizing agent had become increasingly acute. His ideas on the *drame bourgeois* had already been successfully realized by Sedaine and others while, to his delight, his own *Père de famille* enjoyed a mild success, having been received with some enthusiasm in Marseilles and, in 1761, performed several times at the prestigious Théâtre Français in Paris.

In the summer of 1773 Diderot found himself lingering in Holland, his head as usual teeming with a great variety of notions, and making new friendships while summoning up courage for what would soon be the longest and most momentous journey of his life. During this first stay at The Hague he took time out to compose the short, diverting essay, *Satire première,* that demonstrates how a person's mannerisms and vocabulary help to reveal his profession and his position in society. Balzac and other nineteenth-century writers were to take tips from its pages.

But Diderot was otherwise busy as well. On 18 August he wrote Mme d'Epinay, "I have not completely wasted my time while here. I have rather interesting notes on the inhabitants. I've splattered Helvétius' last work with marginal comments. A certain pamphlet on the actor's art has almost grown into a book" (*Corr,* 13:46). This final reference is to the famous *Paradoxe sur le comédien,* sometimes translated as *The Paradox on Acting* and *The Actor's Paradox.*

Just as the author had turned a book review for Grimm's *Correspondance Littéraire* into the *Supplément au voyage de Bougainville,* he now turned his review of Antonio Fabio Sticoti's mediocre study on "David Garrick or the English Actors" into a work of perennial controversy. Presented in dialogue form, it appears—as is frequently so with Diderot—as the written record of at least two voices that stimulate and respond to one another. The technique makes for a lively give-and-take as well as for flexibility of thought—a seemingly endless series of tests and challenges.

Were we to judge by the title alone, we would be inclined to believe that the work is devoted exclusively to the actor and the art of acting. But a glance at its pages reveals that it also deals with the creative artist in general as well as with the Diderot of the *Père de famille,* of the *Salons,* of the *Rêve,* and of everyday life. Another brilliantly controversial essay of the philosophe, *Le Paradoxe,* at times, leads the unsuspecting reader far afield.

In the *Discours sur la poésie dramatique* (1758) and in the *Salon de 1767* Diderot had already expounded on the concept of the *modèle idéal.* For the superior actor this ideal model will be the character he has studied, inventively imagined, and seized upon chiefly through his intelligence but partly through his intuition. The result is that the final product will remain steadfastly the same whatever the vicissitudes of the actor's life as the performances follow one another night after night, week after week. The great actor or actress guided by intelligence, not by emotion, will have complete mastery of the role at hand just as the great playwright has already chosen and realized his ideal model in the creation of the convincing and exceptional personages in his theater. Sometimes the actor's ideal model transcends that of the author, we are reminded, as Diderot relates how Voltaire, upon seeing Mlle Clairon in one of his plays, cried out in admiration: "Did I write that?" Diderot remarks that, in this moment, at least, her ideal model as she delivered Voltaire's lines went far beyond the ideal model the poet had in mind when writing them. But, Diderot concludes—and the statement is important—Mlle Clairon and the ideal model she had created were two separate entities ("mais ce modèle idéal n'était pas elle," *AT*, 8:393).

Diderot arrived at the same conclusion concerning Mlle Clairon that Sir Joshua Reynolds had reached concerning the greatest English actor of the day. Garrick's trade, as Reynolds put it, was to represent passion, and not to feel it, and so, Garrick left nothing to chance. Every gesture, every expression of countenance and variation of voice, was settled in his study before he set his foot on the stage.

What, precisely, is the paradox of the actor? Diderot explains that the great performer transmits to the audience through his art the illusion of emotion he himself does not feel. Those actors who do rely upon or are torn by feeling give uneven and unpredictable performances where illusion is often cast to the winds, hence the paradox.

Near the beginning of *Le Paradoxe* the first interlocutor says:

> The actor who follows only the dictates of nature is often detestable, sometimes excellent. But in whatever genre, beware of an unremitting mediocrity. No matter how harshly a beginner is treated, it is easy to foresee his future success. Hoots and jeers stifle only the inept. How should nature without art make a great actor, since nothing happens on the stage exactly as it does in nature, and when dramatic pieces are all composed after a fixed system of principles? And how can a part be played in the same way by two different actors when, even with the clearest, the most precise, the most forceful of writers, the words are not and can never be more than symbols, indicating a thought, a feeling, an idea; symbols which need action, gesture, intonation, expression, and a whole set of circumstances, to give them their full significance? (*AT*, 8:363)

Diderot, who knew Garrick almost as well as did Sir Joshua, marveled at this actor's remarkable theatrical discipline. He refers not once but twice (*AT*, 8:362; 381–82) to a particular instance of it. The version of the incident as related in the *Paradoxe* is as follows:

I myself saw what I am going to tell you. Garrick stuck his head out of a door, and, within four or five seconds his face changed from delirious joy to moderate cheerfulness, from this cheerfulness to serenity, from serenity to surprise, from surprise to astonishment, from astonishment to sadness, from sadness to dejection, from dejection to fear, from fear to horror, from horror to despondency, and from this last emotion back up the ladder to the first. (*AT,* 8:381–82)

To drive his point home, the philosophe gives many anecdotes and examples, in his essay, of actors and others who, through artfulness and deliberation, succeed in gaining their ends. But since Diderot is Diderot, he must try his hand at being naughtily mundane now and then. One illustration should suffice:

"The tears of an actor," he tells us, "fall from the mind while those of a man with feeling rise from the heart. The actor weeps like a priest devoid of faith who preaches on Christ's martyrdom; like a seducer at the feet of a woman he does not love but with whom he wishes to have his way; like a beggar in the street or at the church door who explodes in insults when his pleas are in vain; or like a courtesan who, though feeling nothing, is enraptured while in your arms" (*AT,* 8:370). All of the above are purveyors of illusion as is the actress who, in the eyes of the audience is dying, and with her head on the actor's breast and in the midst of her death throes, whispers: "You smell to high heaven" (*AT,* 8:420).

Diderot examines the question from another point of view, and an extremely important one, with regard to the creative artist:

Is it, he asks, when you have lost your best friend or the woman you love that you will compose a poem on his or her death? No. He tries his talent under such circumstances to no effect. It is when the great sorrow has passed, when intense feeling has abated, when the catastrophe has faded into the distance, that the soul becomes calm, that one . . . is capable of evaluating the loss, that memory mingles with the imagination, memory to recall past happiness, imagination to magnify it. . . . It is said that you weep, but you do not weep when you are striving for a strong characterizing word or phrase that does not come; they say you weep, but you do not weep when you are engaged in making a line of poetry harmonious; or if the tears flow, the pen falls from the hand, you yield to your emotions, unable to compose any longer. (*AT,* 8:386)

Diderot's reasoning here is corroborated by the genesis of some of the best-known French romantic lyrics. It was a year after his nineteen-

year-old daughter had drowned that Victor Hugo could finally write
the profoundly touching poem of grief, "At Villequier." And in "Nuit
de Mai" ("On a May Night") Alfred de Musset says that it is not
in the first despair of overpowering anguish that one can "write on the
sand swept by the North Wind. Anything he might try to say in such
a moment would break his heart as though it were but a reed."

In summing up the philosophe's personal application of these principles, Michael Cartwright says in a well-ordered essay:

> Diderot's own creative effort and the rigours it undoubtedly entailed, indicates
> that he was intimately aware of a species of calm, a sentiment . . . close
> to the Wordsworthian "emotion recollected in tranquillity . . ." He himself
> would never commit himself to the eccentricity of a simple formula or a
> line of Beauty such as that propounded by Hogarth, but there does seem
> to be evidence that may lead us to a clearer understanding of that unity
> and harmony of the aesthetic experience that he knew very well and that
> he tries, not always with perfect clarity, to communicate to his reader.[3]

Though there are many other aspects of the *Paradoxe* that might be
touched upon with profit, there is—by way of conclusion—one point
that should not be neglected. In the dialogue Diderot is employing the
dialectical method against himself. The method explains the extreme
position that is taken against emotionalism. The actor's genius, as we
have seen, is closely associated with the writer's; Diderot's, it has long
been held, was characterized by enthusiastic outbursts that often inspired
others, but that he himself was all too rarely able or willing to control.
It was a view encouraged by the philosophe himself, and in the *Paradoxe*
Diderot openly admits that he is arguing against his own temperament.
Toward the end of his essay he writes: "When I declared that feeling
was the trait of a kind heart and little genius, I made a confession
which is not overly common, for if nature created a spirit sensitive to
the impact of emotion, I am that man" (*AT*, 8:408).

But as certain of his manuscripts have come to light, they have
revealed that he had subjected them to constant revision; this is especially
true of his posthumous works. They do not show an outpouring of
unbridled emotion, but the discipline and intelligence of a superior
mind. Diderot, who so often uses the word "illusion" in the *Paradoxe*,
calls Mlle Clairon "cette incomparable magicienne" (*AT*, 8:403). By
the same token, Diderot, with increasing frequency, is today being called
le grand mystificateur. Perhaps it would be still closer to the truth if
he were called the great illusionist.[4]

A Master of Fiction and His "Determined Fatalist"

As eighteenth-century French fiction went, the *Bijoux Indiscrets* (1746) had been a patchwork affair with two of the better patches added in the 1770s. The *Oiseau blanc* (1748) was a run-of-the-mill tale of fantasy, allegory, and oriental exoticism. *La Religieuse,* begun in 1760, became a brilliant, though unfinished experiment in new fictional dimensions; the *Neveu de Rameau* developed into a devastating satire, but the argument as to whether or not it is a novel has yet to be settled.

Jacques le fataliste, conceived and worked over on the trip to and from Russia (1773–74), was quite another thing. After its first appearance in print posthumously in 1796 Carlyle, with critical acumen equal to his wide-eyed amazement, said that there was nothing like it in the whole range of French literature. Edmond and Jules Goncourt were also among the chosen few of their day to sense the importance of Diderot's last work of fiction. Calling the attention of nineteenth-century France to the novel, they deplored the fact that Voltaire was immortal while Diderot was only famous. Arguing that the patriarch of Ferney was the last spirit of old France, they maintained that Diderot was the first genius of modern France and that it was he who, with *Jacques,* had inaugurated the modern novel (*Journal,* 11 April 1858).

But Voltaire and Diderot had much in common when they wrote their fictional masterpieces, *Candide, ou l'optimisme* and *Jacques le fataliste,* even though now *Jacques* is often referred to as an anti-*Candide.* Both writers had achieved eminence throughout Europe as leaders in the French Enlightenment. Both had reached the height of their intellectual powers and had proven to be exceptionally adept in wielding the pen with censorious, satirical, and ingeniously creative results. Throughout their careers they retained their sly impudence and idealistic rashness in the face of immutable authority and tradition. But years of shrewd experience seasoned their art of subversion with subtlety. In its disposal of facile optimism and its witty, vital preoccupation with the presence of evil in the universe, *Candide,* written when Voltaire was sixty-four, had come to represent the philosophical tale in its purest form. Diderot, too, was in his early sixties when he composed *Jacques,* presumably a ramblingly entertaining inquiry into what Aram Vartanian has called "the question of freedom and its denial."[5] An important aspect of the work is indeed the depiction of a world "where events are seen alternately as belonging to a necessary order and as unfolding with a capricious freedom." But there were other, and equally tantalizing aspects, as posterity would finally discover.

In the recent past there has been considerable agreement that *Jacques* is a pungently witty novel of eighteenth-century mores and thought where one can find a splendid blend of choice, juicy, intellectual, and aesthetic morsels along with a generous portion of the bawdy, explicit libertinage for which the period is duly celebrated. Generally speaking, though, it had been well into the twentieth century before any substantial appreciation of the novel was discernible. The long and widely recognized authority on the history of French fiction, George Saintsbury, lacking the astuteness of Carlyle or of the Goncourt brothers, had fallen into the trap set by Diderot and assumed that *Jacques* was a fictional failure in the form of a romance, a novel, a love story. According to Saintsbury, then, the author had striven in vain to realize the usual and no doubt admirable ambition of novelists in general to entertain and properly divert the reader. Saintsbury was an admirer of the conventional narrative with its carefully ordered plot. This was the sort of novel that Diderot's contemporary, Mme de Riccoboni, knew how to turn out and in *Jacques,* she is gently ridiculed for so doing. This might be another reason why Saintsbury could not suppress his annoyance with *Jacques.* In any event, the distinguished professor wrote on his own behalf as well as that of his compeers when he declared: "It is comparatively of little moment that the main ostensible theme—the very unedifying account of the loves of Jacques and his master is deliberately, tediously, inartistically interrupted and 'put off.' "[6] Saintsbury was unable to throw any meaningful light on *Jacques le fataliste* because he failed to uncover the novel's roots in the past, because he neglected to ascertain its relation to the contemporary literary scene, and because he was bewildered and repelled by Diderot's visionary mind.

The tradition to which Diderot had responded was the satirical realistic genre with its lust for life and its teeming variety, frequently presenting a vast spectacle of customs and mores in a given epoch. Its expression in French literature was most clearly exemplified in *Gargantua and Pantagruel,* in *Francion,* in *Le Roman comique,* and in *Gil Blas,* as the current passed from the sixteenth down into the eighteenth century. Rabelais, Sorel, Scarron, Lesage—these were among the worthy representatives of a great tradition which in the Age of Enlightenment was in danger of being forgotten amidst a mass of new fly-by-night novels.

Diderot, by temperament and by talent, belonged to the older tradition. His mind worked through digression and association rather than through logical pattern. As a writer of fiction as well as a natural scientist, he hewed to the Baconian or experimental rather than to the Cartesian tradition. It is not implausible, then, that, surrounded by readily accepted, tritely conventional forms of fiction in France that left his inspiration fundamentally unrequited, he should with his restless and ever-alert mind, turn toward England. In Richardson, Fielding, and Sterne he found a new and refreshing departure from the eighteenth-century types of French fiction that had pushed the spontaneity and realism of even so relatively recent a novel as Lesage's *Gil Blas* (1724–35) into the background. And yet this newness in no small measure represented to Diderot qualities inherent in the earlier French literature that led him to accept Sterne, for example, as the English Rabelais.

Jacques itself reflected the humor of Sterne's *Tristram Shandy* and, indeed, exploited two or three episodes of that novel. Moreover, like Sterne's bizarre masterpiece, *Jacques* gave the impression of wandering along with its chief characters at the mercy of the fates or of chance. "Digressions," exclaims Sterne, "incontestably are the sunshine; they are the life, the soul of reading."[7] And F. C. Green, in his *Minuet* adds: "One has to read *Jacques le fataliste* to appreciate the justice of this remark."

Because of the deliberate similarity of these features, earlier critics frequently leveled the charge of plagiarism against Diderot. The tide, however, has long since turned, and *dix-huitiémistes* are now generally in agreement with J.J. Mayoux who, in distinguishing between the two practitioners of contrived ease in the art of narration, wrote in 1936: "Sterne was to a great extent Diderot's model in *Jacques;* but the waywardness of narrative and caprice of digression which is Sterne's portrait of the mind as it runs on, is with Diderot a portrait of life, of reality, as it appears: a substantial and significant difference."[8]

The twentieth-century French antinovel, with its antihero, and antiplot, has so often reminded recent critics of Diderot's last novel, that such avant-garde writers as Nathalie Sarraute, Michel Butor, and Alain Robbe-Grillet, for instance, have been bluntly asked to what extent they have been influenced by *Jacques le fataliste.* So far these exponents of the so-called *nouveau roman* have denied any immediate or direct influence. Resemblances with Diderot's literary theories and practices were merely the result of chance or *le hasard*—a governing theme in *Jacques*.

What is the plot or antiplot of the novel? A rapid first reading of the book might not allow for much more than the following anti-summary. The plot presumably is to deal with the love life of Jacques.

After all, love is the main theme of eighteenth-century French fiction. But, in the present instance, we learn about it only in fragments as it applies to our doughty protagonist. As Jacques and his master proceed with their journey on horseback, adventure after adventure, incident upon incident, break into the supposed narrative of Jacques's sentimental experiences. The episodes come in such fast succession that it seems quite impossible to give a satisfactory account of the unfolding of events. A girl falls off a horse, an incident that elicits mildly obscene, pseu-dophilosophic bantering among those present; Jacques and his master meet bandits who are not bandits; there is more than one encounter with a funeral cortège with nightmarish qualities and surrealistic over-tones.

At an inn the two voyagers hear stories including that of Mme de La Pommeraye, perhaps the best-known episode in the book. Mme de La Pommeraye, a serious-minded widow, after persistent persuasion by her late husband's friend the Marquis des Arcis, finally becomes his mistress amidst promises of lasting fidelity on the part of each. When the ardor of the Marquis cools, she avenges herself by maneuvering her inconstant lover into marriage with an alluring prostitute. Mme de La Pommeraye's revenge, however, comes to naught, for des Arcis, at first devoured by chagrin, finally accepts the humble supplications of his courtesan-wife. This he does with dignity and compassion. The reader is left to decide either with Jacques that La Pommeraye is a despicable creature or with the narrator that she is at least partially justified in her act of vengeance.

The master and servant are once again en route, but to where? Diderot had a ready answer for such a question, an answer echoed throughout the narrative: "But for God's sake, author (you beg of me), where were they going?—But for God's sake, reader, I shall reply, do you ever know where you are going?" The two travelers set out again and anecdotes, incidents, and digressions continue to pile up for the characters, the narrator or narrators, and the reader as well as the readers-turned-characters. At the end of the novel Jacques is looking forward to marrying his betrothed. But he already wonders whether his master is not himself in love with her. Yet, true to his philosophy, the servant tells himself that if it is written by fate that his wife is to be unfaithful, she will be, and if it is written that she will not be unfaithful, she will not be, no matter what others may attempt. And with that Jacques—whom Marxist critics have called the first proletarian hero in the history of the French novel—falls sound asleep.

What to do with such a haphazard work of fiction? A few other nineteenth-century critics besides Carlyle and the Goncourts—Goethe and Schiller, for instance—suggested that the novel offered more than casually met the eye. But in general Saintsbury's verdict that Diderot "in an evil moment took it into his head to Shandyise," prevailed.[9]

By 1936, however, J. J. Mayoux whose distinction between *Jacques* and *Tristram Shandy* has already been cited, was able to convey the spell of the novel: "For Diderot's philosophical mind literature is a subtle game, an Indian magic, a means of throwing ropes into the air and holding them there."[10]

Full realization of the fact that *Jacques le fataliste* had something to say for the twentieth century had been slow in coming, although by the 1950s paperback and critical editions of the novel began to multiply rapidly. In 1946 Charly Guyot, a Swiss critic and one of the leading European authorities on the history of French fiction, in the preface to his own edition of *Jacques* gave what is now the generally accepted explanation for the delay in recognition. Emphasizing that this particular novel is a work full of the rarest, the most original fictional contrivances, Guyot adds that its author has long been—and perhaps still is—a victim of mischance. As general editor of the collective enterprise, the *Encyclopédie,* Diderot remained in semidarkness, while the authors of *Candide* and *La Nouvelle Héloïse* enjoyed European renown. Diderot's most personal works, Guyot concludes—those capable of bringing him lasting fame—were posthumous and so would have to be judged by an enlightened posterity.[11]

By 1950, the time was ripe for a whole volume devoted to *Jacques le fataliste:* J. Robert Loy's *Diderot's Determined Fatalist,* a 234-page study which, according to Jean Fabre, "was to lift the veils in which this enigmatic work was shrouded and to propose a coherent, and on some points, an already decisive interpretation."[12] Not only did Loy accomplish this, he inspired a host of specialists to do likewise. Many of these recent studies are rich in substance and provocatively original in interpretation.[13]

Today's readers see Diderot's mind working through digression and the association of ideas. We are also struck by the author's animation, his spirited dramatic dialogue, his irony, and his oddities of mind. André Gide has called his own *Caves du Vatican (Lafcadio's Adventures,* 1914) a *sotie,* that is to say, a dramatic piece of a type particularly in vogue during the fourteenth and fifteenth centuries, in which all the characters are supposedly more or less touched in the head. In recent years it has from time to time been pointed out that *Jacques* falls into the same category, that of the *sotie*.

Shortly after the middle of the twentieth century this particular novel has established itself as a milestone in the evolution of the French novel. By way of brief résumé we could say that it included 1) the old Gallic tradition; 2) superimposed English influences which, at times, had more than a little in common with the Rabelaisian and picaresque genres in France; 3) Diderot's own multifaceted mind constantly striving for new goals in fictional as well as other fields of expression.

Before touching upon *Jacques* in relation to modern aesthetics of the novel, we should consider the question of whether there is a metaphysical or philosophical aim in the work. There are those who say that here Diderot is specifically studying the problem of human liberty, and that he wishes to demonstrate that everything in life is a linking of blind forces that man dominates only in his illusions. Others, more directly to the point, suggest that Jacques's fatalism is a literary counterpart of Diderot's determinism. There is no doubt but that Diderot liked to speculate on moral problems and that the one that concerned itself with human destiny in its various forms was extremely popular in the eighteenth century. Voltaire dealt with the subject from the viewpoints of Christian doctrine and oriental fatalism in his philosophical tale, *Zadig, ou la destinée;* he examined it with regard to Leibniz in *Candide, ou l'optimisme.* Diderot treats the same question in relation to Spinoza or, more exactly, the protagonist's conception of the philosophy of Spinoza. Many twentieth-century readers, wishing to cut immediately to the bone, say that Jacques's attitude is that of Diderot himself; to wit, we are victims of the caprices and quixotic whimsy of a fate we do not control. It is possible, however, that the problem is more involved and that Jean Thomas falls short of the mark when he says in the *Humanisme de Diderot* that the author is depicting through Jacques's adventures a fatalism more implacable than the Spinozan doctrine to which the hero constantly refers.

As we now realize, Diderot intended this great experimental novel of his to be a satire on a number of things,[14] among them Spinoza's metaphysical determinism. In the unfolding of the narrative, in the diversity of adventures that befall Jacques and his master, we find repeatedly the same general comment on the inevitability of fate and man's need to be resigned to it. Through sheer monotony, then, Diderot forces upon the reader the realization that a formula that explains everything, explains nothing. Long before the end of the dialogue the

absurdity of ascribing all events to destiny in whatever form is made
amply clear. For whatever man's destiny may be, it does not alter his
choice of action, which is governed by the search for happiness in
society. And this constitutes his real moral problem.

More than a satire on Spinozistic fatalism, then, *Jacques* may be a
satire against prevalent views on fatalism. Four major positions on the
subject can be seen in the book: 1) that of Jacques the determined
supporter of an unrelenting pseudo-Spinozism; 2) that of Jacques who,
unconsciously, by word and action, revolts against his adopted doctrine;
3) the position of the master, one of oscillation, of fluctuation; 4) that
of the third person, the narrator, who addresses the reader and calls
attention to the inconsistencies in the first three points of view.

Through constant repetition and ironic treatment, however, Jacques's
theoretical position has been reduced to an absurdity and his formula,
écrit là-haut, or, if you will, "written on the great scroll up yonder,"
has, philosophically speaking, become a meaningless catchall. In the
final analysis, then, it would seem that this new Sancho Panza reveals
his ill-defined fatalism under three forms: 1) as a mechanistic materialism
whereby he sees the principles of cause and effect leading to an inevitable
result in the future; 2) his religious fatalism in which he imagines the
future incontrovertibly written in the heavens above (Diderot had been
a great admirer of Milton's *Paradise Lost*); 3) his acceptance of the
indisputable role of chance and caprice, perhaps the most dangerous of
all fatalistic credos.

Diderot had always been obsessed by the tantalizing question of
freedom and its disavowal. As early as 1756 in his well-known letter
to Landois, he had said: "Consider carefully and you will see that the
word liberty is devoid of meaning; that there is not and there can not
be any free existence; that we are only what is suitable to the general
order, to nature, to education, and to cause and effect. . . . What
deceives us is the tremendous variety of our actions, joined to the habit
developed from the moment of birth to confuse what is deliberate with
what is free" (*Corr* 1:213–14). As the aging stoic, Diderot adopts a
broader view that is reflected in his novel, and we can not but agree
with Aram Vartanian's conclusion that "In this crucial text, Jacques is
the personification of a double truth. If there is no decisive proof that
man is free, there is none, either, that he is not. Consequently, as the
occasion demands, Jacques *acts* on the assumption of freedom, but
theorizes on the assumption of necessity. Each principle is valid—because
indispensable—in its appropriate sphere. The philosophical truth of

fatalism and the practical truth of free will constitute a dialectic without synthesis."[15]

If *Jacques* is a satire of a number of things, it is perhaps most explicitly a satire of the conventional romance or novel so popular in Western Europe at the time. This is a point effectively made by Claude Roy in 1950 and emphasized ever since. Roy ingeniously observed: "Just as Pirandello wrote his plays while ridiculing the theater, Diderot achieved his masterpiece [*Jacques le fataliste*] by means of a novel that ridicules novels, through an infinitely complex work which is at once a novel, a critique of that novel and the imaginative treatment of that critique itself."[16] More succinctly, though perhaps less wittily, Yvon Belaval says the same thing: "*Jacques* is a story in which an analysis of the aesthetics of narration constantly interferes with the narrative flow. . . . The narrator places himself among his protagonists."[17]

And indeed almost from the outset of the novel the narrator puts himself squarely among the leading characters. If he were a playwright, we might imagine him calling out over the footlights to us when the opportunity presented itself. And this is precisely what happened when the novel was with great success adapted for the Paris stage in 1962. Diderot himself was depicted on the stage, to the delight of the audience, interrupting the action, arguing and discussing his characters with the director. In the novel, however, the reader is made to participate in the unfolding of the narrative. Diderot calls out to us from the stage setting of the novel, he asks our advice, he makes us share his doubts, he wants us to enjoy with him his aesthetic theories, his literary hypotheses. Then, without pause, he returns to his characters and seems to have forgotten us, only to reappear quite unexpectedly in another dialogue with the reader. Early in the novel we come to the incident of the girl falling off the doctor's horse, followed by quips of the onlookers, and by the philosophizing of Jacques. But in the midst of the jests and Jacques's metaphysical speculations, the narrator chooses to intervene! "What couldn't this adventure become in my hands," he tells us, "if I took it into my head to tease you! I should make that woman an important character—the niece of the neighboring village curate. I should stir up the peasants of that village; I should prepare all sorts of combats and love affairs" (*AT*, 6:13). The narrator even suggests that, in her fall from the horse, the girl has revealed enough hidden charms to have Jacques quite possibly fall in love a second time. But the reader presumably intervenes himself to ask whether the author means that Jacques has already fallen in love with someone else.

Precisely, says Diderot, and then suggests that all this be cut short if the reader wants Jacques to get on with his love story.

Everywhere in the work there is evidence of ambiguity with respect to narrator, narrative technique, and literary intent. In one instance the narrator suddenly reveals that there are two versions of a particular incident and tells the reader to choose whichever version suits him better. At another point the narrator reminds the reader that he is only an editor and so is not able to present part of a conversation between Jacques and his master because of a lacuna in the manuscript. There is also the assertion that we are reading "history" rather than a novel. The self-styled narrator, in refusing to embellish history or compromise his standing as a historian by suppressing an incident, underscores his obligation to the truth. The illusion is created that the story's characters and the narrator exist independently in the same world, since the narrator can pursue one activity while the characters are involved in others. We are repeatedly reminded of the ease with which the narrator can manipulate events. Or again, we are led to believe that perhaps we are not reading a history or a work of fiction after all, but memoirs. There seems no end to the author's ingenuity.

In such instances and throughout, we see Diderot building on the traits of irony and digression, and willfully introducing fortuity to his storytelling. We see him refusing to build a novel—he prefers to let it take place. "How easy it is to fabricate stories!" he tells us on the second page. Another incident coming fast on the heels of the girl on horseback again illustrates Diderot's insistence that his story must unfold, willy-nilly or not. Jacques and his master have left an inn early in the morning, with some dozen brigands locked by Jacques in one room and their clothes in another. Suddenly our heroes notice they are being followed by a band of men. Jacques and his master view with trepidation the troop of horsemen, armed with pitchforks, bearing down upon them. Diderot again intervenes. He sees that the reader may well expect some bloody action, some pistols shot off, some skulls cracked. But narrator-Diderot adds: "It's completely up to me whether it happens or not, but then, goodbye to the truth of this story, goodbye to the history of Jacques's loves." Nothing of moment happens, though, and the author adds: "Our two travelers were not followed at all; I don't even know what went on in the inn after their departure." This last remark is, in itself, of interest because it represents a new stance on an author's part. As a rule in eighteenth-century fiction, the writer is one who has come across a collection of letters (for example, in

Montesquieu's *Lettres persanes,* Rousseau's *Nouvelle Héloïse,* or Laclos's *Liaisons dangereuses*) or the manuscript of someone's memoirs (Marivaux's *La Vie de Marianne,* among the large number of pseudomemoirs of the day); or a story is told to him (Prévost's *Manon Lescaut*); or it is an autobiography (Lesage's *Gil Blas*); or the narrator is omniscient, and is not only everywhere, but knows the innermost unspoken thoughts of each character. Diderot, until the final pages at least, assumes none of these positions.

In fact, he declares in his own terms that he is writing an antinovel: "It is quite evident," he tells us, "that I am not writing a novel, since I avoid using those things that a novelist never fails to employ in his craft. He who takes what I write to be the truth will be less mistaken perhaps than he who takes it for fiction."

It is already clear that one aspect of *Jacques le fataliste,* and an important one, is Diderot's preoccupation with the aesthetics of the novel as a literary genre. In the second chapter he rejects a trick in narration that would have been typical of a novel by Prévost, and cries out: ". . . that would have reeked of *Cleveland,*" and he adds, "The truth, the truth!" Preoccupation with realism is repeatedly emphasized in the pages of *Jacques.* This realism involves the question of truthfulness toward reality as well as that of the illusion of reality. In what may be a highly significant principle of aesthetics, Diderot appears to be saying that fictional writing is on the right path, it is carrying out its proper functions, *when* it mirrors life. But when it intensifies and reveals patterns of life it enhances its possibilities as a work of art.

Philippe Garcin, the French critic, one of many to be strongly drawn to *Jacques,* himself suggests this view when he tells us that of all Diderot's writings, this is the one that most brilliantly emphasizes freedom of tone and inspiration, a freedom which always magnifies the meaning of important books. Then Garcin adds a statement that should perhaps be quoted in its entirety, for we sense that he is bewildered, delighted, shocked, dismayed, and puzzled, like not a few of his fellow critics of the mid-twentieth century. He tells us: "This novel which is not a novel, nor, on the other hand, an antinovel, and which cannot be explained merely as a critique of all novels published before it (of all possible novels), this satire which is not really exhilarating, this experiment which is not very judicious, this overflow of impudent aphorisms and bizarre anecdotes constitutes in fact the most equivocal work in the literature of the Enlightenment."[18]

For Philippe Garcin and numerous other critics who have in the present century rediscovered *Jacques le fataliste,* the work represents the liquidation, the pulverization of the traditional rules of composition. Yet, according to these critics, *Jacques* has a very definite place in the aesthetics of the novel as, in various ways, it leads to a broadening of the art of fiction.

The third aspect of the novel or, if you will, the third general theme besides philosophy and aesthetics is ethics. Here, too, far more questions are posed than can immediately be answered. Diderot dwells, for example, on the equivocal Gousse; his noble gestures on one hand, and his complete lack of principles on the other—Gousse "whose head has no more sense of morality than that of a pike" (*AT,* 6:71). Is there any code of ethics revealed or advocated in the pages of *Jacques?* How much is man a mere victim of deterministic forces? How can a relativistic society set up a workable code of conduct? What about the place of the conformist and the nonconformist in society? And the nonconformists, from the eccentric through the perverse, the criminal, the superman, or the monster—what are their places, their natural functions in society? What about their social behavior in particular and in general? Is Madame de La Pommeraye an iconoclast or a monster? And what moral judgments are we to make about Père Hudson, the handsome, magnetic, intelligent priest with no calling for his office, who breaks without any scruples whatsoever the vows of poverty, chastity, and obedience?

This brings us to one final aspect of the question of morality. Long before writing *Jacques,* Diderot had become an avowed atheist. But he constantly questioned whether a godless universe gives us the right to do whatever we like. In *Jacques,* in the *Entretien d'un philosophe avec la Maréchale de* ***, and elsewhere, he maintained that we must not allow ourselves to be motivated entirely by caprice or by an irresponsible conglomerate mechanically structured by sensory impressions like Condillac's statue. Rather, our *philosophe* sees man consciously torn between an idealistic concept of absolute moral values and the practical concept of fundamental materialistic demands. Man is the one social animal caught up in a reality which alone can make him fully aware of his moral and material self.

In addition to the grand philosophical, aesthetic, and moral themes of *Jacques,* there are a multitude of lesser ones. Many of these have been examined by J. Robert Loy in his pioneer work on the novel, and still others are to be found in Stephen Werner's *Diderot's Great Scroll: Narrative Art in "Jacques le fataliste."* This latter, a study rich in factual information and provocatively original in interpretation, reveals that Diderot's recurrent theme of the great scroll in the sky is, in many ways, central to the novel itself. A concluding paragraph reads:

> *Jacques le fataliste* sums up Diderot's oeuvre in a cascade of parody and ironical disbelief. It announces—some years before Sade—the end of the *Aufklärung.* Indeed it looks forward to that one immense compendium which will bring the whole process of literary amplification and self-analysis to a close. The poignant nihilism of *Finnegan's [sic] Wake*—the text which not only demands that an entire life be spent creating it, but that a whole lifetime be spent trying to understand it—is, to a large extent, the ransom of *le grand rouleau.*[19]

By way of general conclusion to Diderot's involuted tale of fact and fiction it might be said that his proletarian hero, Jacques, is a prerevolutionary figure, as is the aging Diderot in his somber clothes, a Frenchman far removed in dress, manner, and thought from the majority of his countrymen, even from the more gifted members of the Académie Française. Diderot's works, including *Jacques le fataliste,* nurture change—change in the aesthetics of the short story and the novel, change in the psychology of acting or in the poet's creative art, change in education and the political order of the day, and in the approach to biological and psychological man. More clearly in Diderot than in Montesquieu, Voltaire, or Rousseau there is recognition of a dying era, the *ancien régime,* and a premonition of the revolutionary era with the inevitable upheaval already close at hand. "My aim," says the narrator in *Jacques,* "has been to seek out the truth, and I have fulfilled it" (*AT,* 6:239). It is a time when, more than ever before, Diderot is living on the edge of change.

The Man in the Black Suit: The St. Petersburg Interlude

By the middle 1760s, with the formidable task of editing the *Encyclopédie* drawing to a close, Diderot realized that he was no longer young. By eighteenth-century standards he had reached the age of venerability. Yet one thing was certain, Diderot was not then nor would he ever be venerable. His thinking, always complex, varied, original was now more so than ever. With advancing years, his already bold— some would say disorganized—mind became even bolder, more challenging, and, at times, more ambiguous. His ambiguity frustrated and irritated some contemporaries as it still does a number of his twentieth-century critics. He not only appreciated ambiguity, he willfully practiced it in his own works. There is even a hint of this with a touch of self-excuse when discussing Helvétius in the *Réfutation suivie de l'ouvrage d'Helvétius intitulé l'Homme* (1773), Diderot wrote, "There is always something to learn in works based on paradox, such as his and Rousseau's; and I prefer their false reasoning which forces me to think to commonplace truths that have no interest for me" (*AT*, 2:363). In this same *Réfutation,* taking issue with the absolutism of Helvétius's syllogisms, Diderot presented the idea of contradiction through a strikingly dialectical statement. Addressing the deceased Helvétius directly, he said, paraphrasing Descartes: "I contradict you, therefore I exist" (*AT*, 2:310). This is in the nature of Diderot's peculiar dialectic. To present both sides of a problem, he makes the existing contradiction a springboard for new ways of seeing things. It is an important methodology noticeable in almost all of Diderot's works, but especially so in those of his later years. There should, then, be general agreement with Arthur Wilson as to this innovative mode of procedure: "The method of seeking truth through the tension of opposites is as conspicuous a characteristic of Diderot in his aesthetic as it is in his scientific or ethical thought."[20]

With the partial advantage of hindsight, the Marxist critic, Henri Lefebvre, has this to say: "On one hand, Diderot reveals himself as the prudent arbiter between the interests of the bourgeoisie and those of feudalism; on the other he proclaims revolution. Whence the duality of Diderot's narratives and his thought which are in response to the contradictions of the age and the duality of his public's expectation."[21]

No doubt all centuries are prone to tensions between the past, the present, and the future; they are, for the most part, social, economic, and religious tensions. During the Enlightenment, though, they assumed a new coloring through independent thinking, often of a high order. Diderot, among others, had shown that driving spirit, that urge to make his own way to success, a spirit that was part of the eighteenth-century bourgeois heritage. François Arouet, turned Voltaire, had become a world-renowned writer; Marmontel, born in the most modest circumstances, a member of the French Academy; and Buffon had passed from the middle class to the nobility. And now Diderot, the son of a provincial cutler, had turned into an intellectual gadfly of the French Enlightenment. Though alternately scorned, respected, and feared by the authorities of his own country, with time he gained repute abroad

partly through certain of his writings that had drifted into foreign
countries through Grimm's *Correspondance Littéraire,* partly through the
impression he had made on distinguished visitors from England, Germany, Italy, and Russia, but chiefly, perhaps, because the *Encyclopédie*
bore witness in tangible form to this man's erudition and ingenuity.
Jean Vier, with special reference to Bayle and Fontenelle, speaks of the
early years of the Enlightenment as *des brumes d'aurore* (the "mists of
dawn"); the Enlightenment at its zenith in the middle of the century
is referred to by Jean Fabre as *le midi des lumières* or "high noon."
Following this pattern, the period from 1765 to 1780 might be called
the twilight of the Enlightenment (its *crépuscule*).

These latter years beginning with 1765—Diderot had nineteen more
to live—were a period of the late Enlightenment, a time when he was
no longer dazzled by speculation on the brightness of man's future.
On the contrary, he had doubts, sometimes serious, about the ability
of the human race to improve its lot. With growing conviction he
viewed the orthodox underpinning of the authoritative status quo of
his day as a worm-eaten base or perhaps more aptly as a corpse swarming
with the maggots of reaction, intolerance, and tyranny in every form.
But, unlike his fellow philosophes, Diderot was not only witty, he had
a grace-saving sense of humor. He used his active mind—sometimes
with a new intensity—to fight the intellectual and social excrescences
of the moment, knowing full well that he would not see them eliminated.
And he found a certain sense of well-being in his immense range of
writings, in his brilliant and seemingly interminable dialogue with himself
and with others.

One of the early desires of the philosophes had been that there might
emerge from the European Enlightenment a genuine example of Plato's
philosopher-king—a monarch who would rule through the love and
possession of wisdom rather than that of wealth, hollow honor, and
blind lust.

One could hardly look to France for such an example. Louis XV,
with his official mistresses, his courtiers, and scores of pretty nymphets,
seemed interested only in royal banquets, sex, and hunting. Louis XVI,
somewhat underdeveloped mentally, was a well-meaning individual far
more engrossed in the minutiae of running a clock than of running a
state. Nor were the reigning monarchs of Great Britain apt for the
role.

Until the inevitable disillusionment set in, the two most promising
candidates were Frederick II of Prussia and Catherine II of Russia.

Frederick, an enlightened despot, had carefully nurtured his interests and talents in literature, music, and the arts while proving himself to be an able and ruthless warrior and statesman. Voltaire and other intellectuals had become more than disillusioned at Potsdam where, as guests of the king, they were subject to Frederick's unscrupulousness and cynicism. After some three years in Frederick's entourage Voltaire escaped from the king and his court never to return. Diderot was always to remain immune to the blandishments of the Prussian king, and, being well read in Buffon's *Histoire naturelle des animaux,* deemed Frederick as ethical as a Bengal tiger. He was not to be lured to the misnamed castle of Sans Souci and, in consequence, succeeded in incurring the king's wrath.

Catherine offered a slightly different story. Her political principles, inspired to a considerable extent by Montesquieu, the Encyclopedists, and the Italian jurist, Beccaria, were at first surprisingly liberal. This inclination for political change, effectively expressed in her *Nakaz (Directive),* was a serious attempt at political and social reform. She was fully aware, however, that the Russia of her day was dominated by the notion and practice of serfdom, and that she could not remedy the situation, since she had come to power by supporting those of the nobility whose prestige and prosperity depended upon the labor of serfs. In short, she had won and continued to maintain the allegiance of the Russian aristocracy by her fierce consideration for what appeared to be Russia's present interests and the empire's glorious future. She nevertheless remained fascinated by contemporary French intellectual and artistic movements and, when she wished, she could be gracefully munificent by way of appreciation. She showered Buffon with lavish gifts for his volumes on natural science, and he replied in kind by sending his doltish son, "Buffonet," as emissary to the Russian court with a bust of his illustrious father to add to the empress's collection of famous men. Falconet, the sculptor, and other figures of note were, at Diderot's instigation, invited to take the long, wearisome voyage from Paris to St. Petersburg for the privilege of being feted by the tsarina. Catherine conducted a long and pleasantly intimate correspondence with Voltaire and, after his death insisted upon buying his library.

It is more than possible that Diderot had inherited a touch of his father's reverence for royal sovereignty. The myth of the reappearance of one of France's greatest monarchs had a modestly enshrined place in the writings of son Denis who, in *Le Rêve,* muses: "Perhaps a Henri IV will return some day" (*AT,* 2:181). In the years he was directing the *Encyclopédie* what he wrote revealed a stronger bent to free France from the shackles of outmoded religious practices than those of royal prerogative. In 1765 he was no democrat but combined the same mistrust as Voltaire and Rousseau for the swarming, unthinking masses, with a decided uneasiness over the tradition-bound authority of the nobility of the altar, the robe, and the sword. By then Diderot had revealed himself as something of a philosophical idealist, romantic, atheist, and realist. At the time, however, no one could be absolutely sure on any of these points. Still, having in abundance the bourgeois values of resourcefulness and responsibility toward himself and those of his kind, he had become, almost imperceptibly, an important spokesman of the middle class.

As a good bourgeois, who had suffered from impoverishment during his bohemian days in Paris, he had become acutely aware of the importance of material assets so necessary to the physical comforts and the social mobility of the aspiring commoner under the ancien régime. Up to 1765, when Diderot was fifty-two, he had had little or no recognition, honors, and distinctions from the French government or any other. In March 1765 Catherine changed all that. For some time a distant admirer of his versatile, far-reaching and vigorous mind, she bought Diderot's personal library for a handsome sum. This in itself assured him a certain financial independence and could provide a highly respectable dowry for his marriageable daughter, Angélique. But, having bought the philosophe's library, the empress made him its custodian for life with an annual income of one thousand livres. In a letter to General Betski who had informed him of this added gesture on Catherine's part, Diderot expressed pathetic gratitude bordering on the maudlin, and longed, he declared, to throw himself at the empress's feet in fervid appreciation (*Corr,* 6:355).

For the next several years Diderot was, from afar, Catherine's "cultural attaché." The term *attaché culturel* in this context is Paul Vernière's and it neatly applies to the philosophe's activities at the time. He would suggest to the empress gifted French men and women whose stay in St. Petersburg—however long or short—might prove mutually beneficial. He recommended scientific and artistic collections as well as individual paintings she might wish to acquire and, of course, he could always call her attention to what indispensable reading was available.

This was not enough, however. Diderot felt obligated to take the hazardous journey to St. Petersburg to express his gratitude in person. Now the tsarina was no more in the tradition of the philosopher-king

than was Frederick the Great. Both these dedicated political despots
toyed with intellectual playthings much as they did with their constant
stream of lovers. Besides providing diversion, a man of Diderot's stamp
could be excellent propaganda as well. In 1773, with the tribulations
of the *Encyclopédie* only a vague memory, with his daughter now married
for better or worse, and his autumnal romance with Mme de Maux a
thing of the past—there would be no others—Diderot responded to
his sense of duty and Catherine's wishes. It was an appropriate moment.
For the time being, the empress had considerable leisure. As one historian
has tactfully put it, she had lost one constant companion and had yet
to gain another. In reality, this high-spirited, earthy, and intelligent
ruler had dismissed one lover, and had not yet chosen his successor—
who was to be the celebrated Potemkin.

Diderot did not make the customary grand tour of Russia. He felt
no compulsion to flee the routine of Parisian life or to escape from
himself. His was not that fickleness of disposition that is always
dissatisfied with the present. The philosophe's journey was leisurely and
engaging. Away from France, he had time to regale a number of
correspondents, some twenty in all, including, *mirabile dictu,* his wife.
Whether seated in a highway coach swaying along the cobblestones of
Holland or through the forests of Westphalia or strolling through the
imperial winter residence at St. Petersburg, he viewed things with an
alert mind and a fresh perspective.

The Russian trip represented an important period in his life. He had
passed beyond those years of deepest pessimism and darkest discour-
agement but also of *recueillement* when, writing for himself and posterity
alone, he had conceived some of his greatest works. Now well into his
twilight years he was not only an aging Stoic, but one who was unable
or unwilling to shake off some attractively epicurean attitudes that were
so much a part of his nature.

On 15 June 1773 Diderot set out on his travels, a fact that caused
unequivocal reactions among those in France who knew him well. Mme
d'Epinay wrote the Abbé Galiani: "Friday the philosopher left for The
Hague and for Russia. . . . What a droll child this philosopher is!
On the day of his departure he was so full of wonder that he would
have to leave after all, so frightened to have to go farther than Grandval,
so unhappy that he had to pack up and be off. As for friends, I am
convinced that he thinks he will find them wherever he goes. But one
is fortunate to be so constituted" (*Corr,* 13:12). At almost the same
time Mlle de Lespinasse said in a letter to the Comte de Guibert:

"Diderot is in Holland. . . . He is an extraordinary man; he is a social misfit. He ought to be the leader of a sect, a Greek philosopher teaching the young" (*Corr,* 13:17).

The duality of personality that marks us all was always prominent in Diderot, but perhaps no more so than during and following his sojourn in Russia. In the eyes of those who knew him well it often assumed the pattern of naiveté coupled with the wisdom of age. Upon one occasion Catherine was to tell him bluntly, "Sometimes I see you a hundred years old and often I see you as a child of twelve" (*Corr,* 14:105).

But it is to be wondered whether this foreigner, this middle-class Frenchman in his black suit, offered a series of contradictory images to the vast majority of nobles who frequented the empress's winter palace. Benjamin Franklin was to come to France two years after Diderot's arrival in Russia. His wit and intelligence, his prudent moderation, his somewhat homespun dress, and slightly homespun but winning ways made this representative of a new country unreservedly acceptable in France. Perhaps Franklin would have been held in high esteem in St. Petersburg as well. But Diderot was a Frenchman who represented anything but the formal elegance and external sophistication of Louis XV's court, with its social graces, its profusion of silk and lace, its knee breeches and bagwigs that the Russian nobility had been so closely aping since the 1740s.

Diderot made little effort to mingle with those in attendance at the Imperial Court. The man in the black suit generally kept his distance amidst all this finery and ritualistic etiquette, but he was enchanted when the czarina on one occasion invited him to accompany her to one of her lesser palaces, where she made it a point to have the courtiers fined six rubles if they rose when she passed. What a splendid equalitarian principle was being exercised by a crowned head of such grandeur!

Perhaps Diderot hoped to be inconspicuous in his bourgeois garb among the Russian nobles. But the effect was quite the opposite. The suit itself was revolutionary. It subtly expressed a present disquiet and an uncertain future with new values in the air. For some, the philosophe cut an absurdly amusing figure, now jaunty, now careworn, in his somber clothes. For others at Catherine's court he was already the *épouvantable bonhomme,* the "odious old codger" that Barbey d'Aurevilly was to call him a century later. Had Diderot, so attired, gone to Versailles at the invitation of the king, he would have been judged a radical, an eccentric, or a country bumpkin. So, in a sense, the black suit was the crux of the matter. For many it symbolized, not without justification, the unpredictable and the dangerous.

Catherine, however, did not see matters thus. She had perfect confidence in her strong will, her august position, and her shrewd intelligence. During the late months of 1773 and the early months of 1774 Diderot was granted the privilege of spending long hours in her exclusive company. The vivacity of this elderly man was as remarkable as it had been among his most intimate friends back home. The empress herself said that he spoke with warmth, brilliance, and even vehemence. The story goes that, to emphasize his points, he would often lean over and slap her thighs, leaving them bruised black and blue. Rumor had it that the empress was even obliged to put a table between the philosophe and herself to protect her limbs. Such stories may have been the work of malicious tongues, for there were those at court only too happy to cast aspersions upon the frequent tête-à-têtes that Catherine granted this bumbling but scintillating foreigner. For her part, she wrote back to Voltaire that she could talk with Diderot her whole life long without ever growing weary, that he had a prodigious imagination, and that it was a pity that all men did not possess a heart like his.

Thus for five months Diderot was closeted with the empress almost daily. We know the subjects of their discussions for the philosophe wrote them up. Catherine and he then went over them together after which he placed the corrected versions in the czarina's hands. Lost and found several times, the notes and essays experienced many vicissitudes before finding a safe haven and a more or less permanent title as the *Entretiens avec Catherine II*. These memoranda reveal that the philosophe and the empress talked of many things, and certainly of kings.

Having won Catherine's confidence to the point that they could engage in intimate discussion, it now seemed Diderot's earnest wish to win this formidable woman over to the philosophy of the Enlightenment, or at least to bolster up any slumbering liberal convictions she may have had. During one discussion, for example, Diderot noted that no man-made laws were eternal and, in consequence, from time to time, they should be examined and modified when they no longer conformed to the spirit of the times. On another occasion the subject was the administration of justice. Diderot made it clear that his definition of justice included all that each person owes to himself and to others, to his country, to his family, to his mistress, to his friends, perhaps even to animals domestic and other. The philosopher's role, he insisted, was to sift out the laws of reason, to combat political madness, to glorify freedom. It is the philosopher's responsibility, he maintained, to tell the masses that they are the strongest class and that if they go to the slaughter it is because they let themselves be led to it. Small wonder that upon occasion the talks between the imperious ruler and the idealistic bourgeois became heated.

One day he told the empress that, if he were crowned king by her majesty's hands, he would suppress wanton luxury, corruptor of everything. He would reduce the cost of crown and court, he would sell the goods of the church, he would make nobles and army officers pay taxes like everybody else. In this instance, as throughout these discussions, Diderot was most assuredly criticizing France as well as Russia. He added that he would take all his subjects into consideration, giving them instruction in philosophy, painting, the works of sculptors, even Chinese porcelains to fill more profitably their leisure hours. He would—and here he must have had Catherine's willing ear—even extol the charming vices that bring happiness to mankind in this world and damnation in the next.

But Diderot did not let occasional sallies belie his deadly seriousness. All absolute governments tend to be bad, he artlessly and courageously told the empress. The best of despots commits a crime in taking away all sense of freedom from his subjects—thus reducing them to the condition of beasts. He did not make a frontal attack on serfdom, but he did counsel Catherine to create a whole class of small landowners since, one day, she would doubtless be obliged to develop a third estate.

The empress was not averse to proposing topics for discussion, but she had made no mention of that of divorce. This is understandable, for she had no difficulty whatsoever in ridding herself of one male companion for another; even her husband, Peter III, had died under dubious circumstances. Diderot forged ahead, however, saying that he felt no embarrassment in advocating divorce himself, whether on the grounds of natural law or because of the harm that is done when the marriage tie cannot be dissolved. He told Catherine—who presumably was unmoved by and indifferent to the suggestion—that the possibility of divorce renders both marriage partners stricter in observance of the duties they owe each other. And, in effect, divorces help improve morals and increase the population. But, he declared, the divorce must be requested by both partners at once. And so the discussions went.

Foreign emissaries, including the French ambassador and a nobleman Frederick II had sent to spy on Diderot, were visibly uneasy over and inordinately curious about these private talks between the son of a

provincial cutler and one of the most powerful rulers in the world. To
their chagrin, they remained to the end uninformed and steeped in
jealousy and resentment.

During these five months of close give-and-take on philosophical,
political, and sociological levels, Catherine, intrigued by her handpicked
French bourgeois, stressed to others two traits of her interlocutor. She
found he had a prodigious imagination and that he was extraordinary.
Extraordinaire could have, in the empress's mind, referred to a number
of things: his intellectual brashness, his original turn of mind, his offhand
familiarity, his impulsiveness, and a character at once naive and wise
in the ways of the world. Diderot's warmest praise for Catherine was
his repeated assertion that she had the soul of Brutus and the charms
of Cleopatra.

But at last the time for the fatiguing journey back home was at
hand. The long Russian winter had been hard on the health of the
aging philosopher. Catherine gave him a ring from off her finger with
her profile cut in the stone. And she provided him with a carriage in
which he could lie down when overly weary. The conveyance lasted for
some four hundred and fifty miles. Four other carriages were needed,
one after the other, as the lurching course and the deep-rutted roads
took their toll. Lingering along the way, Diderot finally reached Paris
21 October 1774. His farewell letter to Catherine (*Corr* 13:198–201)
gave her great pleasure; it was a fine mixture of gratitude, esteem, and
affection. This amiable old man, as a Russian baron called him, was
also pleased with his letter and he quoted generous extracts from it in
correspondence to his cherished Sophie.

During the conversations at the Hermitage the subject had often
turned to education, and Diderot showed much interest in the empress's
educational reforms, as reflected in the aristocratic schooling for cadets
at St. Petersburg and the School for Noble Girls that Catherine had
established at Smolny. One innovation Diderot wished to introduce for
the young was the opportunity to understand the physiology of the
human body. A scientifically inclined Parisian lady, Mlle Biheron, had
succeeded in reproducing with much success wax replicas of the human
anatomy for this very purpose. Catherine did not accept the philosophe's
recommendation that Mlle Biheron be invited to Russia, but the empress
did purchase her anatomical collection for the further enlightenment of
adolescents among the Russian nobility.

The talks on education often dealt specifically with pedagogy. And
so, back in Paris, with a strong sense of obligation to his benefactress,

Diderot was able to draw up at her instigation a *Plan d'une université*. The plan was replete with ideas as bold as they were new. Besides suggestions for specific curricula, he insisted with renewed fervor upon government-sponsored education for all, regardless of social or economic status. There was to be no religious interference whatsoever, and the students would be taught the fundamentals by the best teachers the state could provide. All should be subjected to discipline and hard work. Basically essential and useful programs of study such as mathematics, physics, and the natural sciences should remain apart from theoretical programs of study like logic, grammar, French, or Latin; the learning of modern languages was, rather surprisingly, spurned. The superior students would be encouraged to pursue their education at a higher level, while for those less intellectually gifted there would be vocational schools where their talents would also be developed in their own interest and that of the state. A plan of education devised along these lines was indeed a drastic criticism of the existing order not only in Russia but throughout Europe.

Diderot had, while in Holland, conceived a fictional Jacques who was a proletarian hero of prerevolutionary vintage. The author himself was a bourgeois of much the same nonconformist, prerevolutionary stamp. Plumagewise, he was in St. Petersburg a slightly ruffled, shuffling old blackbird amidst the strutting peacocks of Catherine's court. The spectacle was a foreshadowing of things to come, and feared as such.

No doubt there is truth in the assertion that Diderot's political education had been largely formulated in the decades of the sixties and seventies. But somewhat earlier there was a pervasive feeling in the writings of Montesquieu, Voltaire, Rousseau, and Diderot himself that something was deeply wrong with the social and governmental organizations and spirit then prevalent in Europe. It is undeniable, however, that Diderot's political education was given its final touches only with the completion of his Russian sojourn.

The *Plan d'une université* was one indication of the heightened audacity of his political thinking, and his *Observations sur le Nakaz*, with its implicit radicalism, its strong emphasis on love of freedom and loathing of political despotism, was another.

Back again in Paris, Diderot could not be entirely at ease with himself. He was well aware that his imposing empress, whose lavish hand and studied attentions had profited him greatly, was one of the great despots of the century. The ambivalence of his position was now plainly evident. He had been the beneficiary of Catherine's cordiality, her generosity, her seeming thoughtfulness and sincerity. All this had caused Diderot to return to France in a euphoric mood, with a new self-confidence and the optimistic notion that he may have helped in the westernization of Russia. But as Paul Vernière has noted, with his voyage over Diderot realized that, because of his relations with Catherine, he had come home with a sullied conscience.[22]

Henceforth he was aware of a new dualism in his heart and soul. He felt commitment toward Catherine the Great for her unfailing courtesies and her material generosity. At the same time he hoped to preserve his own intellectual integrity as a politically committed writer. He would, in his last great work, *Essai sur les règnes de Claude et de Néron,* strive to come to terms with his ideals.

With Diderot's St. Petersburg experiences behind him, Mme Geoffrin wrote her friend, King Stanislas of Poland: "Diderot . . . is a good and decent man, but his head is screwed on so poorly and he is so badly organized that he neither sees nor understands what he does see. . . . He is always like a man who is dreaming and who is convinced that what he is dreaming is real" (*Corr* 13:242), Catherine was of much the same opinion for, after Diderot's death, she spoke of him to the Comte de Ségur saying: "Had I placed faith in him, every institution in my empire would have been overturned; legislation, administration, politics, and finances, would all have been changed for the purpose of substituting some impractical theories. . . . speaking to him freely, I said: 'Monsieur Diderot, I have listened with the greatest pleasure to all that your brilliant genius has inspired you with; but all your grand principles, which I understand very well, though they will make fine books, would make sad work in actual practice.' "[23]

Mme Geoffrin's explicit and the empress's implicit judgment that Diderot was a dreamer is close to the truth. Diderot himself was so aware of the fact that he was willing to leave it to posterity to see whether any of his dreams would materialize.

Chapter Seven
Twilight, Darkness, and Light

By 1777 Diderot had cleared his worktable of such tasks as his intensive and extensive collaboration on the third and ever-popular edition of the *Histoire des deux Indes.* Here he gave life and even fire to the dry but revealing statistics of the Abbé Raynal's work, whose ponderous title in its entirety translates as *The Philosophical and Political History of the European Establishments and Trade in the East and West Indies.* This important and highly successful magnum opus was an anticolonial manifesto based on humanitarian principles close to the hearts of an elderly Diderot and his fellow *encyclopédiste* the abbé.

Precisely what Diderot's contributions were to this impressive work cannot always be positively ascertained. We know he worked on a salaried basis. His daughter tells us that he labored hard and long on the lengthy study, which sets forth our moral obligations to the underprivileged races. The work contains much fascinating information on such topics as slavery, despotism, and religion, and we may assume that Diderot's contribution was vast. If the *Histoire* was widely read, it was also suppressed by the French authorities, and Raynal was forced to flee the country.[1]

Diderot had always been a humanitarian at heart and now, during the last years of his life, his political thinking had taken on an increasingly liberal tinge. Time and again he reacted to the political scene with such writings as *Pages inédites contre un tyran* (Frederick the Great), the *Principes de politique des souverains,* and *Observations* for the possible edification of Catherine of Russia. In many of these writings, political and ethical theory went hand in hand, and in his *Essai sur Sénèque le philosophe* (1779) Diderot continued to pursue—though often in veiled language—his passionate interest in political questions and their far-reaching social implications. The essay on Seneca would be revised and amplified into its definitive form in his last work, the *Essai sur les règnes de Claude et de Néron,* three years later. At this point there were those among his friends who felt they had good reason to be uneasy over the possibility that an even bolder Diderot might, with age, again find himself imprisoned in the fortress of Vincennes or between the blackened walls of the equally formidable Bastille. However, with time passing so quickly, Diderot was persuaded there were other things to attend to before it was too late.

Important Odds and Ends

Among these other things, Diderot pressed on to prepare available manuscripts of his writings in two duplicate batches, one to send to Catherine in Russia and the other for a projected *Oeuvres complètes*. Despite visibly failing health, he continued to collate, edit, and even compose with much of that same energy and enthusiasm that had marked his work in the past.

In 1780 the philosophe was sixty-seven years old. With four years still to live, he had, in many ways, at last become a figure of first consequence on the European scene. For some time he had been writing thoughtfully, and without fear, on the subject of death. Falconet was again urging him to collaborate on a further exchange of correspondence in their longstanding controversy over immediate fame versus recognition by posterity. But, as Diderot wrote Galitzin in October of the same year, more urgent matters required his attention. One of these was the accumulation and ordering of serious scientific notes jotted down between 1774 and 1780. For facts and inspiration he had drawn partly from Albrecht von Haller's magistral *Elementa physiologiae corporis humani* (1757–66), and partly from such other writers of the age as Bordeu, Bonnet, Buffon, and La Mettrie. Added to this was the considerable data he had long before gleaned from his translation of James's *Medicinal Dictionary*, from his conversations and correspondence with eminent physicians like Théodore Tronchin, from the witnessing of autopsies, and from his lasting interest in medical problems and physiology in every form. He had already intimated in the *Rêve de d'Alembert* an essential link between the anatomist, naturalist, physiologist, and physician on one hand, and the philosopher conducting thoughtful inquiry into metaphysics, ethics, and—though the term was not then in use—psychology, on the other.

Diderot's approach is often psychophysiological as, time and again, he moves from the biological and physiological to the psychological which in turn leads to the ethical. "There is only one passion," he tells us, "to be happy," and adds: "It assumes different names according to its violence, the means it employs, and its effects" (*AT*, 9:352).

It has not yet been fully ascertained what sort of work Diderot intended to write from all these notes taken either from his reading or from his poetic and scientific reflections. His procedure seemed to be more that of the painstaking *encyclopédiste* he could at times be. Perhaps had there been more time to assemble these scattered notes with some semblance of continuity, the work might have been his *summa,* showing the creative imagination so evident in the *Interprétation de la nature* and the *Rêve de d'Alembert.* Death did not permit him to complete the task; still, by gathering the odds and ends he had amassed, under headings and subheadings, glimpses of an overall purpose are discernible in this work that is generally referred to as the *Eléments de physiologie.* Aram Vartanian suggests that Diderot's aim may have been "to investigate the diversity of human faculties, temperaments, and conduct in relation to the corresponding diversity of biological structures and physiological processes of which man, in his total being, was the natural product."[2] The grouping of material seems to bear out this dual preoccupation. For instance, under the general heading, *On Man,* we have such subheadings as *On the Perfectibility of Man, On Abstract Man and Real Man,* and *On Life and Death,* plus separate developments on *The Stomach, The Heart, Blood, Glands, The Passions,* and, among others, *Understanding, Imagination,* and *Memory.*

Diderot posited that it is to memory that we owe our sense of the continuity of time and personal history that is basic to self-consciousness and identity. To give support to his views, he wrote this passage in the *Eléments:* "I am inclined to believe that all we have seen, known, perceived, or heard—even the trees of a great forest . . . every concert we have listened to—exists within us and unknown to us" (*AT,* 9:366–67). While still awake he could see the forests of Westphalia, and again, while dreaming, he could see them as vividly colored as though they were on a canvas by Vernet. Then too, "the sound of a voice, the presence of an object, a particular place . . . and behold the object recalled–more than that, a long period of my past—and I am again plunged into pleasure, regret, or affliction" (*AT,* 9:369–70). In such passages the naturalist Diderot joins with the idealist Plato to point the way to the involuntary memory of Baudelaire and Proust, and the conscious and unconscious of Freud.

What are we to conclude from all these unfinished thoughts, these odds and ends of pages whipped into a scant semblance of order? As Jean Mayer has noted, Diderot did not consider himself a scientist. He conceived of his role from an entirely different point of view. Without trying to take the place of inventors or researchers, he was determined, whenever possible, to put them on the right path by helping to establish the methods and laws of research, to use his imagination to broaden the views of men of science.[3]

If Diderot was not himself a man of science in the strictest sense of the word, he was nevertheless taken very seriously by the great Claude Bernard (1813–78), the founder of experimental medicine. It was Bernard's intention to publish an edition of the *Elements of Physiology,* presented in an orderly fashion and annotated by himself. But just as Diderot's death had prevented the completion of the *Elements,* so Bernard's own death prevented him from realizing this new, carefully controlled edition.

Though the work remained unfinished, Diderot had written its conclusion as a moralist, a metaphysician, and a poet: "The world is the abode of the strong. I shall not know until the end what I have won or lost in this vast gambling den, dice-box in hand. . . . What do I perceive? Shapes. And what else? Shapes. I do not know the substance. We walk amidst shadows, and we are also shadows, both to ourselves and to others. . . . There is but one virtue, justice; but one duty, to achieve happiness; only one corollary: not to expect too much of life and not to fear death" (*AT,* 9:428–29).

How Good Is He?

In the *Elements* Diderot had baldly declared: "What we have the least knowledge of is ourselves" (*AT,* 9:346). Since the work, as we have already seen, dealt with the parts, processes, and functions of the human body, including neurology and psychophysiology, we cannot but conclude that his chief aim was to arrive at a better understanding of biological, cerebral, and ethical man in general. But his statement concerning knowledge of ourselves could, at the same time, refer to one of his favorite literary obsessions: self-examination with the desire to comprehend the physical as well as the emotional currents of his being.

Given his forceful personality, his original turn of mind, his habit of not mincing words, it is to be expected that almost everything Diderot wrote bore his individual stamp. There was also the compulsion to portray himself in various situations, under different lights, while using specific techniques in the process.

The pronoun in the first person singular—*moi*—plays an important role in a goodly number of his works. This is true whether one or several facets of Diderot's nature is carrying on a conversation with his father, with Dorval, with Rameau's nephew, or with d'Alembert and others. There are intimate sketches of himself in his correspondence and the famous one in *Regrets sur ma vieille robe de chambre*. There is the double exposure of Diderot-Ariste, first as the unpretentious philosopher in *La Promenade du sceptique,* and then in the *Discours sur la poésie dramatique,* the ideal philosophe and the man he would like to be. Unlike Rousseau, Diderot had no need of spinning out a long, detailed autobiography filled with self-persuasion, self-immolation, and self-justification. His *Confessions* are everywhere in his work, now in the spirit of bonhomie, now serious and reflective, now in deadly earnest.

Est-il bon? Est-il méchant? Diderot's last and by far his best play, deserves a privileged place in this corpus of so-called confessions. The play, written three years before his death, is of considerable interest for a number of reasons. An earlier sketch in 1775 called *Plan d'un divertissement* mildly suggested what Diderot had in mind. This was confirmed by an intermediate step in 1777 entitled *La Pièce et le prologue.* Finally, the finished product appeared in 1781, a four-act comedy, asking the question "Is he good? Is he bad?" of the protagonist, Monsieur Hardouin, who is, in reality, a thinly disguised Diderot. The successive steps, *Plan, Pièce,* and four-act play—showing the unfolding of a subject rich in possibilities—was an example of his creative processes that revealed once again that he often gave much time and thought to his works, resorting far less to facile improvisation than had once been supposed. *Est-il bon? Est-il méchant?* also interests us because in it Diderot jettisoned certain of his dramatic theories along with the stilted moralizing, and the farfetched coincidences that marred *Le Fils naturel* and *Le Père de famille.*

Carol Blum, noting that Hardouin is marvelously adroit in managing other people's affairs through a series of cleverly unscrupulous maneuvers, gives the following account of the day's activities:

He agrees to write a *divertissement* for Mme. de Chépy only upon the request of her pretty servant, humiliating the mistress in her own eyes and those of her maid. He procures the pension for the widow Bertrand's son by implying that the boy was probably his own bastard son when he importunes his friend the Minister. Mme. de Vertillac is induced to give her daughter permission in writing, to marry Crancy when M. Hardouin makes it appear that the girl is pregnant, reminding the mother that her own wedding had taken place a bit later than the event it was supposed to sanctify. At the end of the play, each of the characters has received what he wanted but at the price of a blow to his self-esteem. In each case the humiliation is more or less justified, but a certain residue of subdued resentment nevertheless taints the pleasurable denouement.[4]

Through Hardouin's lips Diderot sums up the past two decades of his own life: "For twenty years I have walked between the complaints of my friends and my own remorse." And he adds, "If I had wanted to I believe I could have been a dangerous rogue" (*AT,* 8:187). The ultimate conclusion of those befriended in the play is that Hardouin-Diderot is, like all of us, good and bad by turn. In the last act the victims of Hardouin's manipulation are first appeased, then full of rejoicing, and finally break out into song.

This little comedy, most unconventional for the time, is swift-moving, replete with amusing confrontations, unexpected witticisms, and spirited dialogue, while now and then—for good measure—a bright thumbnail sketch of both the moral and physical Diderot is deftly drawn.

The play remained in manuscript form quite unknown to his contemporaries. But it was to have a small and enthusiastic number of readers when the manuscript surfaced in the nineteenth century. Paulin, Taschereau, and Champfleury were among the Parisian men of letters, journalists, and erudites who urged the Comédie Française to produce the newly discovered play that bore no resemblance to Diderot's two well-known bourgeois dramas. In this they were abetted by such distinguished actors as Got and Mme Plessy. However, some of the officials of the national theater rejected the comedy without reading it, while others found a play in four acts unacceptable.

The most famous of Diderot's admirers to enter the lists was Charles Baudelaire. Late in 1854 Baudelaire wrote a letter of considerable eloquence to the director of the Gaîté Theater pleading the case of *Est-il bon? Est-il méchant?* But the director, astute businessman that he was, remained convinced that the theatergoing audiences of mid–nineteenth-century France would choose to spend their money on more up-to-date spectacles. It was not until well into the twentieth century that the comedy was performed in Paris and received with éclat by spectators and journals alike.

Among other things this pleasantly entertaining comedy showed how capable Diderot was of laughing at himself, especially his shortcomings—

those of the well-intentioned enthusiast, meddler, and bungler, the all-too-human individual susceptible to the cajoling of his male friends and the appeals of pretty women. Here Diderot was in marked contrast to his fellow philosophes, Voltaire and Rousseau who, when they smiled, usually did so at someone else's expense. "It is Diderot," writes Jean Thomas, "who taught his century the spontaneous love of humanity."[5] In *Est-il bon? Est-il méchant?* this trait is everywhere apparent.

But this amiable and slightly ridiculous portrait Diderot offered of himself was soon to be followed by a more somber one involving serious ethical and political questions. In its final form it would be a long essay ostensibly on the life and death of a Stoic philosopher under the reigns of two Roman emperors, Claudius and Nero.

Philosophical Rectitude and Imperial Tyranny

Like that of ancient Greece, the cultural history of Roman antiquity was an almost inexhaustible source of knowledge and inspiration for Diderot. Lucretius, Virgil, Cicero, Cato the Elder, Tacitus (Diderot was called *le Tacite moderne*), Terence, and especially Horace were returned to time and again for consideration, interpretation, and better understanding of the human condition. He admired the "stiff and stern" Rome of the flourishing Republic, and he was filled with shocked wonder at imperial Rome from the dictatorship of Caesar and Augustus, down through the tyranny of Tiberius, Caligula, Claudius, Nero, Galba, and Caracalla. For Diderot, it has been said, the true mark of antiquity could be summed up in two words, *le noble et le grand*. Among the *noble* were those who had lofty moral qualities, and among the *grand* were those who, like Nero, were illustrious in infamy.

Throughout his life Voltaire had admired and drawn satisfaction from the great authors of antiquity, as did a goodly number of his contemporaries. Like him, they often turned to the Roman Stoic philosopher, statesman, and man of letters, Lucius Annaeus Seneca, for guidance and encouragement.[6]

Diderot varied somewhat from this pattern. "I was early suckled," he wrote in *Plan d'une université pour le gouvernement de Russie* (1775–76) "on the milk of Homer, Virgil, Horace, Terence, Anacreon, Plato, Euripides, mixed with that of Moses and the prophets" (*AT*, 3:478). Seneca was not among these first idols. In fact, in the *Essai sur le mérite et la vertu* (1745) this Roman philosopher seems far more interested in piling up riches through courting the powerful and corrupt than in risking death by speaking out against Nero's ruthless criminality.

And yet it was unquestionably Diderot who, among his compeers, ended up by understanding Seneca best. He felt certain as his life drew to a close that he had at last found a kindred spirit in the Roman philosopher.[7] "After having read Seneca," he exclaimed, "am I the same as I was before—no, that cannot be!"[8]

It was a constant source of regret for the aging Diderot that he had not earlier discovered the *noble* Seneca—Seneca as he no doubt really was. He made up for this dereliction by publishing a vast farewell essay of several hundred pages paying homage to and acknowledging kinship with the great philosopher and humanist who had lived under the heel of Roman despotism at its worst.

Briefly, Seneca (4 B.C.–65 A.D.) had been chosen to be tutor in the art of government to Prince Nero, heir to the imperial Roman throne. He tried to instill in his pupil the virtues of a Stoic philosopher-king. For some time Nero looked to Seneca for counsel and direction. Eventually, however, they grew apart and, for reasons not clearly apparent to historians, a complete break occurred in their relations. Later Seneca was accused of participating in the conspiracy to assassinate Nero. The philosopher, sixty-nine years old, was then ordered by his former pupil to commit suicide. He complied, with Stoic serenity, by having his veins opened.

There are a number of reasons why Diderot, in the final years of his life, should turn to Seneca with ardor and persistence. The youthful translator, Joseph de Chancel de La Grange, having rendered into French the works of the Roman philosopher, died in 1775 before being able to put the finishing touches on his translation. Diderot was urged by his friends, d'Holbach and Naigeon, to follow La Grange's six volumes with a life of Seneca based on Tacitus, Suetonius, and Seneca himself as well as Diderot's own reactions and reflections. Diderot took to the suggestion with relish, consulting a large number of historians both ancient and modern for, as he told Naigeon, "Youth likes happenings; old age prefers meditation" (*AT,* 3:10). He was following a personal predilection as well. But as recent scholarship has not tired of emphasizing, there were other reasons for Diderot's devotion to Seneca once he had read his life and works with care.

First of all, this last ambitious work of Diderot is an essay on moral philosophy, and our philosophe is the same humanist—if older and wearier—that he was some twenty years before when he wrote his cherished Sophie, "I love that philosophy which raises up humanity" (*Corr*, 2:225). In the *Essai sur les règnes de Claude et de Néron* he considers inhumanity as well, while he ponders the relentless malevolence of the rulers, the horrors of the amphitheater, the excesses of the priests, the depravity of the masses, the effete barbarity of imperial Rome.

There is, especially in the second and longer version of the *Essai,* a constant shuttling back and forth between Nero's Rome and eighteenth-century Paris, that cruel world of *La Religieuse* and *Le Neveu de Rameau,* where again we see man's inhumanity to man. But, in each of these two times and places, there was at least one philosopher striving to make life better for everyone. "What is the aim of philosophy?" Diderot writes upon rereading Seneca. "It is to unite mankind through the exchange of ideas and by the exercise of mutual benefaction" (*AT,* 3:210).

There is no doubt that Diderot chose the subject of his final essay partly because his life and that of Seneca offered striking parallels. As Loy, among others, has noticed, Diderot too championed philosophy in an era hardly sympathetic to philosophical speculation; he too was an independent thinker chary of philosophical systems; he too was often obliged to make disturbing concessions the better to accomplish what he thought to be his duty; he too was often tempted to seek out either bald, workaday solitude or prosperity among the chosen few. Moreover, like Seneca, he knew what it was to have prison walls close in about him, and he too had found dialogues, conversations, and essays to be his favorite literary forms for expressing ideas in general and ethical precepts in particular. In short, Seneca was a sort of Diderot of the first century A.D. and so, quite naturally, he became a model for the aging Stoic of the French Enlightenment.

But Seneca was only nominally a Stoic and, like his eighteenth-century disciple, found himself enticed by the less rigorous philosophy of Epicurus and Lucretius as well. Like the Stoics, or at least the Stoics in Diderot's mind, both found virtue in enlightenment, and, like the disciples of Epicurus, they held that the search for happiness, pleasure, and utilitarian interest should be the basis of individual conduct.

There are those who persist in thinking that Diderot's Claudius and Nero are actually Louis XV and Louis XVI, thinly disguised. Yet Frederick of Prussia, whom Diderot had spurned, and Catherine the Great, whose lavish generosity he had accepted, would offer more apt parallels to the Roman imperialism he had in mind. And it is Catherine upon whom Diderot's moral ambivalence centered. Like Seneca, torn between his principles as moralist and philosopher, and his halfhearted concessions to the absolutism of a Claudius and a Nero, Diderot had accepted Catherine's beneficence and intellectual camaraderie while seeing her as the partially enlightened despot—gifted and dangerously ambiguous—that she was. In consequence, Diderot was in a far better position to appreciate Seneca's plight than were Voltaire, Maupertuis, La Mettrie, and d'Alembert, for Frederick's brand of tyranny had made the parting of the ways with him that much easier. Diderot's revised essay on Seneca and his two imperial masters reveals a shade of his own bitterness and disillusionment. "Not only is he distressed with the political and social evils of his time," Douglas Bonneville tells us, "he is also tortured by personal doubts and fearful of his reputation, present and future."[9]

Three components of the essay stand out as very much a part of the French eighteenth century and of Diderot's preoccupations. They include the two perhaps unwise though not entirely gratuitous attacks on Rousseau and La Mettrie, and a brief, eloquent, and warmly acceptable panegyric to a young America that had only recently come into being.

The unprovoked and willful critique of Rousseau appears in the 1778 version of the essay—the year of Rousseau's death. Diderot does not mention Jean-Jacques by name, but he is easily identifiable. Reader reaction was vigorous and prolonged. Diderot was soundly rebuked for the violence of his recriminations against a great man, now unable to defend himself, and who was, perhaps, victim of a touch of madness. Diderot even found himself in the uncomfortable situation of having his remarks attributed to a seizure of *violent délire* (*AT*, 3:8). By way of answer to his critics, in the second or 1782 version of the essay, he devoted seven sub-chapters—some ten pages in all—to even harsher criticism, this time referring to his former friend by name (*AT*, 3:90–100).

With Rousseau's death it was presumed that his dreaded *Confessions* would be promptly released for publication. Diderot denied that it was from fear of being mistreated or slandered in Rousseau's posthumous memoirs that he was expressing himself so vehemently; in fact, he had learned from those who had heard the *Confessions* read aloud in manuscript form that he had "unfortunately been spared" from among the large number of individuals the work had "torn to shreds." Perhaps he was simply acting as the avenger of others (*AT*, 3:93).

This, however, does not explain the savagery of the attack. J. Robert Loy lays its violence to Diderot's hatred of hypocrisy in all its forms, and astutely observes that what is sincerity for Jean-Jacques immediately turns into hypocrisy for Diderot.[10] Arthur Wilson, noting the obsession that this *frère ennemi* had become, suggests that it could have been "Rousseau's impenetrability, his invulnerability, his inaccessibility" that had irritated Diderot through the years to the point of impairing his judgment.[11] Doubtless both Loy and Wilson are right.

If Diderot went out of his way to discredit Rousseau, the transition leading to his deep-seated disapproval of La Mettrie is carried out more smoothly. In ancient Rome there had been perverse men whom enemies of the philosophers deliberately associated with philosophers in an effort to sully their reputation through the moral turpitude of the former. In the same way, Diderot tells us, there are those contemporaries who, motivated by a desire to slander the philosophes, have placed La Mettrie in their midst, La Mettrie who, utterly devoid of judgment as usual, wrote the *Anti-Sénèque* without knowing the first principles of Seneca's philosophy. By extension, then, as the author of the *Homme machine*, he is "dissolute, impudent, a clown, and a flatterer, totally lacking in any moral sense" (*AT,* 3:247–48).

Diderot thus takes a final and excellent opportunity to show his contemporaries and posterity that, though La Mettrie's ideas on philosophical materialism bore a close resemblance to his own, the two men had nothing in common in the realm of ethics; of the two only Diderot had the humanist's concern for men's ethical relationships.

The third contemporary matter in hand was the newborn American republic, a symbol for Diderot and others that had now become a reality and promised much for the future. Despite the merits of the *Histoire des Deux Indes* (1772), the work had often given a confused account of the non-European world. Something else was needed to explain the spirit of the new America.

France in the 1770s and the 1780s was the center of European Enlightenment. Benjamin Franklin himself, with his arrival in Paris as ambassador from America, excited enthusiasm of all sorts, and Turgot coined for him—with the approval of the philosophes—the Latin epigram, *Eripuit coelo fulmen, sceptrumque tyrannis* ("He seized the lightning from the heavens and the scepter from the tyrant"). Franklin had already become a mythical figure who had led a rebellion of humanity and who had bestowed enlightened law upon the rude Americans. The role of the lawgiver was a status of particularly high repute in the Enlightenment, which explains in considerable measure Diderot's respect for Moses,[12] and his appreciation of the civic and moral lessons in the writings of Seneca. Moreover, in his work for

Catherine, Diderot had assumed for himself the role of the exalted figure of lawgiver.

It was both natural and fitting that Diderot should devote chapter 72 of the *Essay on the Reigns of Claudius and of Nero* to the thirteen English colonies that had, with a united front, broken off from an oppressive motherland. With the persuasion of a Tacitus or a Suetonius, he began his encomium as follows:

Following centuries of constant oppression, may the revolution that has just come to pass beyond the seas, by offering all the inhabitants of Europe a refuge against fanaticism and tyranny, teach those who govern their fellowmen the legitimate use of their authority! May these worthy Americans, who have preferred to see their wives ill-used, their children killed, their houses destroyed, their fields laid waste, their cities burned, and themselves shed their blood and die, rather than lose the smallest part of their freedom, may they forestall the enormous increase and the unequal distribution of wealth, luxury, indolence, the corruption of morals, and see to the maintenance of their freedom and the preservation of their government. (*AT,* 3:324)

This is followed by a prophetic warning to the new nation to prolong as much as possible its time of vigor before inevitable decadence sets in. May America not engage in civil wars or let itself fall under despotic rule. General welfare is the result of necessity, and it is in times of prosperity, not adversity, that a country is in danger of extinction. It is not with gold or even with large armies but through its morals that a state endures (*AT,* 3:324–25).

This premonition of things to come is a testimony to Diderot's historic vision. But in this tribute to a youthful America—as well as in other pages throughout the *Essay*—there is also hidden emphasis on the dangers of the abuse of political power by an arrogantly presumptuous monarchy in those years of the ancien régime directly prior to the French Revolution.

In a two-page conclusion, largely made up of a series of questions, Diderot seeks justification for his *Essay,* for Seneca, and for himself. Among these questions are the following. After so many unfavorable reactions to the work, what is the reader's final judgment? Was Seneca an upright man or a cowardly flatterer? Did he have genius, or was he merely a false *bel esprit?* Did he speak of virtue as one who was appreciative of its merits, or as a hypocrite whose conduct and writing remain equally questionable?

Then, turning to himself, he asks: Am I a decent man, or a vile apologist for Seneca? If someone defended me as I have defended the Roman philosopher, would he risk universal scorn and indignation? Do I reason honestly or am I a sophist? Is there logic in my ideas or am I self-contradictory? Have I written a good book or a bad one?

In reply to this last question, it could be said that—with the possible exception of the *Bijoux indiscrets*—no work of Diderot's had come in for such sharp criticism either in the eighteenth century or in the twentieth as this, his last and longest of many essays. The author has been chided for his verbosity, his vindictiveness, his hypocrisy, his inordinate self-justification, and his frequent manipulation of historical facts to suit his own purposes. The work has been criticized for being confusedly disjointed, eloquent in the wrong places, injudicious, and overly subjective.

And yet, if a thinking person were obliged to spend a month or a year on a desert isle with no other reading than one of Diderot's works, he could do far worse than to have the *Essay on the Reigns of Claudius and of Nero* as his first choice. For as a few have noted, in this superb essay—written with old age upon him—Diderot found in Roman history a pretext for an immense intellectual and moral last will and testament.[13]

With Few Regrets

Diderot was old and famous and he was, at long last, well-to-do, when his essay on Claudius and Nero appeared. Word was spread that it caused royal displeasure, chiefly because of certain religious overtones, and Diderot had reason to fear the Bastille. But late in May 1782 he wrote a note of apology to Le Noir, the commissioner of police, and the latter gave his assurance to higher authorities that, following instructions, "the philosopher has been let off with a severe reprimand" (*Corr*, 15:303). The author of the *Essay* could once again feel safe, and his godson, writing from Paris on 5 October of the same year, reported: "Papa Diderot complains, but eats, drinks, and sleeps well" (*Corr*, 15:509). Early in 1784, though, his health showed marked signs of deterioration, a fact he took stoically. On 22 February his beloved Sophie died, leaving him a set of Montaigne's *Essais* bound in red morocco.[14] By February 1784 Diderot was only too well aware of the fragility of human life, and because of his knowledge of physiology, gave himself some five more months to live; in this he was correct.

His daughter, Mme de Vandeul, calling upon her father the day before his death, relates the visit as follows " 'the first step towards philosophy is disbelief.' This is the last thing he said to me; it was late, I left him, I hoped to see him again" (AT, 1:lvii).

His very last morning he spent in the sumptuous ground-floor apartment in the Rue Richelieu that Catherine II had given him, presumably chatting with his friend d'Holbach, his doctor and his son-in-law. He then sat down cheerfully to a noonday repast and ate heartily. During dessert Mme Diderot asked him a question, but he did not answer; he had abruptly stopped thinking, suffering, and living. It was Saturday 31 July 1784. Thus died a philosophe who was at once a skeptic, an Epicurean, and a Stoic.

Interment was in the Chapelle de la Vierge in the Eglise Saint-Roch, within walking distance of his home, of the Bibliothèque Nationale, of d'Holbach's town house, the Palais Royal, the Café de la Régence, and the present Comédie Française. Diderot would have been surprised could he have foreseen that, following a Christian funeral, his remains were to repose in a church, the same church that was the final resting place of the brilliant scientific theorist, Maupertuis, and the great playwright, Corneille. He would have been far less surprised that, years later, interested parties could find no trace whatsoever of his mortal remains.

At the age of seventy-two with heart at last still, Diderot had taken that first essential step into the future. His physical being would shortly lose its individuality and return to that state of flux he had always insisted was so much a part of the universe. It was a step he had calmly foreseen for some time—the moment when peace would settle over a throbbing body and a restlessly inquiring mind.

The immortality Diderot sought was not that offered by Christianity or that of a passive marble bust by Houdon, but, rather, the appreciation of posterity. Edmund Burke, scoffing at French Enlightenment in the name of British traditionalism, declared: "We are not the converts of Rousseau; we are not the disciples of Voltaire; Helvétius has made no progress against us. Atheists are not our preachers; madmen are not our lawgivers."[15]

Burke did not consider Diderot to be of sufficient importance to be named in this subversive company. And, to be sure, it was altogether too soon for him to be placed on the same level with Voltaire and Rousseau—or even, it seems, with Helvétius. He was still too poorly known by the British, and such outstanding works as Le Neveu and Le Rêve were not known by the French until well into the nineteenth century. But Diderot died with few regrets and with confidence in the future. He was convinced that his thoughts would be esteemed by, as well as furnish impetus, to those individual and collective minds that were to constitute posterity. And so it has indeed come to pass.

Conclusion

Here was a man who in fact liked to live on both sides of the looking glass, constantly in search of elusive truth and a better understanding of human reality. Such problems as virtue and vice, good and evil, free will and determinism, materialism and spirituality, democracy and absolutism, were well-worn subjects for debate. But Diderot pursued them in new ways. He was equally fascinated by the irrational and the rational, sanity and madness, talent and genius. He added substantially to the order and disorder of aesthetics. He gave new dimensions to time and distance, to psychophysiology and to art criticism. Moreover, as sexologist in an age when Christian oversimplifications prevailed, he foreshadowed Sade by discussing the darker appetites of human nature.[1] Indeed, he left no appetite unturned. His approach to every subject was nearly always fresh and challenging.

If, for instance, we take the problem of virtue—frequently a stumbling block for students of eighteenth-century thought—we see that what Diderot calls virtue is, in reality, the loftiest possible expression of sociability, for morality in a social context is the only kind of morality Diderot recognized. In his complex ethic, virtue is not all of a piece, an end in itself, an abstract goal, but a function necessary to man's social condition, and subject to the contingencies thereof. As Jacques Proust has remarked, "Diderot would appear as an immoralist if his work . . . were not almost completely an apology for social virtue."[2]

As the multilayered complexities of his thought continue to come to light it is difficult not to agree with the American historian Peter Gay, a present-day authority on the Enlightenment, who writes: "Diderot is one of the most difficult among the philosophes to capture: versatile, volatile, erotic, experimental, profoundly original, he belongs to no single category, and puzzled everyone who knew him. He even puzzled himself."[3]

But perhaps the last word should be given to that eminent nineteenth-century philosopher, critic, and historian Hippolyte Taine who, in the majestic sweep of his *Ancien Régime,* found time to pause in double-edged tribute to Diderot. According to Taine, Diderot, unlike Voltaire or Rousseau, was a volcano in eruption that, for forty years, discharged ideas of every order and kind, boiling and fused together.

After expressing shock at the open and hidden crudities that so marked Diderot's work, Taine concludes: "On the other hand, among so many superior writers, he is the only genuine artist, the creator of souls, the mind in which objects, events, and personages are born and become organized of themselves, through their own forces. The composer of the 'Salons,' the 'Petits Romans,' the 'Entretiens,' the 'Paradoxe du comédien,' [*sic*] and especially the *'Rêve de d'Alembert'* and the 'Neveu de Rameau' is a man of unique species in his time."[4]

Sainte-Beuve had given Diderot to the neighbors across the Rhine with the famous specious remark that he alone, among the French, had "la tête allemande." Taine restored him to his own and to the world at large where he had belonged all along. The French had only to open their arms to receive him.

Notes and References

Preface

1. H. G. C. Grierson, *Classical and Romantic and Other Collected Essays and Addresses,* 2d ed. (London: Chatto & Windus, 1950), 55–56.
2. Otis E. Fellows and Norman L. Torrey, eds., *The Age of Enlightenment,* 2d ed. (New York: Appleton-Century Croft, 1971), 1.

Chapter One

1. Edna C. Frederick, *The Plot and Its Construction in Eighteenth-Century Comedy* (Bryn Mawr, Pa.: Bryn Mawr Press, 1934), 74–75.
2. Robert Niklaus in *A Literary History of France. The Eighteenth Century 1715–1789* (London and New York: Ernest Benn, 1970), 23.
3. References to Thomas Carlyle's turgidly brilliant piece on Diderot are taken from the *Critical and Miscellaneous Essays. Collected and Republished* (Boston, 1884), 3:83–151.
4. See Elizabeth Potulicki, "L'Expérience poétique de Diderot," *DS* 16 (1973):107–228.
5. See Marx W. Wartofsky, "Diderot and the Development of Materialist Monism," *DS* 2 (1952):279–327.
6. Emanuel Chill in *New York Times Book Review,* 17 September 1972, 6, 7, 14.
7. The reader may wish to bear in mind that Professor Miller has had occasion to revisit the Soviet Union since the publication of his *Diderot in Soviet Criticism, 1917–1960* and, in consequence, like others, has fresh insights to offer.
8. See Blake T. Hanna, "Diderot théologien," *RHLF* (1978):19–34.
9. See R. Trousson, "Les Circonstances d'un Centenaire: Diderot en 1884," *Europe* (May 1984): 94–106.
10. Otis Fellows and Donal O'Gorman, "A note concerning Diderot's Mathematics," *DS* 10 (1968):47–50.
11. For further information on the Lewinter edition see Eve Sourian, "Diderot retrouvé," *DS* 18 (1975):169–87.
12. I would like to set the record straight on *Diderot Studies:* I conducted the first seminar on Diderot ever offered at Columbia University during the spring term of 1948. Syracuse University Press accepted seven papers written by students in the seminar and an introduction by myself on condition that Professor Norman L. Torrey (a well-known *dix-huitiémiste*) be coeditor. He kindly accepted for the sake of the struggling students and their instructor.

It was a beginning and at first rather poorly received both at home and abroad. Torrey accepted responsibility for the introduction to the second volume and encouraged such scholars as the already-eminent Herbert Dieckmann to contribute to what was to be the first periodical or series devoted to Diderot. The university press refused to publish a third volume. Fortunately, Droz of Geneva assumed responsibility and Professor Gita May became coeditor. In considerable measure through her efforts, such notable specialists as Yvon Belaval, Jean Fabre, Georges May, Arthur Wilson, and Herbert Dieckmann, among others, contributed manuscripts. The series was launched! Droz offered to buy the copyright for the first two volumes, but Syracuse University Press flatly refused and in 1971 granted permission to Greenwood Press to release a second printing of both. Professor May turned to other scholarly pursuits, and I continued to edit the series up to volume 8. I then invited Diana Guiragossian Carr to be coeditor, and *Diderot Studies,* now in its twenty-fourth volume, is nationally and internationally known because of her unstinted devotion to the series.

13. For a more complete understanding of this epistolary debate with one preferring the esteem of his contemporaries and the other aspiring to posthumous fame, see chapter 5 of this book and especially Maurice Posada's "An Introduction to the textual Problem of the Diderot–Falconet Correspondence on Posterity," *DS* 16 (1973):75–96.

14. Jacques Barzun, "Doing Research," *Columbia* (1987):22.

Chapter Two

1. References to Diderot's letters will be drawn from Denis Diderot, *Correspondance,* ed. Georges Roth and Jean Varloot, 16 vols. (Paris: Editions de Minuit, 1955–70); hereafter abbreviated *Corr,* plus volume and page; here, *Corr* 2:207.

2. Generally, quotations from Diderot's works will be taken from the conventional Assézat-Tourneux *Oeuvres complètes de Diderot* (Paris: Garnier, 1875–77). References to this edition will be given as *AT,* plus volume and page, here, *AT* 17:335.

Chapter Three

1. For these early years, however, see Jean Pommier, *Diderot avant Vincennes* (Paris: Boivin, 1939).

2. None of this correspondence gave the slightest inkling that some day he would be regarded as one of the great letter writers of the age.

3. The complete title is revealing as regards the broad scope of this work: *A Medicinal Dictionary; including Physic, Surgery, Anatomy, Chymistry, and Botany, in all their Branches relative to Medicine. Together with a History of Drugs; and an introductory Preface, tracing the Progress of Physic, and*

explaining the Theories which have principally prevailed in all Ages of the World, 3 vols., 1743–45.

4. Scientific inquiry of the day is handled in detail in Jean Mayer, *Diderot homme de Science* (Rennes: Imprimerie Bretonne, 1959), and Jacques Roger, *Les Sciences de la vie dans la pensée française du XVIII siècle* (Paris: Armand Colin, 1963).

5. Franco Venturi, *La Jeunesse de Diderot* (1713–53) (Paris: Skira, 1939), 66.

Chapter Four

1. Assézat assumes Barclay to be a certain John Barclay, and not George Berkeley whose name was often spelled "Barclay" on the Continent.

2. See Otis Fellows, "George Berkeley, His Door, and the Philosophes," *FLRN,* 53–66.

3. Pommier, *Diderot avant Vincennes,* 117.

4. Carlyle's remarks on the philosophe—some utterly disparaging, others reflecting unabashed admiration—may be found throughout his essay "Diderot," first appearing in the *Foreign Quarterly Review* 11 (1833) and republished in his *Critical and Miscellaneous Essays* (London: Chapman & Hall, 1897).

5. For other reactions to the novel, pro and con, past and present, see Otis Fellows, "Metaphysics in the *Bijoux indiscrets:* Diderot's Debt to Prior," *SVEC* 56 (1967):509–40.

6. For which see Lester Crocker and Raymond L Krueger, "The Mathematical Writings of Diderot," *Isis* 33 (1941):219–32.

7. Notable is the memoire *Sur les probabilités* Why it has puzzled historians of mathematics is explained by Otis Fellows and Donal O'Gorman in "A Note Concerning Diderot's Mathematics," *DS* 10 (1968):47–50. This represents the primary source. The original manuscript in Diderot's hand was discovered and here published by these two scholars.

8. See Elie Fréron's review of Rameau's *Nouvelles Pièces de Clavecin, distribuées en six suites d'airs de différents caractères* in *L'Année littéraire* 7 (1757):45.

9. Sidney Hook, "Diderot's Great Legacy," *New Leader,* 2 January 1961, 25.

10. The preceding translation is from Denis Diderot's *The Encyclopedia, Selections,* ed. and trans. Stephen J. Gendzier (New York: Harper & Row, 1967). This volume gives the general reader an excellent idea of the *Encyclopédie,* its contents, its tribulations, and final triumph. The more specialized reader will want to consult such works as Jacques Proust, *Diderot et l'Encyclopédie* (Paris: Armand Colin, 1962), 621.

11. See Charles C. Gillespie's introduction to *A Diderot Pictorial Encyclopedia of Trades and Industry* (New York, 1959). These two volumes,

representing a choice of the ten original volumes of printed plates, make for fascinating perusal.

12. See Paul H. Meyer's introduction to his critical edition of the *Lettre sur les sourds et muets,* in *DS* 7 (1965):232. The same volume has a prefatory essay by Georges May entitled "A l'usage de ceux qui lisent la *Lettre sur les sourds et muets,*" which presents and situates admirably the complexities of the work.

13. See Shelby T. McCloy, *Eighteenth-Century Inventions* (Lexington: University of Kentucky Press, 19), 131–32, for indications concerning Père Castel's color-organ.

14. For a very good idea of Diderot's general impact as an art critic in the nineteenth century, see Gita May, *Diderot et Baudelaire, critiques d'art,* 3rd ed. (Geneva: Droz, 1973), 187.

15. *DS* 7:7–8.

16. Herbert Dieckmann, "The Influence of Francis Bacon on Diderot's *Interprétation de la nature,*" *Romanic Review* 34 (1943):329; see also Lilo K. Luxembourg, *Francis Bacon and Denis Diderot, Philosophers of Science* (Copenhagen: Munksgaard, 1967), 127.

17. "Jeune homme, prends et lis. . . . Un plus habile t'apprendra à connaître les forces de la nature; il me suffira de t'avoir fait essayer les tiennes. Adieu." *AT* 2:6.

18. Arthur Wilson, *Diderot* (New York: Oxford University Press, 1972), 187.

19. There has been a curious and interesting attempt on the part of certain twentieth-century scholars to speak authoritatively on Diderot, and yet, when possible, to denigrate his insights into the aesthetics and the sciences of the future. The Marxists feel that he was moving in the right direction but had been born too soon. The anti-Marxists, forgetting they are standing on Diderot's shoulders, often adopt the condescending tone.

20. George Havens, *The Age of Ideas; from Reaction to Revolution in 18th-Century France* (New York: Colliers Books, 1962), 315.

21. Wilson, *Diderot,* 328.

22. Lenore R. Kreitman, "Diderot's Aesthetic Paradox and Created Reality," *SVEC* 102 (1970):157–72.

23. For an interesting account of this love-hate relationship, see Jean Fabre, "Deux Frères ennemis: Diderot et Jean-Jacques," *DS* 2:155–214.

24. The complete text of the *Tablettes,* along with related correspondence, may be found in *DS, 309–20,* "Les Tablettes de Diderot," by John Pappas and Georges Roth.

25. Fellows and Torrey, *The Age of Enlightenment,* 501n.42.

26. Hilde H. Freud, "Palissot and 'Les Philosophes,' " *DS* 9 (1967):243.

Chapter Five

1. Posthumously published in 1798.

2. See, for instance, Jean Pommier, "Les Salons de Diderot et leur influence au XIX siècle et le Salon de 1846," *Revue des Cours et des Conférences*

37 (1936):289–303, 437–52; and May, *Diderot et Baudelaire, critiques d'art,* 197.

3. Jean Seznec, *Salons. Texte établi et présenté par Jean Seznec et Jean Adhémar,* 4 vols. (Oxford: Clarendon Press, 1957–67; 2d ed., 1975). This edition has a new introduction and an updated bibliography.

4. Gita May, "Denis Diderot: The Emergence of an Unconventional Philosophe," in *European Writers. The Age of Reason and the Englightenment* (New York: Charles Scribners Sons, 1984), 4, 488.

5. Abbé Morellet, *Mémoires,* 1:134.

6. Carol Blum, *The Virtue of a Philosopher* (New York: Viking Press, 1974), 65. "What this book conveys so well is the exciting quality of Diderot's mind and temperament, one brilliant, the other complex," says J. H. Plumb in "Strong Appetites, Insatiable Curiosity," *Book World,* 17 November 1974, 3.

7. For those wishing a detailed and, indeed, fascinating account of the Delamarre incident, and especially of Diderot's novel, Georges May's study, *Diderot et "La Religieuse"* (New Haven: Yale University Press, 1954), would be required reading.

8. Nedd Willard, *Le Génie et la folie au dix-huitième siècle* (Paris: Presses Universitaires de France, 1963), 33. Willard has an interesting chapter, "La Folie et le génie vus par Diderot à travers ses oeuvres," which could easily be expanded.

9. Herbert Dieckmann, "The *Préface-Annexe* of *La Religieuse,*" *DS* 2:31.

10. The observations in this section have surfaced through the research of June S. Siegel, "Diderot and Richardson: A Confluence of Opposites," (Ph.D. diss., Columbia University, 1963); "Grandeur Intimacy. The Dramist's Dilemma," *DS,* 4; "Diderot and Richardson: Manuscripts, Missives, and Mysteries," *DS,* 18; "Lovelace and Rameau's Nephew: Roots of a Poetic Amoralism," *DS,* 19.

11. Typical is Paul Vernière's remark in his introduction to the *Eloge:* "Nous n'avons plus aucune raison de partager cet enthousiasme." *Oeuvres esthétiques* (Paris: Garnier, 1959), 26.

12. Only very recently has Richardson criticism begun to drop its psychosocial bias, and show some awareness of the author's stylistic gifts. While Diderot admittedly contributed much to the fatal identification of Richardson's art with social reality, it is not the sole preoccupation of the *Eloge.* According to Dr. Siegel's initial study, which includes perhaps the first extended consideration of Richardson's poesis, Diderot did not go too far at all in his praise of Richardson's art per se.

13. Jean-François Rameau, son of an eccentric but talented organist of Dijon, had won fleeting success with his *Nouvelles Pièces de clavecin,* published in 1756 at Bertin's expense, but now unfortunately lost. This windfall and the acquisition of a number of distinguished ladies as pupils led him to marriage and an effort to establish a home. Ill luck followed, for his wife

died shortly before our dialogue takes place, and his son was to die soon after. Moral collapse and dependence on friends followed.

14. Carlyle, *Critical and Miscellaneous Essays*, 3:148.

15. *Denis Diderot. Le Neveu de Rameau. Edition critique avec notes et lexique*, ed. Jean Fabre (Geneva: Droz, 1950), lxxxvii. This work, with its introduction some ninety pages in length, offers a wealth of information, rich in erudition, interpretation, and suggestion.

16. This subject has been studied in some detail; see Otis Fellows, "The Theme of Genius in Diderot's *Neveu de Rameau*," *DS* 2:168–99.

17. Gilbert Highet, the classicist, first informed me that such is in spirit a faithful rendering of the line: *"Vertumnis quotquot sunt, natus iniquis."* We have seen Diderot using Vertumnis, the Roman god of change, in another context.

18. June S. Siegel, "Lovelace and Rameau's Nephew: Roots of Poetic Amoralism," *DS* 19:167–68.

19. *"Rameau's Nephew" and d'Alembert's Dream*, ed. L. W. Tancock (London and Baltimore: Johns Hopkins University Press, 1966), 16.

20. Donal O'Gorman, *Diderot the Satirist: "Le Neveu de Rameau" and Related Works, an Analysis* (Toronto: University of Toronto Press, 1971). By "Related Works" Dr. O'Gorman refers to *Satire I, sur les caractères et les mots de caractère, de profession, etc.* and a brief dialogue between the author *(Moi)* and an insolent young man with literary pretensions *(Lui)*. Among other things, O'Gorman studies the interrelationships of the three satires.

21. Etienne-Maurice Falconet, "Avertissement," in *Le Pour et le contre: correspondance polémique sur le respect de la postérité, Pline et les anciens auteurs qui ont parlé de peinture et de sculpture* by Diderot and E.-M. Falconet, ed. Yves Benot (Paris, 1958), 366. See Herbert Dieckmann and Jean Seznec, "The Horse of Marcus Aurelius," *Journal of the Warburg and Courtauld* (1952), 201; and *Le Pour et le contre*, ed. Benot, 17.

22. Letter to Falconet, 15 February 1766, *Corr* 6:58–59.

23. Letter to Falconet, January 1766, *AT* 18:91; *Corr* 6:16; *Le Pour et le contre*, ed. Benot, 60; Diderot and E.-M. Falconet, *Correspondance: les six premières lettres*, in *Analecta romanica, Beihefte zu den romanischen Forschungen*, ed. Herbert Dieckmann and Jean Seznec (Frankfurt: Klostermann, 1959), 7:56.

24. Letter to Falconet, April or May 1767, *Corr* 7:54.

25. For a fuller account of this controversy and its editions, see Maurice Posada, "An Introduction to the Textual Problem of the Diderot–Falconet Correspondence on Posterity," *DS* 16 (1973):175–96.

26. This letter, dated 20 October 1760, was written nine years before *Le Rêve* (*Corr* 172–73).

27. *Le Neveu, Le Rêve*, ed. and trans. L. W. Tancock (London: Penguin Books, 1966), 137–38.

28. See Otis Fellows, *From Voltaire to "La Nouvelle Critique": Problems and Personalities* (Geneva: Droz, 1970), 120–23.

29. He was also to suggest that man was the monster of the woman and woman the monster of the man.

30. Wilson, *Diderot,* 559.

31. See Eleanor M. Walker, "Towards an Understanding of Diderot's Esthetic Theory," *Romanic Review* 35 (December 1944):277–87.

32. Aram Vartanian, "Diderot and the Phenomenology of the Dream," *DS* 8:237.

33. Havens, *Age of Ideas,* 348.

Chapter Six

1. The *Entretien* first appeared in Grimm's *Correspondance Littéraire* and was published as a posthumous work of the Italian poet Tomasso Crudeli.

2. *Diderot's Selected Writings,* ed. Lester G. Crocker (New York: Macmillan, 1966), 252.

3. Michael Cartwright, "Diderot and the Idea of Performance and the Performer," *FLRN,* 33.

4. Douglas Bonneville, in a challenging article, "Diderot's Artist: Puppet and Poet," in *Literature and History in the Age of Ideas,* ed. Charles G. S. Williams (Columbus: University of Ohio Press, 1975), 245–52, treats the *Paradoxe* not as a turning point in Diderot's aesthetic thinking but as a crystallization of his thoughts on artistic inspiration, creation, interpretation, and criticism.

5. Aram Vartanian, *"Jacques le fataliste:* A Journey into the Ramifications of a Dilemma," ed. John N. Pappas, *DEOF,* 325.

6. George Saintsbury, *A History of the French Novel* (London, 1917), 1:404.

7. In *Tristam Shandy,* bk. 1, chap. 22. See especially Alice Green Fredman, *Diderot and Sterne* (New York: Columbia University Press, 1955), where she discusses the use of digression in both authors: pp. 126, 141, 142–43, 144–45, 161, 163.

8. J. J. Mayoux, "Diderot and the Technique of Modern Literature," *Modern Language Review* 31 (October 1936):523.

9. Saintsbury, *History of the French Novel,* 1:404.

10. Mayoux, "Diderot and Technique," 523.

11. Charly Guyot, "Avant-propos, *Jacques le fataliste,"* 10.

12. Jean Fabre's statement appears in the introduction to *Essays in Honor of Otis Fellows,* 27. The title of the Loy book (New York: Kings Crown Press, 1950) was a partial inspiration for the title of this section.

13. A far from complete listing of those who have made a contribution to a better understanding of *Jacques* would include Yvon Belaval, Lester Crocker, Herbert Dieckmann, Jean Ehrard, Jean Fabre, Alice Green Fredman,

Robert Mauzi, Georges May, William Moore, Vivien Mylne, Jean A. Perkins, Gabrijela Vidan, Aram Vartanian, Paul Vernière, and Stephen Werner.

14. William Moore, in discussing the functions of satire in *Jacques,* notes that the keys to understanding the work as a satire lie in the most difficult passages, the narrative interruptions, and he concludes in his unpublished manuscript that "we are confronted in *Jacques* with a satire in the Menippean tradition. But these ramblings also accentuate certain questions of morals and manners, and attack the complacent *Lecteur,* arguing in a vein decidedly reminiscent of Rousseau. While appropriating a point of view that causes the greatest incongruities in the text, the Narrator urges us to go beyond parody to examine issues of the greatest political and moral moment." In "Functions of Satire" (Ph.D. diss., Columbia University, 1975), 186.

15. Vartanian, *"Jacques le fataliste,"* 345.

16. Claude Roy, "Sur Diderot," *Europe* 28 (1950):26.

17. *Jacques le fataliste,* ed. Yvon Belaval (Paris, 1953), 3.

18. Philippe Garcin, "Diderot et la philosophie du style," *Critique* 15 (1959):204.

19. Stephen Werner, *Diderot's Great Scroll: Narrative Art in "Jacques le fataliste"* (Banbury: The Voltaire Foundation, 1975).

20. Wilson, *Diderot,* 531.

21. Henri Lefebvre, *Diderot: Hier et aujourd'hui* (Paris: Les Editeurs réunis, 1949), 307.

22. *Oeuvres politiques de Diderot,* ed. Paul Vernière (Paris: Garnier, 1963), xxvi.

23. Louis-Philippe Ségur, *Memoirs and Recollections* (London, 1825–27), 3:34–35.

Chapter Seven

1. In this respect the *Histoire* bears comparison with another work on which, years before, an equally reckless and far younger Diderot may have collaborated, with the result that the work itself was banned and its principal author had to find safety in exile. This was the Abbé Jean-Martin de Prades's thesis, "Jerusalem coelesti," which had first been defended before the Faculty of Theology of the Sorbonne (1751). In any event, in 1752 Diderot wrote a *Suite de l'Apologie de l'abbé de Prades,* and the whole affair was partly responsible for the suppression of the first two volumes of the *Encyclopédie* in the same year. For a thoroughgoing account, see Yves Benot, *Diderot de l'athéisme à l'anticolonialisme* (Paris: François Maspero, 1970).

2. Aram Vartanian, "The Enigma of Diderot's *Eléments de physiologie, DS* 10:299.

3. See Jean Mayer, *Diderot homme de science* (Rennes: Imprimerie Bretonne, 1959), 21, as well as Jacques Roger, *Les Sciences de la vie dans la pensée française du XVIIIe siècle* (Paris: Armand Colin, 1963), 676.

4. Blum, *Diderot: The Virtue of a Philosopher*, 143–44.

5. Jean Thomas, *L'Humanisme de Diderot* (Paris, 1938), 71.

6. See Jean Seznec, "Diderot and Neo-Classicism," *Listener*, 26 October 1972, 535–36.

7. See Stephen Werner, "Voltaire and Seneca," in *SVEC* 67 (1969):29–44.

8. Herbert Dieckmann, *Inventaire du fonds Vandeul et les inédites de Diderot* (Geneva: Droz, 1951), 257.

9. Douglas Bonneville, *Diderot's "Vie de Sénèque," A Swan Song Revised* (Gainesville: University of Florida Press, 1966), 50.

10. J. Robert Loy, "L'Essai sur les règnes de Claude et de Néron," *Cahiers de l'Association internationale des études françaises, Diderot*, 1961, 13:245.

11. Wilson, *Diderot*, 692.

12. Nicolas Fréret, not Diderot, was author of *La Moïsade*, the anti-Semitic mock epic of Moses and his people. On various occasions Diderot portrayed Moses as an exalted figure.

13. To do full justice to this work, one should turn to Diderot's "Essai sur les règnes de Claude et de Néron," ed. and annotated by Jean Deprun, Jean Ehrard, and Annette Lorenceau, in *Oeuvres complètes*, vol. 25, ed. H. Dieckmann and J. Varloot (Paris: Hermann, 1986).

14. A love of Montaigne was one more thing they had in common during the thirty years of their mutual attachment; see Jerome Schwartz, *Diderot and Montaigne* (Geneva: Droz, 1966).

15. Edmund Burke, *Reflections on the Revolution in France*, ed. Thomas H. D. Mahoney (New York, 1955), 97.

Conclusion

1. Jenny Batlay and Otis Fellows, "Diderot et Sade: Affinités et divergences, *L'Esprit Créateur* 15, no. 4, (1976):449–59.

2. Jacques Proust, *Diderot et l'Encyclopédie*, 273.

3. Peter Gay, *The Enlightenment: A Comprehensive Anthology* (New York, 1973), 287.

4. Hippolyte Taine, *The Ancient Regime*, trans. John Durand (New York, 1962), 268.

Selected Bibliography

PRIMARY SOURCES

Oeuvres complètes. Edited by Assézat-Tourneux. 20 vols. Paris: Garnier, 1875–77. Standard but somewhat obsolete edition.

Oeuvres complètes. Edited by Roger Lewinter. 15 vols. Paris: Le Club français du livre, 1970–73. Chronologically presented.

Oeuvres complètes. Edited by Herbert Dieckmann, Jacques Proust, Jean Varloot, et al. 33 vols. Paris: Hermann, 1975–. Definitive edition.

Oeuvres philosophiques. Edited by Paul Vernière. Paris: Garnier, 1956.

Oeuvres esthétiques. Edited by Paul Vernière. Paris: Garnier, 1959.

Oeuvres romanesques. Edited by Henri Benac. Paris: Garnier, 1962.

Oeuvres politiques. Edited by Paul Vernière. Paris: Garnier, 1962.

Mémoires pour Catherine II. Edited by Paul Vernière. Paris: Garnier, 1966.

Correspondance générale. Edited by Georges Roth and Jean Varloot. 16 vols. Paris: Les Editions de Minuit, 1955–70.

Le Neveu de Rameau. Edited by Jean Fabre. Geneva and Lille, 1950.

Le Rêve de d'Alembert. Edited by Jean Varloot. Paris: Editions Sociales, 1962.

Eléments de physiologie. Edited by Jean Mayer. Paris: Didier, 1964.

Lettre sur les sourds et muets. Edited by Paul H. Meyer. *Diderot Studies* 7 (1965).

La Religieuse. Edited by Roland Desné. Paris: Garnier-Flammarion, 1968.

Les Salons. Vols. 1–4. Edited by Jean Seznec. Oxford: Clarendon Press, 1957–67.

Essais sur la peinture. Edited by Gita May. Paris: Hermann, 1984.

SECONDARY SOURCES

Adams, D. J. "An English Printing of *Les Bijoux indiscrets.*" *DS* 22 (1986):13–15.

———. *Diderot, dialogue and debate.* Vinaver Studies in French, vol. 2, Liverpool: Francis Cairns, 1986. Perceptive treatment of Diderot, philosopher and writer.

Barzun, Jacques. "Why Diderot?" In *Varieties of Literary Experience,* edited by Stanley Burnshaw, 31–44. New York: New York University Press, 1962. Stresses the philosophe's modernity.

————. "The Mystery in *Rameau's Nephew*." *DS* 17 (1973):109–16. Underscores complexities of this lively dialogue.

————. "Diderot Made Art Reviews into An Art." *New York Times*, 28 August 1983, Arts and Leisure section.

————."Diderot as Philosopher." *DS* 22 (1986):17–25. Excellent little discussion and summary.

————. "Doing Research." *Columbia* (1987), 22.

————. "Diderot. *Lettre sur le commerce de la librairie*." *DS* 24 (1988):169–71.

Batlay, Jenny, and Otis Fellows. "Diderot et Sade: Affinités et divergences." *EC* 15 (Winter 1976):449–59. Emphasizes Diderot's intellectual, psychological, and aesthetic superiority over Sade.

————. "De l'amour et des amours dans *Jacques le fataliste*." *AIOW* (1977):1–17.

Beco, Annie. "Diderot, historien de l'art." *DHS* 19 (1987):423–38.

————. "La Réflection sur la dissonance chez les philosophes du XVIII, siècle, D'Alembert, Diderot, Rousseau." *Revue des Sciences humaines* 205 (1987):13–25.

Belaval, Yvon. *L'Esthétique sans paradoxe de Diderot*. Paris: Gallimard, 1950. An expert's digressive views on aesthetics.

————. "Les Protagonistes du *Rêve de d'Alembert*." *DS* 3 (1961):27–53. Diderot's reasons for choice of characters in the dialogue.

————. "Trois Lectures du *Rêve de d'Alembert*." *DS* 18 (1975):15–32. Analyzes opposing views of three authorities on the *Rêve*.

————. "Sur l'addition aux *Pensées philosophiques*." *DEOF* (1974).57–70. The *Addition* is more moralizing than the *Pensées*.

Benot, Yves. *Diderot, de l'athéisme à l'anticolonialisme*. Paris: François Maspero, 1970. Sees Diderot's most vital works as a reaction to his age.

Besse, Guy. "Observations sur la *Réfutation d'Helvétius* de Diderot." *DS* 6 (1961):29–45. Interesting presentation of clash between Diderot's views and those of Helvétius.

Blum, Carol. *Diderot: The Virtue of a Philosopher*. New York: Viking Press, 1974. Spritely study containing original ideas.

————. "Fesser et confesser: deux impulsions de Diderot envers la femme." *CID* (1985):99–104.

Bonneville, Douglas. *Diderot's "Vie de Sénèque."* Gainesville: University of Florida Press, 1966. Diderot's last essay.

————. "Diderot's Artist: Puppet and Poet." *LHGH*, 245–52. Columbus: Ohio State University Press, 1975. Unravels strands of Diderot's controversial *Paradoxe*.

Brewer, Daniel. "Diderot and the Image of the Other (Woman)." *EC* 24 (1984):53–65. No desire, we are told, is more basic than the desire to know.

Bukdahl, Else Marie. *Diderot, les salonniers et les esthéticiens de son temps*. Vol. 2 of *Diderot, critique d'art*. Copenhagen: Rosenkilde et Bagger,

1982. Diderot remains the most knowing, scrupulous art critic of his day.

Camp, Wesley D., and Agnes G. Raymond. *Jack the Fatalist and His Master*. New York: Peter Lang American University Studies, 1984. Translated from the French with preface, postface, selected bibliography and name index. A new and lively translation of Diderot's famous novel.

Carr, Diana G. "The image of Diderot in the British Periodical Press from 1750 to 1800." Diderot a Bicentennial Tribute: *French Forum Monographs* 58 (1986).

———. *"Le Père de Famille* et sa descendance anglaise." *ESLC* (1979):49–58.

———. Coeditor of *DS*.

Cartwright, Michael. "Diderot critique d'art et le problème de l'expression." *DS* 13 (1969). Solid grasp of Diderot's principles in art criticism.

Casini, Paolo. "Le hasard, la nécessité et 'un diable de philosophie.' " *ESLC* (1979):59–70.

———. "Diderot et les philosophes de l'antiquité." *CID* (1985):33–43.

Catrysse, Jean. *Diderot et la mystification*. Paris: Nizet, 1970. Long-needed study on Diderot's love of mystification.

Chouillet, Anne-Marie. "Actualité materielle de Diderot (En marge bibliographie concernant les ouvrages de/sur Diderot paru depuis (1972)." *Bulletin de la Société française d'étude du XVIII*, no. 22 (July 1977).

———. "L'anecdote Diderot-Euler ou Dieu prouvé par A=B." *DHS*, no. 10 (1978):319–28. On the anecdote's origin.

Chouillet, Jacques.

———. *La formation des idées esthétiques de Diderot, 1745–1763*. Paris: A. Colin, 1973.

———. *L'Esthétique des Lumières*. Paris: Presses Universitaires de France, 1975. Collection SUP.

———. *Diderot*. Paris: Société d'Edition d'Enseignement supérieur, 1977. Excellent introduction to the man and his work.

———. "Le Mythe d'Ariste, ou Diderot en face de lui-même." *RHLF* 64 (1964):565–88. Besides the aesthetics, perhaps the person Diderot would like to become.

———. "Le personnage du sceptique dans les premières oeuvres de Diderot (1745–1747)." *DHS* 1 (1969):195–211.

———. "Le message est-il de notre temps?" *DS* 21 (1983):33–44. Good question interestingly handled.

———. *Denis Diderot—Sophie Volland. Un dialogue à une voix*. Documentation and bibliography by Anne-Marie Chouillet. Paris: Champion 1986. Subject handled with mastery.

———. "La Promenade Vernet." *RDE* 2 (April 1987):123–63.

———. "Le rôle de la peinture dans les clichés stylistiques et dramatiques de Diderot." *Europe* (May 1984):150–58. Yes, they are there!

Cohen, Huguette. *La Figure dialogigue dans Jacques le fataliste.* SVEC 162 (1976). One of the first book-length studies in French; analyzes the various "couplings" that confirm the underlying structure.

———. "Jansenism in Diderot's *La Religieuse.*" *Studies in Eighteenth-Century Culture* 11 (1982):75–91. One of several recent revisionist studies linking Jansenism and the Enlightenment in their struggle against arbitrary authority.

———. "Diderot's Machiavellian Harlequin: Ferdinando Galiani." *SVEC* (forthcoming, 1989). Evaluates the extent of Diderot's debt to the Abbé Galiani, vastly underestimated until now.

———. "Diderot et les limites de la littérature dans les *Salons.*" *DS* (in press). Another revisionist study; attempts to give a new explanation for Diderot's gradual estrangement from art criticism.

Coulet, Henri. "Diderot et le problème du changement." *RDE* 2 (April 1987):59–67.

Creech, James. "Diderot and the Pleasure of the Other: Friends, Readers, Posterity." *Eighteenth-Century Culture* 11 (1977):439–56. Need of others to express his ideas on death, the future, etc.

———. "*Us* and Them: Le Paradoxe sur le Comédien." *EC* 24:33–42. The appeal of Diderot's dialogues.

Crocker, Lester. *The Embattled Philosopher. A Biography of Denis Diderot.* East Lansing: Michigan State College Press, 1954. A slightly romanticized life of Diderot; agreeable reading.

———. *An Age of Crisis. Man and World in Eighteenth-Century French Thought.* Baltimore: Johns Hopkins Press, 1959. A sweeping and provocative reinterpretation of the French Enlightenment.

———. *Diderot's Chaotic Order. Approach to Synthesis.* Princeton, N.J.: Princeton University Press, 1974. "Is this confusion appealing to Dr. Crocker?" one asks.

———. "The Idea of a 'neutral' universe." *DS* 21 (1983):45–76.

Daniel, Georges. "Autour du *Rêve de d'Alembert*: Réflexions sur l'esthétique de Diderot." *DS* 12 (1969):13–73.

———. *Le Style de Diderot. Légende et structure.* Genève: Droz, 1986. Impressive.

———. "Visages d'Uranie." *DS* 23 (1988):9–38.

Davison, Rosena. "Diderot, Galiani et Vico: un itinéraire philosophique." *DS* 23 (1988):39–54.

Dédéyan, Charles. "A propos d'un centenaire: les Goncourt juges de Diderot et de Voltaire." *Droit et liberté* 3 (April 1952):24–32.

———. *Diderot et la pensée anglaise.* Florence: Leo S. Olschk, 1987. Same book greatly expanded over the first version, *L'Angleterre dans la pensée de Diderot,* Paris: 1958.

Delon, Michel. "La beauté du crime." *Europe* (May 1984):73–83. Where Diderot differs from his successors.

Desne, Roland. "Recherches nouvelles sur *La Religieuse*." *DS* 6 (1964):197–214.

Didier, Béatrice. "Contribution à un poétique du leurre: 'lecteur' et narrataires dans *Jacques le fataliste*," *Littérature* (Octobre 1978):3–21.

————. *La musique des lumières: Diderot—L'Encyclopédie*. Paris: Presses Universitaires de France, 1985.

————. "L'opéra fou des bijoux." *Europe* (May 1984):142–50. "Le désir aboutit à sa satisfaction amoureuse ou musicale."

————. "L'Ecoute musicale chez Diderot." *DS* 23 (1988):55–74.

Dieckmann, Herbert. "Inventaire du fonds Vandeul et inédits de Diderot." Geneva: Droz, 1951. Invaluable for criticism and further research.

————. The *Préface-Annexe* of *La Religieuse*." *DS* 2 (1961):21–40. Throws important light on this novel.

————. "The Metaphoric Structure of the *Rêve de d'Alembert*." *DS* 17 (1973):15–24.

————. "Natural History from Bacon to Diderot: A few Guideposts." *AIOW* (1977):93–112.

Dolle, Jean-Marie. *Politique et pédagogie: Diderot et les problèmes de l'éducation*. Paris: J. Vrin, 1973. The education of girls, for instance.

Doolittle, James. *Rameau's Nephew: A Study of Diderot's "Second Satire."* Geneva: Droz, 1959. Controversial but interesting independent study of the famous dialogue.

Dulac, Georges. "Diderot et la *Civilisation* de la Russie." *CID* (1985):161–71.

Edmiston, William F. "Sacrifice et innocence in *La Religieuse*." *DS* 19 (1978):67–84.

Etiemble René. "A Mademoiselle Sophie Volland, 31 juillet 84." *Europe* 661 (May 1984):119–32. Étiemble/Diderot writes an ingenious, thought-provoking letter to Sophie some two centuries after her death.

Fabre, Jean. "Deux frères ennemis: Diderot et Jean-Jacques." *DS* 3 (1961):155–214.

————. "Actualité de Diderot." *DS* 4 (1963):17–39.

————. *Lumières et Romantisme*. Paris: Klincksieck, 1963. Includes four essays on Diderot by a great *Diderotiste*.

————. "Sagesse et morale dans *Jacques le fataliste*." *AETB* (1967):171–87.

Fellows, Otis E. *From Voltaire to la Nouvelle Critique*. Geneva: Droz, 1971. Three of the essays bear on interpretations of Diderot's novels.

————. "George Berkeley, His Door and the *Philosophes*." *FLRN* (1975):53–66. The Irish idealistic philosopher influenced Diderot and his compeers more than is generally supposed.

————. "Diderot's *Supplément* as Pendant for *La Religieuse*." *LHGH* (1975):229–43. *La Religieuse* reflected in the *Supplément*.

————. "Diderot and the Mystery of Woman." *Forum* (University of Houston) 16, no. 1 (Winter 1978):23–29. Structural analysis of *Sur les femmes*.

————. "Diderot's *Est-il bon?* rediscovered." *ESLC* (1979):87–109.

————. "The Facets of Illegitimacy in the French Enlightenment." *DS* 20 (1981):77–97. Main emphasis on Diderot.

————. Founder of *Diderot Studies* (1949–present). Coeditors: Norman L. Torrey (1 and 2), Gita May (3), and Diana Guiragossian (8 to present). (Syracuse, N.Y. for first two vols. only; Droz of Geneva for the rest of the series.) Wide range of contributions from Diderot scholars.

————. and Stephen Milliken. *Buffon*. New York: Twayne, 1972. Insights into philosophico-scientific speculations of the day.

Fink, Beatrice. "Ceci n'est pas un compte rendu." *Europe* (May 1984):107–11. Certain of today's aspects of Diderot brought up.

————. "A parasitic reading of Diderot's *Neveu de Rameau*." *Forum* (University of Houston) 16, no. 2 (Spring 1978):19–25. Ingenious analysis with chess table and dinner table as points of departure.

————. "L'Amour, la faim et la femme comestible." *CID* (1985):115–23.

Fontenay, Elizabeth de. *Diderot, ou le Materialisme Enchanté*. Paris: Grasset, 1950. The appeal of Diderot's multiplicity.

Fredman, Alice G. *Diderot and Sterne*. New York: Columbia University Press, 1955. Reassessment of Sterne's influence on Diderot.

Freud, Hilde. "Palissot and 'Les Philosophes.' " *DS* 9 (1967). The enemy confronts Diderot and compeers.

Fried, Michael. *Absorption and Theatricality: Painting and the Beholder in the Age of Diderot*. Berkeley: University of California Press, 1980, 108–22. The title is a fine summary of an enlightening essay.

Funt, David. Foreword by Richard Kuhns. *Diderot and the Esthetics of the Enlightenment*. *DS* 11 (1968). A trained academic philosopher, Funt shows how through philosophy and aesthetics one can come closest to Diderot's thought.

Garagnon, Jean. "Diderot et la méditation sur l'inconstance de *Jacques le fataliste:* 'Je ne sais de qui sont ces réflexions. . . .' " *DS* 22 (1986):57–62. Diderot's system of triangular repetitions.

Garcin, Philippe. "Diderot et la philosophie du style." *Critique* 15 (1959):195–213. Noteworthy article on Diderot's subtlety in general and love of ambiguity in particular.

Garnier, André. "La séquestration arbitraire de Denis Diderot en janvier 1743." *RDE* 2 (April 1987):46–52.

Gendzier, Stephen J. *Denis Diderot's The Encyclopedia*. New York: Harper & Row, 1967. Introduction, notes, and translation of selected articles give excellent idea of this vast compendium.

Gilman, Margaret. "Imagination and Creation in Diderot." *DS* 2 (1952):200–220. New light on Diderot's aesthetic principles.

Gordon, Douglas, and Norman Torrey. *The Censoring of Diderot's "Encyclopédie."* New York: Columbia University Press, 1947. Careful study of the Encyclopedia's deletions and censored proofs.

Goulemot, Jean Marie. "Figures du pouvoir dans *Jacques le fataliste.*" *Stanford French Review* (Fall 1984):321–34.

Grava, Arnold. "Diderot and Recent Philosophical Trends." *DS* 4 (1963):73–103.

Grimsley, Ronald L. "L'Ambiguité dans l'oeuvre romanesque de Diderot." In *Cahiers de l'Association internationale des études françaises.* Paris: "Les Belles Lettres," 1961, 223–37. Ambiguity in Diderot's fictional procedures.

Guyot, Charly. *Diderot par lui-même.* Paris: Editions du Seuil, 1959. Ingenious introduction and expert editing of texts.

Hanna, Blake. "Diderot théologien." *RHLF* (1978).

Havens, George R. "Diderot, Rousseau and the *Discours sur l'inégalité.*" *DS* 3 (1961):219–62. Scrupulous scholarship.

————. *The Age of Ideas: From Reaction to Revolution in Eighteenth-Century France.* 2d ed. New York: Collier Books, 1962. Excellent introduction to figures of the Enlightenment.

Hayes, Julia C. "Diderot and the Problem of Authority in the *Discours sur la poésie dramatique.*" *DS* 23 (1988):75–84.

Hayward, Susan. "Two Anti-Novels: *Molloy* and *Jacques le Fataliste.*" *FLRN* (1975):97–107. Similarities: Diderot and Beckett.

Hill, Emita B. "The role of 'le Monstre' in Diderot's Thought." *SVEC* 97 (1972):148–261. One aspect of Diderot's varied interests treated in depth.

Hytier, Adrienne. "Diderot et Molière." *DS* 8 (1966):77–103.

Jean, Joan de. "Insertions and Interventions in *Le Neveu de Rameau.*" *Eighteenth-Century Studies* 9 (1976):511–22.

Josephs, Herbert. *Diderot's Dialogue of Gesture and Language: "Le Neveu de Rameau."* Columbus: Ohio State University Press, 1969. Adroitly offers an added dimension to an appreciation of *The Nephew.*

————. Co-editor with Jack Undank of *Digression and Dispersion. A Bicentennial Tribute. French Forum.* Lexington: University of Kentucky Press, 1984. Nineteen North American essays, some presenting new critical methods of interpretation.

————. "Diderot's *Eloge de Richardson:* A Paradox on Praising." *AIOW* (1977):169–82.

Kafker, Frank A. "Some Observations on Five Interpretations of the *Encyclopédie.*" *DS* 23 (1988):85–100.

Kavanagh, Thomas M. "Language as Deception: Diderot's *Les Bijoux indiscrets.*" *DS* 23 (1988):101–14.

Kempf, Roger. "Des bijoux et de l'opinion." *CID* (1985):239–44. Those indiscreet jewels again.

Laborde, Alice M. "Le paradoxe de *La Religieuse.*" *Pacific Coast Philology* 2 (1967):28–31. On the stability of Suzanne's virtue.

Lafarge, Catherine. "Le déclin de l'amour." *CID* (1985):125–33. La fin d'une affaire.

Langdon, David. "The Message of Diderot's *Entretien d'un père avec ses enfants.*" *DS* 23 (1988):115–28.

Lee, Vera. *The Reign of Women in Eighteenth-Century France.* Cambridge: Schenkman, 1976.

————. *Love and Strategy in the Eighteenth-Century French Novel.* Cambridge: Schenkman, 1986.

Lefebvre, Henri. *Diderot.* Paris: Les Editeurs réunis, 1949. Important overstudy from the French Marxist point of view.

Lewinter, Robert. "L'Exaltation de la vertu dans le théâtre de Diderot." *DS* 8 (1966):119–69. Another example of Lewinter's fertile mind.

————. *Diderot ou les mots de l'absence; essai sur la forme de l'oeuvre.* Paris: Edition Champ libre, 1976. Analyzes Diderot psychologically and studies his chief works by means of existential formalism.

————. *Oeuvres complètes* of Diderot. 15 vols. Paris: Club français du livre, 1969–73. Useful introductions to individual works by Lewinter plus Belaval, Kempf, Meyer, Varloot, Starobinski et al.

Lough, John. "Who were the *Philosophes?*" *FLRN* (1975):139–50.

Loy, J. Robert. *Diderot's Determined Fatalist.* New York: Kings Crown Press, 1950. A pioneer study in depth of Diderot's greatest novel.

————. "L'Essai sur les règnes de Claude et de Néron." *Cahiers de l'Association internationale des études françaises* 13 (1961):238–54. The political and ethical importance of this essay to an aging Diderot.

————. "Reminiscence and Inspiration: Diderot and Rousseau." *DEOF* (1974):151–61. Ruminations on a passage in *Jacques.*

————. "Richardson and Diderot." *ESLC* (1979):145–50.

Luc, Jean. *Diderot, l'artiste, le philosophe.* Paris: Editions sociales internationales, 1938.

Luppol, I.K. *Diderot: Ses Idées philosophiques.* Paris: Editions sociales, 1936. The best-known Marxist book translated from the Russian.

Luxembourg, Lilo K. *Francis Bacon and Denis Diderot: Philosophers of Science.* Munksgaard, Denmark, 1967. Diderot's debt to Bacon.

Marcu, Eva. "Pensées sur la femme. *DS* 20 (1981):331–43. A useful commentary on Paul Hoffmann's substantial *La Femme dans la pensée des Lumières.* Paris: Editions Ophrys, 1977.

Mat-Hasquin, Michèle. "Diderot et Horace." *DS* 19 (1978):103–27.

Mauzi, Robert. *L'Idée du bonheur au XVIIIe siècle.* Paris: Armand Colin, 1960. Masterly study of the Enlightenment's search for happiness.

May, Georges. *Quatre Visages de Diderot.* Paris: Hatier-Boivin, 1951. Four excellent portraits of Diderot in the form of essays.

————. *Diderot et "la Religieuse."* New Haven: Yale University Press, 1954. Essential work, well-documented.

————. "L'Angoisse de l'échec et la genèse du *Neveu de Rameau.*" *DS* 3 (1961):285–308. A moment of emotional and intellectual crisis in Diderot's life.

————. "Le Maître, la chaîne et le chien dans *Jacques le fataliste*." *Cahiers de l'Association internationale des études françaises* 13 (1961):269–82. The role of liberty in this novel.

————. "*Le Rêve de d'Alembert* selon Diderot." *DS* 17 (1973):25–39. Judiciously presented.

————. "Une certaine Madame Madin." *LHGH* (1975):255–71.

May, Gita. *Diderot and Baudelaire, critiques d'art*. Geneva: Droz, 1957. Diderot rehabilitated as art critic; important.

————. "Diderot devant la magie de Rembrandt." *PMLA* 74 (1959):387–97. Diderot's appreciation of Rembrandt's genius.

————. "Diderot and Burke: A Study in Aesthetic Affinity." *PMLA* 65 (1960):527–39. Diderot's debt to Edmund Burke.

————. "Denis Diderot (1713–1784)." In *European Writers: The Age of Reason and the Enlightenment*, edited by George Stade, 4:475–509. New York: Scribner's, 1984. Outstanding, clear, compact essay on Diderot's life and works.

Mayer, Jean. *Diderot, homme de science*. Rennes: Imprimerie Bretonne, 1959. Important but flawed study on Diderot and science.

McLelland, Jane B. "Changing his Image: Diderot, Vernet and the Old Dressing Gown." *DS* 23 (1988):129–42.

Mésavage, Ruth M. "Dialogue and Illusion in *Jacques le fataliste*." *DS* 22 (1986):79–87. Dialogic formulations in *Jacques*.

Meyer, Paul H. *The "Lettre sur les sourds et muets" and Diderot's Emerging Concept of the Critic*. *DS* 8 (1965). Interesting inquiry into Diderot's marked hostility toward academic criticism of his time.

————. "The Unity and Structure of Diderot's *Neveu de Rameau*." *Criticism* 2 (1959–1960):362–86. Significant addition to the present maze of studies on Diderot's great dialogue.

————. "Diderot's *Prince*: 'Principes de Politique des souverains.'" *DEOF* (1974):162–81. An aging Diderot's political ambivalence.

Miller, Arnold. *The Annexation of a Philosophe: Diderot in Soviet Criticism, 1917–1960*. *DS* 15 (Geneva, Droz: 1971). Impressive study of Soviet Marxist critics' reactions to Diderot.

Mortier, Roland. *Diderot en Allemagne*. Paris: Presses Universitaires de France, 1954. A brilliantly comprehensive monograph on Diderot and German culture.

————. "L'Original selon Diderot." *Saggi e Ricerche di Lettera Francese* 4 (1963):141–57. The eccentric character according to Diderot.

————. "A propos du sentiment de L'existence chez Diderot et Rousseau." *DS* 6 (1964):183–95. Arresting parallels between Diderot's essay, *Délicieux*, and Rousseau's writings.

Moureaux, José-Michel. "Le rôle du fou dans *Le Neveu de Rameau*." In *Siècle de Voltaire: Hommage à René Pomeau*, edited by C. Mervaud and S. Menant, 675–91. Oxford: The Voltaire Foundation, 1987. "When

I spend my time playing with my cat," says Montaigne, "who knows whether it's more of a pastime for her or for me."

Nikagawa, Hisayasu. "Universalité de Diderot." *RDE* 2 (April 1987):123–63.

Niklaus, Robert. "Presence of Diderot." *DS* 6 (1964):13–28. Valuable analysis of the nature of Diderot's thought.

———. *A Literary History of France: The Eighteenth Century 1715–1789.* London: Ernest Benn, 1970. A fine panoramic view of the Enlightenment and its writers.

———. "Diderot and Education." *ESLC* (1970):205–19. Delivers more than title suggests.

———. "The Pursuit of Peace in the Enlightenment." *DEOF* (Geneva: Droz, 1974):231–45.

O'Gorman, Donal. *Diderot the Satirist: "Le Neveu de Rameau" and Related Works, an Analysis.* Toronto: University of Toronto Press, 1971. Presently a controversial work many of whose original insights will stand the test of time.

Osso, Jannette Geffriaud. *"Jacques le fataliste": L'Amour et son image.* Pisa: Golliardica, 1981. Illustrations. Woman according to Diderot: reality or fantasy.

Pappas, John, and Georges Roth. "Les 'Tablettes' de Diderot." *DS* 3 (1961):309–20. Diderot's specific charges against Rousseau.

———. "D'Alembert and *Le Fils naturel.*" *DEOF* (Geneva: Droz, 1974):246–55. One aspect of the theme of illegitimacy.

———. "Diderot, d'Alembert et l'*Encyclopédie.*' "*DS* 4 (1963):191–208.

———. "L'Esprit de finesse contre l'esprit de géométrie: débat entre Diderot et d'Alembert." *SVEC* 79 (1972):1229–53.

———. "The Identity of Lui and Moi in Diderot's *Le Neveu de Rameau.*" *Studies in Burke and his Time,* no. 49 (Winter 1973–74):175–87.

———. "Dans les registres de l'ancien régime: des réponses officielles à Rameau, Diderot et Voltaire." *DHS,* no. 7 (1975):217–21.

———. "Voltaire et le drame bourgeois." *DS* 20 (1981):225–43.

———. "L'Opéra français contre l'italien: la solution de Diderot dans *Le Neveu de Rameau.*" In *Diderot, les beaux arts et la musique. Actes du Colloque international tenu à Aix-en-Provence* (1986):233–40.

Parker, Alice. "Did/Erotica: Diderot's Contribution to the History of Sexuality." *DS* 22 (1986):57–62. On Diderot and human sexual behavior; most informative.

Perkins, Jean A. "Diderot's Concept of Virtue." *SVEC* (1963):77–91. Traces the development of Diderot's theory of virtue.

———. *The Concept of Self in the French Enlightenment.* Geneva: Droz, 1969. Authoritative study of a complex problem.

———. "Gardening in the *Encyclopédie.*" *DS* 19 (1978):145–62.

Perkins, Merle L. *Diderot and the Time-Space Continuum: His Philosophy, Aesthetics and Politics. SVEC,* vol. 211. Oxford: The Voltaire Foundation, 1982. Diderot prescient in his questions.

Perol, Lucette. "De L'importance d'une soupente cassée." *RDE* 3 (October 1987):71–78. Story becomes painting and vice versa.

Posada, Maurice. "An Introduction to the Textual Problem of the Diderot-Falconet Correspondence on Posterity." *DS* 16 (1973):175–96.

Proust, Jacques. *Diderot et "L'Encyclopédie."* Paris: Armand Colin, 1962. This monumental work is indispensable to *dix-huitiémistes.*

———. "Recherches nouvelles sur *La Religieuse.*" *DS* 6 (1964):197–214. New evidence of Diderot's familiarity with eighteenth-century convents.

Pucci, Suzanne. "The Vision of the 'I' of the Beholder." *EC* 24 (1984):108–22. The title is a fine summary of an enlightening essay.

———. "The Art, Nature, and Fiction of Diderot's Beholder." *Standford French Review* (Fall 1984):273–94. Shows how complex relations between audience and narrator work for a mimetic principle throughout Diderot's works.

———. *Diderot and a Poetics of Science.* New York: Peter Lang, 1986. Constructs a model for reading Diderot across the disciplines of philosophy, aesthetics, language theory, and fiction.

———. "Metaphor and Metamorphosis in Diderot's *Le Rêve de d'Alembert.*" *Symposium* 25 (Winter 1981–82):325–39.

Riffaterre, Michael. "Diderot et le philosophe esclave: de Diogène Laërce à Victor Hugo." *DS* 3 (1961):347–67. Deft scholarship, rich in detail on Diderot's use of theme drawn from antiquity, and subsequently appropriated by Victor Hugo.

Roger, Jacques. *Les Sciences de la vie dans la pensée française du XVIIIe siècle.* Paris: Armand Colin, 1963. Diderot firmly situated in the mainstream of French eighteenth-century scientific thought.

———. "Diderot et Buffon en 1749." *DS* 4 (1963):197–216. Good beginning to a complex subject.

Schapiro, Meyer. "Diderot on the Artist and Society." *DS* 5 (1964):5–11. Much is relevant two centuries later.

Schober, Angelika. "Aspects du génie chez Diderot et d'Alembert." *DS* 23 (1988):143–50.

Sherman, Carol. *Diderot and the Art of Dialogue.* Geneva: Droz, 1976. The various forms of dialogue in Diderot.

———. "Diderot et la rhétorique du rococo." *Saggi e ricerche di letteratura francese* (Milano) (1978):247–73.

Siegel, June. "Grandeur-Intimacy: The Dramatist's Dilemma." *DS* 4 (1963):247–60. Diderot's strength lies in intimate style of his fiction and correspondence, not in illusions of theatrical grandeur.

———. "Diderot, Richardson, Manuscripts, Missives, and Mysteries." *DS* 18 (1975):145–67. New light on the Diderot-Richardson rapport.

———. "Diderot and Richardson: A Confluence of Opposites." Ann Arbor, Mich.: University Microfilms, 24 (1963–64): 5327. An outstanding dissertation that should have been published.

————. "Lovelace and Rameau's Nephew: Roots of Poetic Amoralism." *DS* 19 (1978):163–74. Significant rapprochement.

Singh, Christine M. "The *Lettre sur les Aveugles:* Its debt to Lucretius." *FLRM* (1975):233–42. The real extent of Lucretius's influence.

Smiley, Joseph Royall. *Diderot's Relations with Grimm.* Urbana: University of Illinois Press, 1950.

Sourian, Eve. "Diderot retrouvé." *DS* 18 (1975):169–87. The first chronological edition of Diderot's *Oeuvres complètes.*

Souviron, Marie. "Les Romans de Diderot: Une conception philosophique de l'homme." *Europe,* no. 661 (May 1984). Aspects of the human condition in Diderot's three novels brilliantly treated; most informative.

————. *Le malheur d'un vicieux, dialogue socratique: hypothèse de lecture pour "Le Neveu de Rameau."* Paris: Centre d'études et de recherches marxistes, 1972.

Spear, Frederick A. *Bibliographie de Diderot. Répertoire analytique international.* Geneva: Droz, 1980. Indispensable.

————. "Bibliographie de Diderot." Supplement no. 3, *DS* 23 (1988):151–68. These "supplements" will be added to the monumental volumes of the Diderot bibliography.

————. Guest editor of panel discussion on the *Rêve de d'Alembert. DS* 17 (1973):15–106. Other participants: Herbert Dieckmann, Georges May, Aram Vantanian.

Starobinski, Jean. "Le moulin sur le torrent." *EC* 24 (1984):3–12. The figure of the narrator as spectator.

Strugnell, Anthony. *Diderot's Politics: A Study of the Evolution of Diderot's Political Thought after the Encyclopédie.* The Hague: Martinus Nijhoff, 1973.

Sumi, Yoichi. "L'été 1762. Apropos des lettres à Sophie Volland." *Europe* (May 1984):113–19.

Thielemann, Leland. "Thomas Hobbes dans *l'Encyclopédie." RHLF* 51 (1951):133–46. Careful scholarship.

————. "Diderot and Hobbes." *DS* 2 (1952):221–78. The best word on the Diderot-Hobbes relationship.

————. "Diderot's Encyclopedic Article on Justice: Its Sources and Significance." *DS* 4 (1963):26–83. Source is Grotian school of natural law, at least in part.

Thomas, Ruth. "Diderot and Rousseau as literary critics." *Modern Language Review* 73 (1978):51–60. Aesthetic resemblances between the two authors.

Thomson, Ann. "L'unité matérielle de l'homme chez La Mettrie et Diderot." *CID* (1985):99–104.

Topazio, Virgil W. "Diderot's Supposed Contribution to Helvétius's Works." *Philological Quarterly* 33 (1954):313–29. Casts convincing doubt on extent of Diderot's hand in Helvétius's writings.

————. "Culture and the Age of the Enlightenment." *Rice University Studies* 63, no. 1 (1977):125–33. Appraisal of Voltaire's, Montesquieu's, Rousseau's, and Diderot's contributions to Enlightenment thought.

Torrey, Norman. L. "Voltaire's Reaction to Diderot." *PMLA* 50 (1935):1107–43. Voltaire holds Diderot in admiration despite differences.

————. "Diderot, Denis 1713–1784." *The Encyclopedia of Philosophy*, 2:397–403. New York and London: Macmillan, 1972. Splendid brief essay on life and works.

————. *The Censoring of Diderot's "Encyclopédie"* (1947): see Gordon and Torrey.

————. "Rousseau's Quarrel with Diderot and Grimm." In *Essays in Honor of Albert Feuillerat*, edited by French Department, 163–82. New Haven: Yale University Press, 1950. Significant contribution to a still controversial subject.

———— "L'Encyclopédie de Diderot: une grande aventure dans le domaine de l'édition." *RHLF* 51 (1951):306–17.

    , and Otis Fellows, eds. *The Age of Enlightenment*. 2d ed. New York: Meredith Corp., 1971. Introductions, texts, and notes give good idea of the age.

Trousson, Raymond. "Diderot et l'antiquité grecque." *DS* 6 (1964):215–45. Excellent essay on Diderot, Hellenist.

————. *Socrate devant Voltaire, Diderot et Rousseau: la Conscience en face du mythe*. Paris: Minard, 1967. Painstaking scholarship.

Undank, Jack. *Diderot: Inside, Outside, and In-Between*. Madison, Wis.: Coda Press, 1979. Thoroughly original, suggestive, and witty study of the literary transactions among readers, narrators, and characters in Diderot's work.

————. and Herbert Josephs, eds. *Diderot: Digression and Dispersion. A Bicentennial Tribute. French Forum*. Lexington: University of Kentucky Press, 1984. Nineteen North American essays, some introducing new critical methods of interpretation.

————. "The Open and Shut Case of *Est-il bon? Est-il méchant?*" *DS* 22 (1985):143–70. Ingenious, wide-ranging philosophical meditation on the attempt, from Diderot to modern American poetry, to capture "ordinary" life.

————. "On Being 'Human': Diderot's *Satire Première*." *Eighteenth-Century Studies* 20 (Fall 1986):1–16. Persuasive argument linking this satire and its reflexivity to the structure and themes of *Le Neveu de Rameau*, *Jacques*, and *Le Paradoxe*.

————. "*Jacques le fataliste* and the Uses of Representation." *MLN* 101 (1986):741–64. Astutely arguing, against contemporary nonreferentialists, for Diderot's use of a pragmatic and socially engaged language.

Van Den Abbeele, Georges. "Utopian Sexualities and its Discontents: Exoticism and Colonialism in the *Supplément au Voyage de Bougainville*." *EC* 24 (1984):43–52. Title summarizes contents.

Varloot, Jean. "La Copie Naigeon: Prolégomènes philologiques au *Rêve de d'Alembert.*" *DEOF* (1974):302–24. Scrupulous scholarship.

————. "Le poète Diderot: vers inconnus ou méconnus." *Europe* (1963):504–5.

————. Secrétaire général. 33 vols. *Diderot: Oeuvres complètes.* Paris: Hermann, 1975–89.

Vartanian, Aram. "From Deist to Atheist: Diderot's Philosophical Orientation, 1746–1749." *DS* 1 (1949):46–63. Pinpoints change in Diderot's religious convictions.

————. *Diderot and Descartes: A Study of Scientific Naturalism in the Enlightenment.* Princeton, N.J.: Princeton University Press, 1953.

————. "Eroticisme et philosophie chez Diderot." *CAIEF* 13 (1961):238–54. The bond between Diderot's eroticism and his scientific materialism.

————. "The *Rêve de d'Alembert:* A Bio-Political View." *DS* 17 (1973):41–64.

————. "*Jacques le fataliste:* Journey into the Ramifications of a Dilemma." *DEOF* (1974):325–47. *Jacques* is a vindication of the principle of freedom, but here, in its metaphysical dimension.

————. "La Mettrie, Diderot, and Sexology in the Enlightenment." *AIOW* (1977):347–67.

————. "Diderot and the Phenomenology of the Dream." *DS* 8 (1966):217–53.

————. "The Politics of *Les Bijoux indiscrets.*" *ESLC* (1979):249–76. "Political criticism disguised and implicit."

Venturi, Franco. *Jeunesse de Diderot* (1713–1753). Paris: Skira, 1939. Indispensable for partial understanding of Diderot's early works.

Vesely, Jindrich. "Diderot et le roman réaliste du XVIII siècle." *CID* (1985):255–65.

Waldinger, Renée. "Diderot as Dramatist: Dramatic Prose? Prosaic Drama?" *DS* 20 (1981):287–97.

Weisz, Pierre. Le Réel et son double: La Création romanesque dans *Jacques le fataliste. DS* 19 (1978):175–87.

Werner, Stephen. "Diderot's *Supplément* and the Late Enlightenment Thought." *SVEC* 86 (1971):229–92. Sound and provocatively interesting scholarship.

————. *Diderot's Great School: Narrative Art in "Jacques le fataliste." SVEC* 88 (1975). New, valid insights into Diderot's *roman philosophique.*

Whatley, Janet. "Nun's Stories: Marivaux and Diderot." *DS* 20 (1981):299–319.

Williams, Charles G. S., ed. *Literature and History in the Age of Ideas: Essays on the French Enlightenment Presented to George R. Havens.* Columbus: Ohio State University Press, 1975.

Wilson, Arthur M. "The Development and Scope of Diderot's Political Thought." *SVEC* 27 (1963):1871–1900. Excellent analysis of evolution of Diderot's political ideas.

————. *Diderot.* New York: Oxford University Press, 1972. The most complete book on Diderot's life and works.

————. "Diderot: The Verdict of Posterity, 1784–1852." *DEOF* (1974):400–22. Arrestingly important account of Diderot's posthumous rise to fame.

————. "A Festschrift for Otis Fellows." *DS* 19 (1978):197–209.

————. "The Concept of *moeurs* in Diderot's social and political thought." *AETB* (1967):188–99. Fine summation.

Winter, Ursula. *Der Materialismus bei Diderot.* Geneva: Droz; Paris: Minard, 1972. Her astuteness in noting the differences between Diderot and other materialistic thinkers of the age is especially impressive.

Index

185